Teacher Evaluation in Second Language Education

ALSO AVAILABLE FROM BLOOMSBURY

Developing Materials for Language Teaching, edited by Brian Tomlinson
Experimental Research Methods in Language Learning, Aek Phakiti
Key Ideas in Educational Research, David Scott & Marlene Morrison
Key Terms in Second Language Acquisition, Bill VanPatten & Alessandro G Benati
Language in Education, edited by Rita Elaine Silver & Soe Marlar Lwin
Reflective Language Teaching, Thomas S. C. Farrell
Reflective Teaching, Andrew Pollard
Second Language Acquisition, Alessandro G Benati & Tanja Angelovska
Teaching Teachers, Angi Malderez & Martin Wedell
The Bloomsbury Companion to Second Language Acquisition, edited by Ernesto Macaro

Teacher Evaluation in Second Language Education

EDITED BY
AMANDA HOWARD AND
HELEN DONAGHUE

Bloomsbury Academic
An imprint of Bloomsbury Publishing Plc

B L O O M S B U R Y
LONDON · NEW DELHI · NEW YORK · SYDNEY

Bloomsbury Academic

An imprint of Bloomsbury Publishing Plc

50 Bedford Square   1385 Broadway
London   New York
WC1B 3DP   NY 10018
UK   USA

www.bloomsbury.com

BLOOMSBURY and the Diana logo are trademarks of Bloomsbury Publishing Plc

First published 2015

British Library Cataloguing-in-Publication Data
A catalogue record for this book is available from the British Library.

ISBN: HB: 9781-4725-0994-9
PB: 9781-4725-1182-9
ePDF: 978-1-4725-1161-4
ePub: 978-1-4725-0690-0

Library of Congress Cataloging-in-Publication Data
A catalog record for this book is available from the Library of Congress.

Typeset by Integra Software Services Pvt. Ltd
Printed and bound in India

CONTENTS

ACKNOWLEDGEMENTS

We would like to thank all those who have shared their experience and research with us while compiling this book and for their interest and enthusiasm in addressing the boundaries of teacher evaluation in second language education. We would especially like to thank Tania Pugliese and Nick Howard for their invaluable assistance towards production.

TRANSCRIPTION CONVENTIONS

The following transcription symbols appear in the book, although the way in which they have been used varies according to individual authors:

Symbol	Meaning
bold	Speaker emphasis
[	Overlap
- or ...	Interrupted turn
()	Very short untimed pause
(1.0)	Length of timed pause
(xxxx)	Unclear or unintelligible speech
[laughs]	Transcriber interpretation of interaction

NOTES ON CONTRIBUTORS

Fiona Copland is Senior Lecturer in the School of Languages and Social Sciences in Aston University, Birmingham, UK. She has worked as a teacher and teacher trainer in Nigeria, Hong Kong, Japan and Birmingham and has been a CELTA and DELTA course director. Fiona's research interests include the discourses of the feedback conference, teaching English to Young Learners and pedagogies using L1 and L2, and she has published work in these areas. She is interested in methodologies that combine linguistic ethnographic approaches and is currently convenor of the Linguistic Ethnography Forum.

Helen Donaghue is Senior Lecturer in English Language Teaching at Sheffield Hallam University, UK. She has worked in TESOL and teacher education in Hungary, the United Arab Emirates and the UK. Her teaching interests include EAP, teaching L2 reading and language testing and her research interests focus mainly on institutional interaction in educational settings. She is currently researching the co-construction and negotiation of face and identity in post observation feedback meetings.

Marion Engin has been involved in teaching and teacher education for 26 years. She has worked in the UK and Turkey and is currently teaching at Zayed University in Dubai, United Arab Emirates. Her particular interest lies in the field of sociocultural theory and its application to teacher learning and teacher training.

Amanda Howard has worked as an English language teacher, teacher developer and lecturer for a number of institutions and universities both in the Middle East and the UK, most recently as TESOL Coordinator in the Faculty of Education at the British University in Dubai. Her research interests include observation and feedback in educational settings, English language teaching pedagogy, analysis of classroom interaction and Young Learner education. Her most recent book is *Participant Voices: Observation in Educational Settings*, co-edited with Helen Donaghue.

Neil Hunt is a teacher educator working at the Higher Colleges of Technology in Al Ain, UAE. He is interested in post-structural research into the development of teacher identities and the applications of critical theory to English Language Teaching.

Radhika Iyer-O'Sullivan is an independent specialist in teaching, training, mentoring, learning and development, and has recently set up her own academic and educational consultancy. Her professional experience includes teaching English as a Second Language, English as a Foreign Language, English for Academic Purposes, teacher training and mentoring at tertiary level in Malaysia and the UAE. She has also developed curriculum and resources for provision of academic support to postgraduate students. Her research interests include the development of teaching strategies aimed at deterring plagiarism and teacher development within the contexts of ESL, EFL and EAP.

Mick King's twenty-five-year career in education has involved teaching, lecturing, managing, researching and presenting in Europe and the Arabian Gulf. He currently lectures educational leadership and management at Middlesex University Dubai and co-chairs the TESOL Arabia Teacher Training and Development Special Interest Group.

Steve Mann is Associate Professor at the Centre for Applied Linguistics at the University of Warwick and is Director of MA ELT programmes. He previously lectured at both Aston University and the University of Birmingham. He has experience in Hong Kong, Japan and Europe in both English language teaching and teacher development. His most recent book *Innovations in Pre-service Teacher Education* (2013) is part of the British Council's new *Innovation Series*. Steve supervises a research group of PhD students who are investigating teacher education and development. The group's work considers aspects of teacher development, reflective practice and teacher beliefs.

Leonardo A. Mercado, MEd, MBA, originally from Queens, New York, is the Academic Manager at the Instituto Cultural Peruano Norteamericano (ICPNA) binational centre in Lima, Peru. He has been an ESL/EFL teacher, teacher trainer, certified proficiency rater and programme administrator for almost 20 years.

Phil Quirke is currently Executive Dean of General Studies and Education at the Higher Colleges of Technology in the UAE. He has been in ELT Leadership positions for fifteen years and has published in areas as diverse as face, action research, appraisal and journaling. Recent publications include his book *An Exploration of Teacher Knowledge*.

Mick Randall was formerly Dean of the Faculty of Education at the British University in Dubai where he is currently an honorary research fellow and honorary senior lecturer at Birmingham University. He has had experience of teacher training in a number of different countries in the Middle East (Oman, Egypt and the UAE) as well as Singapore and the UK. He gained his master's in Second Language Learning and Teaching and his doctorate from Birkbeck College, London University. He is interested in providing feedback, counselling and cross-cultural interaction in pedagogic situations and has published a book related to this interest, *Advising and Supporting Teachers* with Cambridge University Press.

Wayne Trotman has been involved in ELT for over thirty years, working in the UK, the USA and Portugal. He is at present a teacher educator at Katip Çelebi University in Izmir, Turkey, where he coordinates teacher-research projects in the ELT Department of the School of Foreign Languages and teaches discourse analysis on the MA Language and Literature course. He is currently carrying out research into what motivates researchers.

Steve Walsh is Professor of Applied Linguistics and Director of Postgraduate Research in the School of Education, Communication and Language Sciences at Newcastle University. He has been involved in English Language Teaching for more than 20 years and has worked in a range of overseas contexts, including Hong Kong, Spain, Hungary, Ireland, Poland and China. Steve's research interests include professional discourse, classroom discourse, teacher development, second language teacher education, educational linguistics and analysing spoken interaction. He has published extensively in these areas and is the editor of the journal *Classroom Discourse* published by Routledge.

Introduction

Helen Donaghue and Amanda Howard

Definitions and terms

Teaching is a personal, social, complex activity and most teachers would agree that they continue to learn and develop this skill throughout their careers. Institutions often carry out different forms of teacher evaluation to help teachers develop and improve the teaching and learning experience for students and also to monitor and remediate poor practice. They collect data on which to base decisions, for example, about curriculum design and change, professional development focus and staffing. The evaluation process is complex and often daunting for those involved. Much has been written about the way teacher evaluation in mainstream education generates a great deal of pressure and this is no less true for second language education (SLE) contexts. English language teaching in particular has become a highly lucrative industry and as a result various stakeholders have developed interest in the individuals upon which the effectiveness and success of an institution rests: the teachers.

Much discussion about teacher evaluation originates in the USA where appraisal procedures are constantly under review as participants seek continuous improvement (see Chapter 12, this volume). Our book contributes to this discussion, first, by adding a wider, international perspective, second, by exploring the experiences of participants (observers, pre- and in-service teachers and learners) and, finally, by drawing on research related to teacher evaluation. Although the terms *evaluation, appraisal* and *assessment* are often used interchangeably, the overall focus of this volume is on *teacher evaluation*, a general term which is used to describe an activity carried out by an institution where the quality of provision is the result of systematic study (Department of Education, 1985). Evaluation can also be defined as *'the systematic gathering of information for purposes of decision making'*

(Richards et al., 1992, p. 130) where the data obtained can be used for either appraisal or research purposes. In this volume, different forms of teacher evaluation are investigated: self- and peer observation (Mann and Walsh, Trotman), mentoring (Mercado and Mann), observation for feedback (Randall, King, Howard), critical incidents (Iyer-O'Sullivan), scaffolding (Engin) and a system for teacher appraisal (Quirke). There are also chapters focusing on the discourse of the feedback event (Donaghue, Copland, Hunt) as well as discussions relating to participant responses to teacher evaluation processes (King, Trotman, Howard). As such, this book provides a working sample of many of the ways in which teachers are evaluated. Although it is not representative of all possible methods (e.g. there is no discussion of the three-minute classroom walkthrough (Downey et al., 2004)), what makes this volume relevant and unique is that the chapters have been written by researchers and practitioners involved in teacher evaluation.

How teachers are evaluated and supported throughout their careers through observation and feedback

Teacher evaluation is most often realized by means of observation and feedback, elements which have a symbiotic partnership: there is little point in having one without the other. Observation and feedback are incorporated in all the teacher evaluation systems discussed in this book, whether directly or indirectly, and provide a key focus for the discussion. Although much has been written on various aspects of observation, feedback seems to be an undervalued and neglected area in recent literature. For the purposes of this introduction, observation can be defined as '*the purposeful examination of teaching and/or learning events through the systematic processes of data collection and analysis*' (Bailey, 2001, p. 114), and feedback as the locus of '*help-giving and receiving*' (Wajnryb, 1994).

Observation is certainly a fundamental part of teaching and learning, starting from a very early age: Rinvolucri (2002, p. 90) claims that '*the main pre-service training course that teachers receive lasts around 12,000 hours – the hours they spend in the thrall of teachers between when they start school aged 6 and when they leave it at 18*'. However, teaching in a classroom requires rather more active participation. It could therefore be argued that evaluation has its greatest value in the early, training stages of a teaching career when the progression of instruction, classroom observations and tutor feedback can be '*exciting, confusing and traumatic all at the same time*' (Copland, 2008, p. 5). Trainee teachers and observers have scheduled meetings to discuss observed lessons in detail, reflecting on the teaching that has taken place and planning how to move forward. Teaching in the presence of an experienced observer can be daunting, but the trainee anticipates that the feedback will have elements of judgement and that this will inform his/her future classroom practice. Therefore, at this initial stage, observation and feedback have a clearly instructional and supportive role and in an ideal context trainer and trainee work together to use learned pedagogic theory to inform classroom practice, a process which is of mutual benefit.

Once qualified, new graduates leave the protected confines of training courses and organized teaching practice to join the working community as novice teachers. Those who have moved into supportive institutions may still be observed on a formative basis by a mentor or coach with whom they can reflect on their classroom experiences during feedback meetings. Others may need to make their own way in the teaching and learning environment, experiencing evaluation of a more summative nature. As accountability in the workplace has grown over the last few decades, increasing numbers of working teachers are experiencing highly complex evaluation processes on a regular basis and observation often features significantly as the chosen instrument to measure practice. However, as Edge and Richards argue, *best practice* as a term can be unhelpful within the context of teacher education, applying only to situations where '*for all practical purposes, procedures are precisely specifiable and outcomes predictable*' (1998, p. 569). As demonstrated by the range of contexts included in this book, education is a multifaceted process, so specifying procedures and predicting outcomes will differ in contexts as diverse as early childhood and tertiary education. It is therefore important to remember that perspectives on observation and feedback may vary because of different educational contexts, as well as the stage that a teacher has reached within her/his career and also because learners differ in aspects such as age, language level, skills or motivation.

The value and potential of observation and feedback in teacher evaluation

Observation and feedback have considerable potential in terms of pre-service teacher education, as, for the vast majority of teachers, this is their grounding in effective classroom practice. For practising teachers, observation and feedback can also have much value, especially when linked to concepts of formative evaluation and professional development. Guides to teacher evaluation often present the process in a positive light; however, writing from a less optimistic perspective, Watson-Davis comments:

> Observation plays a fundamental role in improving the quality of teaching and learning. It is the most exciting and dynamic engine for whole-school renewal and change, and it's a powerful way to inspire and motivate. Unfortunately, for many teachers – perhaps because in their schools it's

only ever linked with performance review or inspection – observation is about as welcome as a poke in the eye with a sharp stick. (2009, p. 5)

Establishing that evaluative practice can be viewed negatively, Watson-Davis sets out to counter this with useful suggestions for classroom practice and the delivery of feedback. Other writers are equally aware of potential problems but also advocate the use of observation and feedback as a measure of quality (Danielson and McGreal, 2000; Kennedy, 2010; Montgomery, 1999; Pollock, 2012), contending that if evaluation is carried out according to clear parameters, positive appraisal can be achieved. Teachers can learn and develop during such quality assessment exercises, providing their relationship with the assessor/s allows a sharing of information between the parties involved and any existing power relationships are not used in order to influence outcomes. Because it relates to school and individual accountability, teacher evaluation is generally management-driven and has value for the institution in that it allows access to the working classroom environment which might not be available on a daily basis. Classroom observation can also have a great deal of value for the observers who, it is hoped, having received suitable and relevant training, are able to learn from each lesson observed.

Although fewer books seem to have been written in relation to observation and feedback in an SLE context, the principles above generally seem to apply. Randall with Thornton's book (2001) is a well-cited resource that is frequently used by those who advise and support teachers, and they, along with others such as Rea-Dickins and Germaine (1992), who introduced some early ideas relating to teacher evaluation from a teacher education perspective, all provide useful insights into observation. However, with the notable exception of Farr (2010) there are few books focusing on feedback in SLE, although a number of articles (e.g. Copland, 2008; Kurtoglu-Hooton, 2008) advise on the best way to use feedback as a teacher education tool. It seems that the only volume currently in publication that investigates research into observation and feedback with clear links to SLE is Howard et al. (2014) which responds to participants' voices and advocates ways in which the process can be made a more positive experience for all those involved.

One of the key points to take away from the ongoing debate concerning observation and feedback is that it forms an important learning process for those involved, and, if viewed as such, can be of inestimable value to observers, observees and learners. For example, writing from an American mainstream education perspective, Wei and Pecheone claim that teaching performance assessments (TPAs) have innovative appeal and a *'formative impact on teacher learning and instructional practice'* (2010, p. 71), stating that observation during teaching placements is indispensable to programmes where teachers gain credentials, with their strength lying in the evaluation instruments used. Assuming that these instruments have been developed with the individual appraisee in mind and that the process focuses on professional development rather than judgement, such views should transfer to the evaluation of in-service and SLE teachers.

Problems of observation and feedback

Sykes and Winchell (2010, p. 201) confirm that there is much variation between teachers and their degree of effectiveness, claiming that it is important to be able to evaluate them so that ineffective teachers can be '*deselected*'. However, despite the importance of teacher appraisal, Kennedy (2010, p. 1) suggests that the process is not necessarily effective: '*probably no other profession is subjected to more assessments with less effect than is the teaching profession*'. Kennedy argues that school administrators have long been trying to find ways of discriminating between good and bad teachers and suggests that there are two central problems (2010, p. 226):

1 Current criteria for defining teacher quality sometimes contradict; for example, teachers are supposed to be role models in the classroom at the same time as being '*efficient and goal-oriented*'.

2 Classroom events are difficult to capture on paper, and must be '*inferred from sequences or patterns of events*'. Wragg et al. (1996) refer to this as being high inference, where it is important that the observer exercise subjective judgement.

To these more holistic problems can be added other key concerns, such as the use of often inappropriate observation schedules where teachers are judged on a subjective basis by ticks on a form (Peterson, 2000) which can potentially distract, requiring the observer to focus on criteria which may have little relevance to a particular setting. Evaluation systems are also seen as being elaborate and inapplicable (Tusting, 2012) adding difficulties generated by extensive paperwork.

A further problem in relation to the use of classroom observation during teacher evaluation is the Observer's Paradox (Labov, 1972): the reason for observation is to watch people as they operate in their natural environment, but the presence of an observer causes fundamental changes to that environment, particularly in a restricted classroom context. However, not everyone agrees that this is problematic, as, in a discussion about ethnographic research, Monahan and Fisher argue that there are benefits of '*observer effects*', stating that:

> Staged performances should be warmly accepted as gifts from informants; they are valuable treasures of meaning, abundantly wrapped in abundant layers of interest, assumption and concern; they are alluring conceits overflowing with interpretive possibility. (2010, p. 12)

They claim that it is the observer's task to analyse and interpret such a performance thoroughly because of the volume of information it provides about how participants wish to be viewed and understood and anecdotal evidence does indeed suggest that this may be the case. Monahan and Fisher (2010) also suggest that self-censorship and participant behaviour modification can be used to advantage, while data triangulation should effectively address incidences where such practices are apparent. However, there is still a very distinct possibility that classroom observations are geared towards the observer (Howard, 2008) and are not an accurate reflection of a teacher's regular pedagogic practice. As such they could be viewed as an unrepresentative snapshot of the events that take place in the classroom, where the teacher may favour safe, low-risk classroom activities which he/she has used many times previously.

Feedback also has attendant problems. There is much at stake in the feedback meeting for the teacher whose lesson is being assessed and who risks failure or even loss of job and for the observer, who has a dual role of supporter/advisor and evaluator, this is a considerable responsibility. Unlike other professions, such as counselling, which require extensive training in how to interact with clients, there is a lack of formal training for supervisors in how to conduct feedback in SLE contexts (Bailey, 2006 p.3). Many SLE observers find themselves ill-equipped for the task, as often they are placed in supervisory positions because of their teaching experience which does not always equate to supervisory expertise (Farr, 2011 p. 23). A key concern is that feedback should be delivered in such a way as to support the learning experience (Copland, 2008; Kurtoglu-Hooton, 2008) and various studies have highlighted the multifaceted complexity of negotiating the discourse of the feedback event (Copland, 2011; Donaghue, this volume; Vasquez and Reppen, 2007; Wajnryb, 1998). Pollock's (2012) description of feedback as the hinge that joins teaching and learning is apt because unless it is delivered carefully, feedback can potentially sever the teacher from the classroom.

Organization of the book

We originally intended to organize this book according to the people involved in the evaluation process, that is, evaluators, pre-service teachers, in-service teachers and students. As we read the chapters, however, we realized that the strength of themes emerging suggested an alternative arrangement. All chapters in this volume are united by one dominant and underpinning theme: the importance of reflection and self-evaluation in allowing teachers scope to make choices about changes to their practice. Other emergent themes suggested the four sections: exploring different approaches to evaluation; tools to promote investigation and collaboration; a focus on the discourse of feedback and participants' responses to evaluation. We believe that this organization provides a useful orientation because it supplies readers with ways of looking at evaluation from different perspectives.

Part 1: Approaches to SLE evaluation

The chapters in Part 1 of this volume offer different approaches to teacher evaluation which, by affording opportunities for dialogic reflection, maximize the potential for development and learning in teacher evaluation processes. In Chapter 1, Steve Mann and Steve Walsh argue that reflection is essential in promoting professional development, contending that ongoing and systematic spoken, collaborative, data-led forms of reflection are likely to be more successful in negotiating institutional appraisal and will give teachers the chance to make choices about changes to their practice. The authors suggest a number of tools and processes which can be used to stimulate self- and-peer evaluation and provide examples of two in particular: cooperative development and stimulated recall interview. Cooperative development is shown to be productive as the authors analyse extracts from a group of teachers discussing a master's assignment and illustrate how one of the participants talks herself to a clearer sense of focus and direction through dialogue with others. Discourse extracts from teachers engaged in stimulated recall show how videoed lessons give teachers the opportunity to engage in dialogue and to reflect and fine-tune their thinking. Mann and Walsh show how these processes enable collaboration and self-evaluation, resulting in engagement and learning, a powerful combination for teacher evaluation.

The importance of reflection, collaboration and self-evaluation is extended in Chapter 2 as Leo Mercado and Steve Mann consider the role of mentoring in teacher evaluation and development. Focusing on novice teachers with little training, the authors propose an innovative and systematic mentoring approach aimed at creating opportunities for self- and peer-evaluation to help beginner teachers learn about their new roles. They argue that teachers must be central in an integrated and multidimensional evaluation process and contend that by participating in an action-orientated approach to appraisal, teachers will develop autonomy and self-efficacy. Data extracts show how professional development opportunities catering for new teachers' needs and preferences were created and how dialogic opportunities were set up between mentees, mentor teachers and mentor supervisors, affording mutually beneficial learning opportunities. The result was teachers who enjoyed their work, met their students' needs and stayed in the teaching profession.

In Chapter 3, Mick Randall concentrates the focus on observation and feedback, a process central to teacher development and evaluation and one which he believes has a primary function of enabling change and growth. Randall discusses approaches to observation which have been influenced by educational research and teacher management, maintaining that the central concept which has fuelled observation practice is the desire to be 'objective,' resulting in a voluminous bank of instruments designed either to record what happens in the classroom or to rationally identify strengths and weaknesses. While Randall believes the underlying motivation for objectivity is sound, he argues that taking a non-judgemental stance, listening and empathy are more important in providing opportunities for teacher support and development.

Part 2: Tools to promote investigation and collaboration

Reflection and dialogue again emerge as dominant themes in Part 2, although the focus of this section is on specific tools to foster reflection and learning during the evaluation process. In Chapter 4, Radhika Iyer-O'Sullivan proposes that the teacher and observer focus should be on critical incidents during feedback meetings rather than on the perhaps more common approach of narrating events chronologically, which can often lead to participants focusing solely on negative aspects of the observed lesson. Critical incidents are moments or events that occur unexpectedly during a lesson and which can have either a positive or negative impact on the subsequent progress of that lesson. The author contends that when an incident is critically examined and probed, the entire process of planning and teaching the lesson is discussed and this depth of analysis can produce deep reflection on teaching. The chapter explores the use of critical incidents with both novice and in-service teachers, illustrated by data extracts from feedback meetings which show that teachers and observers can use critical incidents to explore and understand their teaching.

In Chapter 5, Marion Engin examines how objects and artefacts such as lesson plans, running commentaries and transcriptions of feedback sessions can mediate and scaffold teacher learning. The discussion in this chapter views learning as sociocultural in that it takes place through mediation between a more competent other (the trainer), the trainee and the object to be learnt (knowledge about teaching). Drawing on research carried out into scaffolding in a pre-service teacher training context, the author examines how construction of knowledge can be mediated and scaffolded through objects and artefacts, considering specifically the role of physical artefacts in the learning process. Research data show a clear relationship between artefacts and talk, with the artefact acting as a catalyst for stimulating thinking and talk about teaching, which is vital for the construction of knowledge. Engin also discusses areas for further research into using physical artefacts as scaffolding objects in teacher evaluation.

In Chapter 6, Phil Quirke outlines a seven-stage teacher appraisal programme which focuses on appraisal and professional development, a scheme which aims to enhance teacher practice through reflection in a structured framework. The programme involves teachers collecting data from multiple sources in the form of portfolios or dossiers over the course of an academic year and discussions with a supervisor in a systematic cycle of development and appraisal. The centrality of the teacher and the concern with the teacher's professional and personal well-being that this scheme foregrounds echo themes in other chapters of this volume.

Part 3: A focus on discourse

Part 3 of this volume reflects the importance of both the feedback event itself and the discourse with which it is constructed. Feedback is arguably central to the evaluation process as this event affords opportunities for talk and reflection. However, as discussed earlier, feedback discourse is often difficult to manage and negotiate, a fact highlighted in all three chapters of this section. In Chapter 7, Helen Donaghue focuses on supervisors' talk in post-observation meetings, looking specifically at variance between supervisors' espoused style of supervision and their actual talk. The author suggests that this is largely due to contextual factors and constraints and recommends that teacher evaluation processes be monitored in order to identify if institutional processes are limiting or changing the way that supervisors give (or want to give) feedback.

In Chapter 8, Fiona Copland draws on a linguistic ethnographic study of group feedback conferences on in-service courses, focusing on evaluative talk and illustrating a number of approaches used by trainers and trainees to deliver positive and negative evaluation. Although evaluative talk is mostly straightforward criticism or praise, Copland demonstrates how a questioning phase supports a different kind of evaluative talk, one that provides affordances to the trainer and trainees to discuss aspects of the lesson in more detail and to tease out trainees' understandings of the weaknesses in their teaching practice and how it can be improved. Copland suggests, therefore, that questions are a particularly valuable resource for identifying trainees' understandings of weaknesses in their lessons and that developing trainers' proficiency in asking questions, particularly when these questions develop dialogic talk, is a potential area for development in trainer training and one which could support more effective feedback.

In Chapter 9, Neil Hunt contests the view of observation and feedback as an unassailable tool in the process of teacher education. Recognizing that for student teachers the experience of the observation–feedback cycle can be a useful aspect of teacher education, Hunt suggests that it can also produce a sense of intense stress and tension, perhaps because of an unspoken recognition by student teachers that the main aims of the cycle are disciplinary in nature. Hunt uses observation notes and transcripts of feedback discussions to explore how the author (as mentor) and a student teacher co-construct her teacher identity. He looks at the way in which the discursive emphasis on organization of space, teacher speech and the construction of relations produces a restricted teacher identity. Results lead the author to argue that the central role of lesson observation is to normalize, assess and position student teachers within a regulatory framework.

Part 4: Participant responses

In the last section of this volume, participants in the evaluation process are given a voice. The three chapters in this part report on research carried out among teachers and appraisers in different contexts providing recommendations to make the evaluation of SLE teachers more meaningful for all involved. In Chapter 10, Mick King reports on research carried out with appraisers and experienced teachers. Although the respondents in his study found the evaluation process stressful, the majority believed it to be valuable in that it provides quality assurance and useful information for management, encourages personal development and enhances the quality of teaching in an institution. Despite this positive overall view, many respondents described problems such as unskilled and biased appraisers, inappropriate appraisal systems and unrepresentative observations. Respondents also raised issues such as administrative inaction which allowed poor teachers to remain in their posts unchallenged. King encourages a review of current evaluation practices to determine what changes need to be implemented to encourage teacher support and concludes the chapter by recommending proper training in appraisal.

In Chapter 11, Wayne Trotman proposes the use of peer observation as an alternative to the more hierarchical trajectory common to teacher evaluation. Trotman believes that peer observation is a form of research activity as it can enhance teachers' understanding of teaching and result in positive change to classroom practice. The focus of peer observation is on observing a colleague's lesson to gain an understanding of a specific aspect of teaching, learning or classroom interaction and the process is less judgemental and more about self-reflection and awareness. Trotman draws on research carried out with SLE teachers in a tertiary institution who were involved in a peer observation scheme. Analysis of participants' written descriptive and reflective accounts of peer observations shows that professional development occurred in the form of learning outcomes from observation of peers. The author concludes the chapter with two main conclusions: first, participants in his study preferred observing and being observed by peers to being observed by an 'expert' and second, teachers acquired knowledge from peer observations.

Finally, in Chapter 12, Amanda Howard argues that it is important to give all participants in the evaluation process a voice. Drawing on research into observation with in-service teachers, Howard finds that observers have a relatively strong voice but that this is not always the case for teachers and learners. Some teachers in her study were fairly passive throughout the evaluation process and did not expect to have a voice. Teachers also aimed to minimize the observer's voice during feedback by teaching a lesson specifically aimed at the preferences of that observer. Some teachers, however, welcomed the opportunity to talk with an observer and felt that they did have a clear voice. The author found that the least vocal group were the learners. Howard concludes by recommending that teachers assume more participatory roles in evaluation in order to give them greater voice and promote professional development. She also recommends that the importance of learner input is recognized and actively sought.

Conclusion

Teacher evaluation is a practice that has a significant impact on the lives of the majority of teachers and the voices of practitioners deserve to be more thoroughly represented in the literature. It is hoped that the description and investigation of current practice and research provided by the authors of this volume will offer greater insight into the evaluation of teachers and the suggestions and recommendations provided in the following chapters will help to maximize the potential of teacher evaluation in SLE.

References

Bailey, K. (2001), 'Observation', in R. Carter and D. Nunan (eds), *The Cambridge Guide to Teaching English to Speakers of Other Languages*. Cambridge: Cambridge University Press, pp. 114–119.

———. (2006), *Language Teacher Supervision: A Case-Based Approach*. Cambridge: Cambridge University Press.

Copland, F. (2008), 'Deconstructing the discourse: Understanding the feedback event', in S. Garton and K. Richards (eds), *Professional Encounters in TESOL: Discourses of Teachers in Teaching*. Basingstoke: Palgrave, pp. 5–23.

———. (2011), 'Negotiating face in feedback conferences: A linguistic ethnographic analysis'. *Journal of Pragmatics*, 43, 3832–3843.

Danielson, C. and McGreal, T.L. (2000) *Teacher Evaluation to Enhance Professional Practice*. Alexandria, VA: ASCD and Educational Testing Service

Department of Education and Science for England and Wales (1985), *Quality Education (Teacher Efficiency) Review*.

Downey, C., Steffy, B. E., English, F. W., Frase, L. E. and Poston, W. K. (2004), *The Three-Minute Classroom Walkthrough: Changing School Supervisory Practice One Teacher at a Time*. Thousand Oaks, CA: Corwin Press.

Edge, J. and Richards, K. (1998), 'Why best practice is not good enough'. *TESOL Quarterly*, 32 (3), 569–576.

Farr, F. (2011), *The Discourse of Teaching Practice Feedback: A Corpus-Based Investigation of Spoken and Written Modes*. Abingdon: Routledge.

Howard, A. (2008), 'Teachers being observed: Coming to terms with classroom appraisal', in S. Garton and K. Richards (eds), *Professional Encounters in TESOL: Discourses of Teachers in Teaching*. Basingstoke: Palgrave, pp. 87–104.

——, Donaghue, H. and Burke, L. (eds.) (2014), *Participant Voices: Observation in Educational Settings*. Abu Dhabi: HCT Press.

Kennedy, M. (2010), 'Approaches to annual performance assessment', in M. Kennedy (ed.), *Teacher Assessment and the Quest for Teacher Quality: A Handbook*. San Francisco, CA: Jossey Bass, pp. 225–249.

Kurtoglu-Hooton, N. (2008), 'The design of post-observation feedback and its impact on student teachers', in S. Garton and K. Richards (eds), *Professional Encounters in TESOL: Discourses of Teachers in Teaching*. Basingstoke: Palgrave, pp. 24–41.

Labov, W. (1972), *Sociolinguistic Patterns*. Pennsylvania: University of Pennsylvania Press.

Monahan, T. and Fisher, J. A. (2010), 'Benefits of "observer effects": Lessons from the field'. *Qualitative Research*, 10 (3), 357–376.

Montgomery, D. (1999), *Positive Teacher Appraisal through Classroom Observation*. London: David Fulton Press.

Peterson, K. D. (2000), *Teacher Evaluation: A Comprehensive Guide to New Directions and Practices*, 2nd edn. Thousand Oaks, CA: Corwin Press.

Pollock, J. E. (2012), *Feedback: The Hinge That Joins Teaching and Learning*. Thousand Oaks, CA: Corwin.

Randall, M. with Thornton, B. (2001), *Advising and Supporting Teachers*. Ambridge: Cambridge University Press

Rea-Dickins, P. and Germaine, K. (1992), *Evaluation*. Oxford: Oxford University Press.

Richards, J. C., Platt, J. and Platt, H. (1992), *Longman Dictionary of Language Teaching and Applied Linguistics*, 2nd edn. London: Longman.

Rinvolucri, M. (2002), 'Fashioned by our students', in J. Edge (ed.), *Continuing Professional Development: Some of our Perspectives*. Canterbury: International Association of Teachers of English as a Foreign Language, pp. 90–96.

Sykes, G. and Winchell, S. (2010), 'Assessing for teacher tenure', in M. Kennedy (ed.), *Teacher Assessment and the Quest for Teacher Quality: A Handbook*. San Francisco, CA: Jossey Bass, pp. 201–224.

Tusting, K. (2012), 'Learning accountability literacies in educational workplaces: Situated learning and processes of commodification'. *Language and Education*, 26 (2), 121–138.

Vasquez, C. and Reppen, R. (2007), 'Transforming practice: Changing patterns of participation in post-observation meetings'. *Language Awareness*, 16, 153–172.

Wajnryb, R. (1994), *The Pragmatics of Feedback: A Study of Mitigation in the Supervisory Discourse of TESOL Teacher Educators*, PhD. Macquarie.

——. (1998), 'Telling it like it isn't – Exploring an instance of pragmatic ambivalence in supervisory discourse'. *Journal of Pragmatics*, 29, 531–544.

Watson-Davis, R. (2009), *Lesson Observation Pocketbook*. Alresford, Hampshire: Teachers' Pocketbooks.

Wei, R. C. and Pecheone, R. L. (2010), 'The assessment for learning in preservice teacher education: Performance-based assessments', in M. Kennedy (ed.), *Teacher Assessment and the Quest for Teacher Quality: A Handbook*. San Francisco, CA: Jossey Bass, pp. 69–132.

Wragg, E. C., Wikeley, F. J., Wragg, C. M. and Haynes, G. S. (1996), *Teacher Appraisal Observed*. London: Routledge.

PART ONE
Key Approaches

CHAPTER ONE

Reflective Dimensions of CPD: Supporting Self-Evaluation and Peer Evaluation

Steve Mann and Steve Walsh

Introduction

This chapter makes the argument that a reflective dimension is essential in promoting continuing professional development (CPD). The professional life of a teacher can easily become dominated by top-down directives, appraisals, changes in teaching materials and assessment criteria. However, despite the various constraints, requirements and standardized procedures, teachers usually have some scope to make choices and changes to their practice. One of the ways in which such changes are brought about is through reflective practice (RP), a process which helps teachers make appropriate adjustments to their methodology, adapt and supplement materials and create as ideal as possible an experience for language learners. Although the emphasis has often been on written processes of RP, this chapter makes the case that spoken and collaborative forms of reflection are equally, if not more, important. It comments on the range of reflective tools available in CPD.

The chapter is divided into three main parts. The first part reviews contributions about the nature of reflective practice and its importance in creating opportunities for self-evaluation. In doing this, we consider research related to CPD support for English language teaching (ELT) teachers and examine whether reflective practice is a key component. The second part of the chapter then provides detail on the range of tools and processes that can promote self- and peer-evaluation, commenting on how a data-led and systematic approach to reflection can make reflective practice less of a vague notion. The third part of the chapter shares two examples of reflection in action in order to exemplify our call for more data-led accounts of how reflection gets done.

This chapter furthers the arguments made in Mann and Walsh (2013) where we propose a more evidence-based and data-led approach to RP. In the 2013 article, we draw on existing examples of systematic approaches to reflection (e.g. Korthagen and Wubbels, 1995; Walsh, 2011) in order to provide examples and comment on the range of possibilities for encouraging reflection and self-evaluation. In this chapter, we use the term *continuing professional development* to encompass the whole spectrum of training, education and development. This ranges from pre-service teacher education that foregrounds a reflective dimension (e.g. Edge and Mann, 2013) to in-service possibilities (e.g. Malderez and Wedell, 2007). In all phases of a teacher's career it is important to maintain and encourage a reflective dimension so that there is both growth and maintenance of an ELT teacher's sense of '*plausibility*' (Prabhu, 1990) and ability to engage in the provision of appropriate methodology (Holliday, 1994).

Reflection, reflective practice and self-evaluation

This section reviews literature related to reflective practice and its importance for encouraging and promoting self-evaluation. It foregrounds two aspects of RP: first, the importance of a data-led focus on local context; second, the importance of collaborative and cooperative processes in connecting various forms of knowledge and experience.

It is worth beginning this section by making clear that there are a number of accounts that question the value of RP and that see problems with its institutional nature (e.g. Akbari, 2007; Gray and Block, 2012; Hobbs, 2007). Mann and Walsh (2013) provide a response to this 'worried' literature; in sum, our position is that RP is still potentially valuable but that it needs to be more systematic, more data-led, less individual and less dependent on solely written forms. We also believe that teacher educators need to set an example by engaging in RP themselves.

Although there have been criticisms of RP, other studies have established that teachers who employ reflective practice are better able to monitor learners and make appropriate, real-time decisions to respond to changing contexts (McMeniman et al., 2003; Yost et al., 2000). The TDTR (Teachers Develop Teachers Research) series of conferences helped provide a platform for reflective practice and self-evaluation and the resulting publications showcase good examples of how teacher research projects fuel reflection, self-evaluation and teacher development (De Decker and Vanderheiden, 1999; Edge and Richards, 1993; Field et al., 1997; Head, 1998). Roberts (1998) also puts forward a strong argument that professional development is only possible through a reflection process that puts self-monitoring and self-evaluation at the heart of things; he sees these processes as *'the only possible basis for long-term change'* (Roberts, 1998, p. 305). However, Raths and Lyman (2003) argue that teacher trainees need guidance in taking on responsibility for self-evaluation. In response to this challenge, Mann (2004) provides an account of how experienced teachers can combine different evaluative lenses (self-evaluation, peer evaluation and learner evaluation) to make sense of their practice.

In recognizing the importance of RP, we concur with Zwozdiak-Myers (2012, p. 3) who states:

> Central to your development as a teacher is your commitment and capacity to analyse and evaluate what is happening in your lessons and to use your professional judgement both to reflect and act upon these analysis and evaluations to improve pupil learning and the quality of your teaching.

The twin poles of reflection ('to reflect') and action ('to act') are at the heart of the CPD enterprise. Julian Edge makes this clear in his most recent book (2011) and he employs a central metaphor based on the individual stories of Icarus and Narcissus. You probably know these stories but, as a reminder, Icarus had wings and flew too close to the sun, despite his father's instructions that he should follow him. Narcissus stayed too long observing himself (a reflection in a pool) and he put down roots. They are both seen as failures. After all, they both display human traits (self-obsession and hubris) against which we need to guard. However, Edge argues that, together, they represent the dynamic twin aspects of our lives and professional practice; it is precisely the dialogue between reflection and action that propels us forward in our professional practice; it is *'the mutually-shaping interactions between our roots and our wings, our self-knowledge and our environmental knowledge'* that provide awareness so that we can *'commit ourselves to future action based on that combined awareness'* (Edge, 2011, p. 17). We need to know ourselves and our context (through reflection) in order to act appropriately in that context. In other words, we need to reflect on our actions and beliefs ourselves in order to take appropriate next steps.

The origins of RP and our current position that reflective practice has value in education can be traced back to Dewey (1933) and Schön (1983). The importance of reflection in an individual's attempts to consciously act on and with his or her environment is fairly well established (see Nunan, 1989). In ELT teacher education, Richards and Nunan (1990) and Wallace (1991) were important in cementing the view that RP was a key process in CPD. Johnson's (2006) paper further consolidated the position that teacher education should recognize and promote the sociocultural and co-constructed nature of both language classrooms and CPD more generally by promoting and developing RP. Some have argued that self-direction and some form of autonomy is as important in teacher development as it is in language learning (see Nunan and Lamb, 1996). We argue here that self-evaluation is a key trait in teachers who are able to take responsibility for personal learning and development (see also Brockett and Hiemstra, 1991). There is a strong sense that it is both important for a teacher's well-being and professional growth to keep reflective practice as a viable and active process in education (Bailey et al., 2001, Stuart and Thurlow, 2000).

However, although it is now a fairly orthodox position to say that we should make space for reflection when we can, teacher education faces a perennial dilemma in that it needs to balance the giving of input and knowledge (theories, concepts, models, taxonomies, empirical studies) with more individual and personal attempts to make sense of all this information. If education falls into the trap of a form of training that 'imposes' received knowledge (from the outside), it cannot hope to create space for reflection working on and with various forms of knowledge. Bowen (2004) and Tomlinson (2003) argue that teachers should not be simply pushed in predetermined directions. This creates a problem where what counts as important knowledge is imposed 'from the outside'. Instead, space needs to be kept for a self-evaluation process where teachers can explore their beliefs as well as the critical, personal and moral dimensions of teaching (see Miller, 2004). The careful consideration of our values and how these play out in our classrooms is an ongoing process of accounting for and making conscious our values (Johnston, 2003) and personhood (Mori, 2003).

Reflection, then, connects our experience with what others tell us about the world (e.g. how language is acquired, what is high frequency lexis, whether we need to teach intonation). If we accept that knowledge is not in any simple way transferred from educators to teachers (Richards, 1998) and that knowledge is co-constructed through engagement with experience, reflection and collaboration (Roberts, 1998), teachers need opportunities and appropriate tools for reflection, so that both received knowledge and experiential knowledge can be acquired (Wallace, 1991).

We said in the introduction that this chapter picks up two of the main themes in Mann and Walsh (2013) in trying to make RP less vague: first, it needs to be more data-led; second, more attention should be given to collaborative opportunities for reflection.

In terms of the first theme, Farrell (2008) argues that systematic data collection has a better chance of helping teachers to reflect and self-evaluate. Ideally this should be the teacher's own data but other teachers' data can also provide a useful basis for reflection. Use of data helps make the invisible aspects of practice more visible. Such engagement helps teachers '*make their beliefs and assumptions about their practice evident in their analysis of their teaching*' (Farrell, 2008, p. 2). Our argument elsewhere (Mann and Walsh, 2011; Mann and Walsh, 2013) has been that reflective practice is potentially vague if teachers are not encouraged to collect and work with data. It is the small details (in the data) that prompt reflection and make it possible for small changes (often at the level of 'tweaks') to be implemented and evaluated (van Lier, 2000). In this chapter we are emphasizing van Lier's view of '*ecological*' research and inquiry, whereby teachers should pay '*attention to the smallest detail of the interaction*' so that '*they can learn to "read" the environment to notice such details*' (Van Lier, 2000, p. 11). Paying attention to small details in the local context is helped through a data-led approach to reflection.

In relation to the second theme, we suggest that RP needs to be rebalanced, away from a reliance on written forms to take more account of collaborative and cooperative processes. Reflection is usually seen as a process of inner dialogue and '*conversation with self*' (Prawat, 1991). This is a kind of in-the-head reflection (a cognitive space where the language teacher develops awareness of practice) but RP is also something that can be done collaboratively (Beaumont and O'Brien, 2000; Bolton, 2002).

Putting the two themes together, we adopt the position that taking greater account of spoken, collaborative forms of reflection allows for a more dialogic, data-led and collaborative approach to reflective practice. Such a process would encourage a view of reflection as an ongoing activity, where teachers are more likely to be successful in negotiating institutional appraisal (in other words 'top down' evaluation of performance), as well as 'day to day' teaching. Collaborative and cooperative processes can also help sustain and invigorate individual reflection and development. They help an individual in the shaping and reshaping of knowledge and provide opportunities for articulating and connecting versions of external knowledge (received knowledge) with the individual's context (situated knowledge) and the individual (personal, practical and usable knowledge).

Teams, critical friends, peer processes and collaborative efforts allow teacher development to become less of a top-down professional process (Mann, 2005) or leave the individual in isolation. Instead those involved with training, education and CPD need to encourage more bottom-up efforts (e.g. Cheng and Wang, 2004). These collaborative bottom-up processes are more likely to sustain viable self-evaluation. Prabhu (2003) argues that a teacher who is engaged in self-evaluation is better able to cope with change and see it as developmental.

Self-evaluation through reflective practice still has the potential to break down the research–practice divide (Clarke, 1994) and help the teacher to narrow the gap between theory and practice. Reflection can lead to more sustained research (e.g. action research) and this also helps provide more bottom-up accounts of teaching.

Reflection and reflective tools

At one level, reflective practice is simply a normal process for good teachers (Wallace, 1991) and what *'caring teachers have always done'* (Bailey, 1997, p. 1). However, more structured or systematic attempts to carry out reflection are different in nature and this is where particular tools have a role to play. There are a number of fairly well-established tools and procedures that teachers can employ such as peer observation (Day, 1990) and journal writing (Gebhard, 1999) that are usually featured in accounts of developing RP. Richards and Farrell (2005) and Bailey et al. (2001) provide useful overviews of other possibilities for the language teacher who is interested in sustained teacher development. Such reflective and critical processes encourage the individual teacher to articulate, understand and evaluate classroom methodology, aspects of the context (e.g. constraints and responses to these constraints), course and materials and the choices and resources that a teacher can employ or utilize.

Reflective tools are important in encouraging, prompting and structuring the connection between different forms of knowledge. They allow the teacher to work with received knowledge and connect this to more experiential, personal and local knowledge (Freeman and Hawkins, 2004). As we have stated earlier, CPD needs to create space for reflection to find a relation between various forms of knowledge. These include personal knowledge (Clandinin and Connelly, 1987), practical knowledge (Golombek, 1998), experiential knowledge (Wallace, 1991), local knowledge (Allwright, 2003) and usable knowledge (Lageman, 2002). Acknowledging and putting emphasis on such diverse local and personal forms of knowledge allows for alternatives to a transmission of knowledge framework to be explored (Fanselow, 1988).

In the paragraphs which follow, we offer a summary and evaluation of the more widely used reflective tools.

Video and audio recording. The use of audio and video can help focus on aspects of teaching. Bailey et al. (2001) provide guidance on how to use video and audio to promote self-evaluation. McMeniman et al. (2003) is an interesting example of how video helps teachers focus on their various knowledge bases. Richards and Farrell (2005) also see the process of using audio or video data as an important element of self-evaluation and they provide useful suggestions (see 2005, pp. 42–47). Richards (2003, pp. 174–230) supplies helpful advice on preparing for video and audio-taping and Ebsworth et al. (2004) show how video analysis can create opportunities for experiential learning.

Stimulated recall. Stimulated recall uses video or audio data to provide particular procedures for the recall of particular changes or events in the language classroom (see Richards, 2004; Walsh, 2011). These recordings are discussed with a *'critical friend'* as a means of developing more fine-grained and subtle understandings of local practices. Such procedures help the teacher distinguish between the teaching event or incident, the recollection of the event and a possible response or future action. Stimulated recall is particularly helpful in bringing tacit understandings and unconscious actions to the surface through articulation. We feature this reflective tool in the following section.

Critical incident analysis. Critical incident analysis (e.g. Tripp, 1993) has some similarities with stimulated recall, but does not usually employ video or audio recordings. Instead, the focus is on problematic or critical incidents, or even more '*commonplace events*' (Richards and Farrell, 2005, p. 114). These commonplace events can still be critical in the sense that they reveal underlying beliefs or motives. Tardy and Snyder (2004) also have procedures for helping teachers recall and work with particular incidents.

Materials analysis. Copland and Mann (2012) provide materials and tasks which encourage novice teachers to reflect on coursebooks and other teaching materials including the Internet. Changes in course design and materials can be developmental if there is time for evaluation (Tomlinson, 2003).

Questionnaires. The use of questionnaires in a process of ongoing self-evaluation is described by Smith (2005). In particular, she recommends the use of self-evaluation questionnaires in order to provide insight into evaluative processes.

Narratives. Narrative inquiry (Johnson and Golombek, 2002) prizes reflective writing and storytelling (Hazelrigg, 2005) and both written and spoken forms can provide the basis for reflective inquiry (Olson, 1995). Maley (2004) has employed narrative analysis as a useful reflective tool and Johnson and Golombek (2002) feature a wide range of teachers exploring their practice through range of techniques, as teachers use diaries and journals to develop personal and individual processes of self-evaluation.

Portfolios. Tucker et al. (2003) argue for the use of portfolios to challenge language teachers' reliance on summative evaluation. Velikova (2013) focuses on the importance of reflection promoted through a portfolio development framework where novice teachers record their experiences. Velikova shows how different aspects of the course (e.g. the interactions between novice teachers) are made more reflective experiences through the adoption of EPOSTL (the European Portfolio for Student Teachers of Languages). Pre-service teaching is necessarily a space that is dominated by evaluation but here the portfolio offers at least some possibilities for self- and peer evaluation. In other words, it can provide a balance where individuals and peers can assess their own competences and skills.

Team teaching. Team teaching can help establish collaborative partnerships (Wada and Brumby, 1994) and also opportunities for peer and self-evaluation. Johnston and Madejski (2004) give guidance for establishing collaborative team-teaching lessons. Bailey et al. (2001) provide a questionnaire (2001, p. 186) that can be used to foster discussion about the roles and expectations of team teaching.

Peer observation. Peer observation is a well-established aspect of many CPD programmes but is less common when teachers start work. Day (1990) and Bailey (2001) provide useful contributions in this area. Lengeling (2013) reminds us that we need to consider how such an observation process is managed. Her account is useful because she provides concrete suggestions for borrowing techniques from ethnography (the use of ethnographic notes). Mentor teachers (observers) are encouraged to use these ethnographic notes innovatively to enable the novice teachers to focus on the up-close detail of this lesson. Such a process encourages greater '*objectivity*' and '*estrangement*' for all parties. It is also worth looking at Roberts et al. (2003) for other ideas about how to employ ethnographic notes.

Interviewing. Interviewing other teachers can be a developmental process. Allen (2000) puts forward a strong argument that ethnographic interviewing can facilitate the development of peer understanding and self-awareness.

Focus groups. Focus groups create opportunities for evaluative discussion of learners, materials and methodology where understanding is co-constructed through groups and learning communities in schools (Roberts and Pruitt, 2003). Gibson (2002) provides advice on moving interaction away from moans and complaints to more focused discussion. Such groups might use books and articles as a catalyst for professional conversation (see Mahoney, 2005).

Critical friendship. Farrell (2001) promotes '*critical friendships*' (colleagues who help each other develop in a variety of ways) and supplies comment on how colleagues might develop sustainable critical friendships. This involves establishing ground rules such as timing and participant roles.

Collaborative peer conversations. Hawkins and Irujo (2004), Oprandy (2002) and Edge (2002) provide examples of collaborative peer conversations that are non-evaluative in nature. Edge (2002) demonstrates how '*cooperative development*' puts the focus on self-development and self-evaluation. This is achieved through adopting and becoming familiar with set agreed '*understander moves*' and we feature this reflective tool in the following section.

Individual writing. We have deliberately left this until last. This is because, for many, RP is presented as solely an individual and written practice. We absolutely agree that individual writing is a valuable tool and would not want readers to think that we are denigrating this choice in any way. Our purpose in this chapter is simply to give more attention to other more neglected aspects of RP. The individual reflective practitioner can find space and purpose through writing (see Appel, 1995). The process can prompt introspection, reflection and self-evaluation. Autobiographical writing can be a tool for growth and change for the teacher (see Shin, 2003). Richards and Farrell (2005, pp. 68–84) demonstrate a variety of forms of writing that offer a useful overview of the value of keeping a journal where notes and descriptions can promote reflection and self-evaluation. Journals and diaries (in private/paper form) are the preferred form for many. However, blogging (e.g. Siemens, 2004) and online journals (Towndrow, 2004) might allow for wider readership opportunities for collaboration and peer interaction as they are more public documents. Recently there has been increasing use of online social networking sites (e.g. My Space, Facebook, Ning) that function as mechanisms for interaction and support for teachers (see Hart and Steinbrecher, 2011).

Two examples of reflective tools in action

The following is an example of reflection and self-evaluation using cooperative development (Edge, 2002). In this extract, teachers are using cooperative development (CD) as a tool to make progress with teaching ideas related to a master's assignment. The reflection itself is not being assessed and the process is a vehicle for clarifying ideas.

One of the teachers (Jo) is speaking about her inability to decide on a specific topic focus for her assignment. In the following extracts we can see the process of speaking, understanding and '*hearing back*' (Mann, 2002, p. 199). Jo has been articulating her '*biggest challenge*' and does not see how she can produce anything meaningful in 3,000 words. In Extract 1 we hear her working on this puzzle:

Extract 1:

Jo:	I don't know how to (0.5) narrow it down because I think (.) how do you actually cut something down without (2.0) I think just looking at it within CLT so ignoring the post-method and audio-lingualism (.) but to be fair, you could kind of include those quickly with just a sort of a statement (.) you know not very much (.) so I suppose the main focus will be on CLT.
Gifty:	So now you are also probably looking at probably focusing on CLT?
Jo:	I think I have to because (1.0) I think that's one way of narrowing the focus.

Here we have an example of Jo '*talking herself into understanding*' (Mann, 2002, p. 199). However, we should also note Gifty's contribution in keeping the focus on Jo's emerging ideas. It enables Jo to keep working on her partial understandings and developing position. Jo continues to talk about different possible areas of focus and explores the potential pitfalls in each of her ideas. In expressing herself she is bringing together different forms of knowledge and experience. Finally, Jo talks herself to a clearer sense of focus and arrives at a possible interesting topic for the assignment:

Extract 2:

Jo: The history and literature of where grammar has (.) you know (1.0) the importance of grammar through different methods and approaches, current situation, a bit of a questionnaires and a potential for action research in terms of trying out different approaches with the group learners and seeing what they liked. That would work (.) let me write that down before I forget because that is actually **quite good!**

Here Jo works through the structure of the possible assignment and it is interesting to note the emphasis and perhaps surprise in her ringing positive evaluation. In this form of talk it is not the '*understander*' (Gifty) who does the evaluation. By concentrating on listening and trying to understand the Speaker's viewpoint, the Understander keeps the energy and concentration on the emerging idea. In fact, cooperative development explicitly asks understanders to resist their natural impulse to make evaluations or make suggestions in order to concentrate energy on the Speaker's self-evaluation. This might be difficult (for the Understanders might have ideas of their own). However, the discipline is to contain suggestions and ideas. Jo concludes this particular session by telling the Understanders how helpful the session has been. It has helped her develop her ideas and this is explicit in the final few words:

Extract 3:

Jo: Thank you! Thank you! That has actually quite helped! That really has helped (.) I'm surprised (.) because I came to this with (.) I mean I'd been thinking about this for some time and I'd been (.) and this week, since about Monday I've been trying to focus on this and I did. I mean I thought I'd focused a bit clearer, you know I thought I had some focus. But that has actually really helped. It was nice, thank you (.) thank you.

The second example employs data from a stimulated recall interview (see, for example, Lyle, 2003), which has the immediate advantage of allowing both parties to watch or listen to a segment of teaching and comment on it together. It is an excellent means of raising awareness about specific features of a teacher's professional practice. In its purest form, it is used to get practitioners to actually recall specific incidents and comment on them, but it can also be used as a stimulus to provide 'talking points' and promote discussion.

Here, we see the teacher, John, working with a group of adult learners and eliciting information about various pop-stars. The classroom interaction data are presented in the left-hand column, the teacher's reflective commentary in the right-hand column.

Extract 4:

(Teacher stops the activity)

T: so you can help me because I don't know some of these people er who's that who's that person in picture A?

I'm asking referential questions here because I didn't really know the answer to some of these. They just told me. These are genuine questions.

L: Mei Chung

T: Mei Chung. What does she do?

L: she's a pop singer=

T: =she's a a pop singer … from?

L: from Taiwan=

T: =Taiwan is she famous in lots of countries?

L: I think Taiwan and Hong Kong=

T: =uh uh and in Malaysia too?

L: yes

As John's own comments reflect, he is asking genuine or referential questions here in which there is a real exchange of information. As we can see from the interaction, in many respects the extract resembles casual conversation. Turn-taking is rapid (indicated by latching =) and there are requests for clarification (e.g. from?) and acknowledgement tokens (uh uh). It is not immediately evident who the teacher is: this could be two friends chatting and roles are fairly symmetrical. Perhaps one of the things John could have mentioned in his commentary is the fact that there are opportunities here for extending learner contributions and for eliciting further information. We might even argue that learning opportunities, in the form of speaking practice, have been missed in this short extract. Nonetheless, what this and other extracts show quite clearly is the relationship between classroom interaction and teachers' comments on it; this kind of data is both highly revealing and highly suited to the promotion of reflective practice.

It is clear from this short extract that stimulated recall is potentially a very powerful approach which has much to offer reflective practice, providing as it does an opportunity for teachers to use data to inform their reflections and then engage in dialogue to fine-tune their thinking. Even without the transcripts, much can be learned by participants and it is a methodology which brings together very nicely the various elements, which, we have argued, are necessary for RP to work effectively: tools, data and dialogue.

Stimulated recall is relatively easy to organize and relatively inexpensive; yet its potential for influencing professional development is enormous.

Conclusion

The purpose of this chapter was to make an argument for the importance of self-evaluation and how RP can enable this through the use of appropriate tools. We have considered literature which provides an insight on the importance of self-evaluation and RP in a teacher's growing sense of autonomy. In addition, the chapter has developed arguments established in Mann (2005), Walsh (2011) and Mann and Walsh (2013) that reflective practice has an important role to play in sustaining ongoing self-evaluation, especially through the constructivist nature of *'collaborative small groups'* (Bailey and Willet, 2004, p. 15). More collaborative types of RP have not been given the recognition that they deserve. We believe that teacher education and its predictable diet and the transfer of information can at least be supplemented by more formative evaluation and a sustained and ongoing dialogue (see Holland and Adams, 2002) based around data extracts. If this is the case, then teachers are more likely to end up being able to reflect and self-evaluate. However, there is a need for further empirical research into how teachers develop and build knowledge bases, including the influences and sources of these bases and the role RP has to play in this process. Such accounts will help to reveal personal, contextual, pedagogical, linguistic, institutional, intercultural and interpersonal knowledge and the way this is supported by various RP tools. Ideally, studies need to follow this development over a number of years.

We have argued that CPD programmes need to introduce teachers to the range of reflective tools and processes in order to encourage teacher-learning and engagement. Bottom-up teacher reflective practice is not only important for the individual language teacher but for the TESOL profession as well. Such CPD activities may renew commitment and interest in teaching and thereby help to prevent burnout (Maslach, 1982).

Our final comment is that teacher educators working in TESOL also need to show that they are committed to RP themselves. There are accounts by teacher educators that show such commitment. We would recommend Trappes-Lomax and Ferguson (2002) and Bartels (2005) as useful collections from language teacher educators who are committed to researching their own practice and reflecting on underlying principles.

References

Akbari, R. (2007), 'Reflections on reflection: A critical appraisal of reflective practices in L2 teacher education'. *System*, 35, 192–207.

Allen, L. Q. (2000), 'Culture and the ethnographic interview in foreign language teacher development'. *Foreign Language Annals*, 33 (2), 51–57.

Allwright, R. (2003), 'Exploratory practice: Rethinking practitioner research in language teaching'. *Language Teaching Research*, 7 (2), 113 – 114.

Appel, J. (1995). *Diary of a Language Teacher*. Oxford: Heinemann.

Bailey, K. (1997), 'Reflective teaching: Situating our stories'. *Asian Journal of English Language Teaching*, 7, 1–19.

———. (2001), 'Observation', in R. Carter and D. Nunan (eds), *The Cambridge Guide to Teaching English to Speakers of Other Languages*. Cambridge: Cambridge University Press, pp. 114–119.

Bailey, F. and Willet, J. (2004), 'Collaborative groups in teacher education', in M. Hawkins and S. Irujo (eds), *Collaborative Conversations among Language Teacher Educators*. Alexandria, VA: TESOL, pp. 15–32.

Bailey, K., Curtis, A. and Nunan, D. (2001), *Pursuing Professional Development: The Self as Source*. Boston, MA: Heinle and Heinle.

Bartels, N. (2005), *Applied Linguistics and Language Teacher Education*. New York: Springer.

Beaumont, M. and O'Brien, T. (2000), *Collaborative Research in Second Language Education*. Stoke-on-Trent: Trentham Books.

Bolton, G. (2002), *Reflective Practice, Writing and Professional Development*. London: Paul Chapman.

Bowen, T. (2004), Continuous professional development. *The One Stop Magazine*. http://www.onestopenglish.com/News/Magazine/Archive/continuous.htm. Checked 25 July 2005.

Brockett, R. G. and Hiemstra, R. (1991), *Self-direction in Adult Learning: Perspectives on Theory, Research, and Practice*. New York: Routledge.

Cheng, L. and Wang, H. (2004), 'Understanding professional challenges faced by Chinese teachers of English'. *TESL–EJ*, 7, 4. http://www-writing.berkeley.edu/tesl-ej/ej28/a2.html. Checked 25 July 2005.

Clandinin, D. J. and Connelly, F. M. (1987), 'Teachers' personal knowledge: What counts as 'personal' in studies of the personal'. *Journal of Curriculum Studies*, 19, 487–500.

Clarke, M. A. (1994), 'The dysfunctions of the theory–practice discourse'. *TESOL Quarterly*, 28 (1), 9–26.

Copland, F. and Mann, S. (2012), *Developing Materials: Inside and Outside the Coursebook*. Tokyo: ABAX Publishing.

Day, R. R. (1990), 'Teacher observation in second language teacher education', in J. C. Richards and D. Nunan (eds), *Second Language Teacher Education*. New York: Cambridge University Press, pp. 43–61.

De Decker, B. and Vanderheiden, M. (eds) (1999), Proceedings of the TDTR4 conference. CD–ROM available from: Centrum voor Levende Talen, Dekenstraat, B–3000 Leuven, Belgium.

Dewey, J. (1933), *How We Think: A Re-statement of the Relation of Reflective Thinking to the Education Process*. Boston: DC Heath and Co.

Ebsworth, M., Feknous, B., Loyet, D. and Zimmerman, S. (2004), 'Tape it yourself: Videotapes for teacher education'. *ELT Journal*, April 2004, 58 (2), 145–154.

Edge, J. (ed.) (2002), *Continuing Cooperative Development*. Ann Arbor, MI: University of Michigan Press.

———. (2011), *The Reflexive Teacher Educator in TESOL: Roots and Wings*. London: Routledge.

————. and Mann, S. (eds) (2013), *Innovations in Pre-service Education and Training for English Language Teachers*. London: British Council Brand and Design, Innovation Series.

————. and Richards, K. (eds) (1993), *Teachers Develop Teachers Research*. Oxford: Heinemann.

Fanselow, J. F. (1988), 'Let's see: Contrasting conversations about teaching'. *TESOL Quarterly*, 22 (1), 113–130.

Farrell, T. S. C. (2001), 'Critical friendships: Colleagues helping each other develop'. *ELT Journal*, 55 (4), 368–374.

————. (2008), 'Reflective practice in the professional development of teachers of adult English language learners'. *CAELA Network* (2008), 1–4.

Field, J., Graham, A., Griffiths, E. and Head, K. (eds) (1997), *Teachers Develop Teachers Research 2*. Whitstable: IATEFL.

Freeman, D. and Hawkins, M. (2004), 'Collaborative education as critical practice in teacher education', in M. Hawkins and S. Irujo (eds), *Collaborative Conversations among Language Teacher Educators*. Alexandria, VA: TESOL, pp. 1–13.

Gebhard, J. (1999), 'Problem posing and solving through action research', in J. Gebhard and R. Oprandy (eds), *Language Teaching Awareness: A Guide to Exploring Beliefs and Practices*. Cambridge: Cambridge University Press, pp. 35–58.

Gibson, B. (2002), 'Talking at length and depth: Learning from focus group discussions', in K. E. Johnson and P. Golombek (eds), *Teachers' Narrative Inquiry as Professional Development*. Cambridge: Cambridge University Press, pp. 91–107.

Golombek, P. (1998), 'A study of language teachers' personal practical knowledge'. *TESOL Quarterly*, 32 (3), 447–464.

Gray, J and Block, D. (2012), 'The marketisation of language teacher education and neoliberalism', in D. Block, J. Gray and M. Holborow (eds), *Neoliberalism and Applied Linguistics*. London: Routledge, pp. 114–143.

Hart, J. E. and Steinbrecher, T. (2011), 'OMG! exploring and learning from teachers' personal and professional uses of Facebook'. *Action in Teacher Education*, 33 (4), 320–328.

Hawkins, M. and Irujo, S. (2004), *Collaborative Conversations among Language Teacher Educators*. Alexandria, VA: TESOL.

Hazelrigg, A. (2005), 'Storytelling into understanding; middle school teachers work with text analysis and second language reading pedagogy', in N. Bartels (ed.), *Applied Linguistics and Language Teacher Education*. New York: Springer, pp. 325–340.

Head, K. (ed.) (1998), *Teachers Develop Teachers Research 3*. Whitstable: International Association of Teachers of English as a Foreign Language

Hobbs, V. (2007), 'Faking it or hating it: Can reflective practice be forced?'. *Reflective Practice*, 8 (3), 405–417.

Holland, P. and Adams, P. (2002), 'Through the horns of a dilemma between instructional supervision and the summative evaluation of teaching'. *International Journal of Leadership in Education*, 5 (3), 227–247.

Holliday, A. (1994), *Appropriate Methodology and Social Context*. Cambridge: Cambridge University Press.

Johnson, K. E. (2006), 'The sociocultural turn and its challenges for second language teacher education'. *Tesol Quarterly*, 40(1), 235–257.

—— and Golombek, P. (2002), *Teachers' Narrative Inquiry as Professional Development*. Cambridge: Cambridge University Press.

Johnston, B. (2003), *Values in English Language Teaching*. Mahwah, NJ: Lawrence Erlbaum.

—— and Madejski, B. (2004), 'A fresh look at team teaching'. *The Language Teacher*, 29, 2–7.

Korthagen, F. A. J. and Wubbels, T. (1995), 'Characteristics of reflective practitioners: towards an operationalization of the concept of reflection'. *Teachers and Teaching*, 1 (1), 51–72.

Lageman, E. C. (2002), *Usable Knowledge in Education Research*. http://www.spencer.org/publications/usable_knowledge_report_ecl_a.htm checked 25 July 2005.

Lengeling, M. (2013), 'Borrowing the use of ethnographic notes from the social sciences for classroom observation in central Mexico', in J. Edge and S. Mann (eds), *Innovations in Pre-Service Education and Training for English Language Teachers*. London: British Council, pp. 63–80.

Lyle, J. (2003), 'Stimulated recall: A report on its use in naturalistic research'. *British Educational Research Journal*, 29, 861–878.

Mahoney, D. (2005), 'Vignette', in J. C. Richards and T. Farrell (eds), *Professional Development for Language Teachers: Strategies for Teacher Learning*. Cambridge: Cambridge University Press, pp. 54–57.

Malderez, A. and Wedell, M. (2007), *Teaching Teachers: Processes and Practices*. London: Continuum.

Maley, A. (2004), '"Once Upon a time..." The conspiracy of narrative'. Major Article 6. *Humanistic Language Teaching Journal* Pilgrims. http://www.hltmag.co.uk/sept04/mart06.rtf checked 25 July 2005.

Mann, S. (2002), 'Talking ourselves into understanding', in K. E. Johnson and P. Golombek (eds), *Teachers' Narrative Inquiry as Professional Development*. Cambridge: Cambridge University Press, pp. 159–209.

——. (2004), 'Evaluation', in H. Harnisch and P. Swanton (eds), *Adults Learning Languages: A CILT Guide to Good Practice*, London: CILT (The National Centre for Languages), pp. 113–129.

——. (2005). 'The language teacher's development'. *Language Teaching*, 38, 103–18.

—— and Walsh, S. (2013), 'RP or 'RIP': A critical perspective on reflective practice'. *Applied Linguistics Review*, 4 (2), 289–312.

Maslach, D. (1982), *Burnout – the Cost of Caring*. London: Prentice Hall.

McMeniman, M., Cumming, J., Wilson, J., Stevenson, J. and Sim, C. (2003), *Teacher Knowledge in Action: The Impact of Educational Research*. Australia: Department of Education, Training and Youth Affairs.

Miller, P. (2004), 'Review of "values in English language teaching" '. *TESOL–EJ*. 7.2, http://www-writing.berkeley.edu/tesl-ej/ej26/r3.html checked 25 July 2005.

Mori, R. (2003), 'Personal growth in teacher development: A case study'. *JALT2003* at Shizuoka Conference Proceedings, 155–161.

Nunan, D. (1989), *Understanding Language Classrooms: A Guide for Teacher–Initiated Action*. New York: Prentice Hall.

—— and Lamb, C. (1996), *The Self-directed Teacher: Managing the Learning Process*. Cambridge: Cambridge University Press.

Olson, M. R. (1995), 'Conceptualizing narrative authority: Implications for teacher education'. *Teaching and Teacher Education*, 11, 119–135.

Oprandy, B. (2002), 'A counseling–learning perspective', In J. Edge (ed.),*Continuing Professional Development*. Whitstable, UK: International Association of Teachers of English as a Foreign Language (IATEFL), pp. 252–264.

Prabhu, N. S. (1990), 'There is no best method – Why?'. *TESOL Quarterly*, 24, 161–176.

——. (2003), 'An interview with Alan Maley'. *The Language Teacher*, 27, 3–7.

Prawat, R. (1991), 'Conversations with self and settings: A framework for thinking about teacher empowerment'. *American Educational Research Journal*, 28 (4), 737–757.

Raths, J. and Lyman, F. (2003), 'Summative evaluation of student teachers: An enduring problem'. *Journal of Teacher Education*, 54 (3), 206–216.

Richards, J. (1998), *Beyond Training*. Cambridge: Cambridge University Press.

——. (2004), 'Towards reflective teaching'. *The Language Teacher*, 33, 2–5.

Richards, K. (2003), *Qualitative Inquiry in TESOL*. New York: Palgrave Macmillan.

Richards, J. C. and Farrell, T. (2005), *Professional Development for Language Teachers: Strategies for Teacher Learning*. Cambridge: Cambridge University Press.

——. and Nunan, D. (eds) (1990), *Second Language Teacher Education*. New York: Cambridge University Press.

Roberts, J. (1998), *Language Teacher Education*. London: Arnold.

Roberts, S. and Pruitt, E. (2003), *Schools as Professional Learning Communities: Collaborative Activities and Strategies for Professional Development*. Thousand Oaks, CA: Sage.

Roberts, C., Byram, M. and Barro, A. (2003), *Language Learners as Ethnographers*. Buffalo, NY: Multilingual Matters. Modern Languages in Practice, 16.

Schön, D. A. (1983), *The Reflective Practitioner*. New York: Basic Books.

Shin, J. (2003), 'The reflective L2 writing teacher'. *ELT Journal*, 57 (1), 3–10.

Siemens, G. (2004), 'The art of blogging'. Presented at MADLAT Conference 22 October 2004. http://www.elearnspace.org/Articles/blogging/artofblogging1.htm checked 25 July 2005.

Smith, K. (2005), 'The use of self-evaluation in teacher training'. *The Language Teacher*, 34, 2–6.

Stuart, C. and Turlow, D. (2000), 'Making it their own: Presevice teachers' experiences, beliefs, and classroom practices'. *Journal of Teacher Education*, 51 (2), 113–121.

Tardy, C. and Snyder, B. (2004), '"That's why I do it": Flow and EFL teachers' practices'. *ELT Journal*, 58 (2), 118–128.

Tomlinson, B. (2003). Developing materials to develop yourself. *Humanising Language Teaching* 5 (3), http://www.hltmag.co.uk/jul03/mart1.htm checked 25 July 2005.

Towndrow, P. (2004). 'Reflections of an on-line tutor'. *ELT Journal*, 58 (2), 174–181.

Trappes–Lomax, H. and Ferguson, G. (eds) (2002). *Language in Language Teacher Education*. Amsterdam: John Benjamins.

Tripp, D. (1993). *Critical Incidents in Teaching: Developing Professional Judgement*. London: Routledge.

Tucker, P. D., Stronge, J. H., Gareis, C. R. and Beers, C. S. (2003). 'The efficacy of portfolios for teacher evaluation and professional development: Do they make a difference?'. *Educational Administration Quarterly*, 39 (5), 572–602.

Van Lier, L. (2000). 'From input to affordance: Social-interactive learning from an ecological perspective', in J. P. Lantolf (ed.), *Sociocultural Theory and Second Language Learning*. Oxford: Oxford University Press, pp. 245–259.

Velikova, S. 2013. 'Using the European Portfolio for Student Teachers of Languages (EPOSTL) to scaffold reflective teacher learning in English language teacher education', In J. Edge and S. Mann (eds), *Innovations in Pre-service Education and Training for English Language Teachers*. London: British Council Brand and Design, Innovation Series, pp. 201–216.

Wada, M. and Brumby, S. (1994). *Team Teaching*. London: Longman.

Wallace, M. (1991). *Training Foreign Language Teachers: A Reflective Approach*. Cambridge: Cambridge University Press.

Walsh, S. (2011). *Exploring Classroom Discourse: Language in Action*. London and New York: Routledge.

Yost, D. S., Sentner, S. M., and Forlenza-Bailey, A. (2000). An Examination of the Construct of Critical Reflection: Implications for Teacher Education Programming in the 21st Century. *Journal of Teacher Education*, 51(1), 39–49.

Zwozdiak-Myers, P. (2012). *The Teacher's Reflective Practice Handbook. Becoming an Extended Professional through Capturing Evidence-Informed Practice*. London and New York: Routledge.

CHAPTER TWO

Mentoring for Teacher Evaluation and Development

Leonardo A. Mercado and Steve Mann

Introduction

This chapter considers the role of mentoring in creating opportunities for self- and peer evaluation in English language teacher (ELT) development for novice teachers. The chapter considers a number of the contextual features that face novice teachers in Peru and provides an overview of a systematic approach to mentoring. In doing so, we pay attention to specific innovative features that have evolved over a number of years and how they promote reflection.

The demand for learning English as a foreign language continues to increase. Although the picture is complex (Graddol, 2006), the needs and expectations of language learners are changing much more quickly than ever before. Learners' needs require an appropriate response, often within contexts of constraint. All this places a higher degree of accountability on ESL/EFL teachers as they seek to promote successful English language learning experiences. Teacher evaluation plays an increasingly vital role in ensuring that novice teachers can succeed in this endeavour (Mann, 2004). Sometimes this is a voluntary process and sometimes it is not. It is easy enough to make the argument that teacher evaluation is important. However, there are two related issues that need consideration. The first is that teacher evaluation is a highly complex and sometimes daunting task which should not be taken lightly. The second issue concerns the question of who gets to do the evaluation. This chapter explores the potential roles that mentors play in Peru in orienting novice teachers to the complex and challenging roles they face. It also considers how mentors can create conditions for self-evaluation and reflection.

Mentoring is an important element of the teacher evaluation process, since it can promote self- and peer evaluation, rather than being a top-down or external evaluative process. Dewey is widely credited for turning attention to the importance of experiential learning and reflective thought as a key method of escape from '*purely impulsive or purely routine action*' (Dewey, 1933, p. 15) and mentoring has the capacity to help the teacher/learner to negotiate and learn from knowledge and experience through interaction. This process of learning from personal experiences establishes internal frames of reference that can serve to improve teaching over time (Salas and Mercado, 2010).

Developing an insider orientation to teacher evaluation

This section of the chapter makes the argument that a participatory and action-orientated view of teacher evaluation should put the language teacher at the centre of things (Farrell, 2008). This can be contrasted with a view of evaluation that places emphasis on a hierarchical or expert evaluation (Mann, 2004). Putting the teacher at the heart of evaluative processes avoids the limiting scenario of an expert (whether from the school hierarchy or from a university) arriving in a classroom to evaluate the strengths and weaknesses of the language teacher. Not only is the visit of an outsider or expert stressful, it may also be counterproductive to teacher development (Freeman, 2004).

One of the key arguments in this chapter, therefore, is that it is important for the continuing development of the language teacher to keep the individual teacher at the centre of the evaluative process. We believe that if teachers develop skills in self-evaluation and peer evaluation then these skills are more likely to be passed onto language learners (Mann, 2005). Autonomy, learner training and self-efficacy are built on an ongoing commitment to reflection and commitment to appropriate methodology (Holliday, 1994). Some kind of audit, monitoring, appraisal or assessment may be an institutional requirement but this should not be an aspect on the agenda. If possible, institutions should aim for a more integrated and multidimensional evaluation. This chapter sets out a possible model for such an integration.

The idea that an insider view is a valuable one in evaluative terms is not a new one. The basis of a whole range of publications (e.g. Roberts, 1998) argues that learning and self-development is only possible through a commitment to reflection, self-monitoring and self-evaluation. Roberts sees these processes as '*the only possible basis for long-term change*' (1998, p. 305). It is well recognized that a process of exploration or investigation in the classroom is one way to promote self-evaluation, self-monitoring and reflection (Burns, 2010). James (2001) and Richards and Farrell (2005) provide a number of procedures for self-evaluation and suggest various forms of lesson reports, checklists and questionnaires. Certainly the importance of reflection and self-evaluation has been established in the last few decades. Naidu et al. (1992, p. 162) talk of '*recovering experience*' through a process of self-evaluation and there have been increasing numbers of accounts of language teaching practice that might be grouped under the headings 'action research' and 'reflective practice'. A number of key themes have emerged from these accounts and movements: the insider view is crucial to understanding the complex world of the classroom and the nature of language learning; the complex world of the classroom is simply not reducible to causal statements; a committed language teacher is not committed to one way of doing things but is committed to a continual process of reflecting on practice. In addition, a process of self-evaluation through reflection and action research has the capacity to reveal the kind of 'invisible' knowledge that is part of our everyday routines. This knowledge is complex. Freeman (2004) talks about the multifaceted nature of knowledge, including received knowledge, personal knowledge, experiential knowledge, and local and situated knowledge. We too believe that knowledge and beliefs about teaching are both complex and often co-constructed.

The role of the mentor

Mentoring can help novice teachers '*adapt to and learn about their roles as teachers*' (Schwille et al., 2007, p. 89) and can be effective in '*providing support from a more experienced person in order to facilitate the growth and learning of another*' (Malderez, 2001, p. 57), especially in terms of the educational context and culture. Mentoring usually takes place within a structured induction process and this can include orientation meetings, subject related collaboration, developmental workshops, reduced workloads, team teaching and extra classroom assistance. Although some studies have warned that the importance of mentoring is not supported by empirical evidence (e.g. Colley, 2002; Ingersoll and Strong, 2011), a variety of other studies have found that mentoring is largely positive and well received by novice teachers (see Hobson et al., 2009 for an excellent overview of relevant studies). Interestingly, some studies also report benefits for the mentor themselves. This typically involves professional growth and job satisfaction, reflection on aspects of practice, professional development and development of leadership skills (Ganzer, 1996; Hobson et al., 2009, Kwan and López-Real, 2010).

The mentor has a key role in developing understanding of the complexity of teaching decisions and how various forms of knowledge can be marshalled to develop an informed and committed insider evaluation. Encouraging self-evaluation and reflection, supported through a mentoring process, can contribute considerably towards viable teacher development (Mann, 2005). Such a process can help the development of an insider view of classroom events. It can also lead to viable and supportive dialogue with peers. Above all, the process can support the development of a teacher's sense of *'plausibility'* (Prabhu, 1990, p. 172). Mentoring needs to have two aspects. It must ensure quality in terms of a teacher's work and it should provide teachers (the intended main beneficiaries) with a practical process to learn from themselves and their peers.

Mentoring within the ICPNA context

This chapter focuses on mentoring at a large binational centre in Lima, Peru, which has a current monthly student enrolment in the tens of thousands and a staff comprised of hundreds of full-time EFL teachers. The centre is thriving, so the institution needs to hire new teachers on an ongoing basis. Despite its overall success, finding qualified teachers with a strong background in the field is consistently challenging, so the institution usually has to resort to hiring candidates with a solid mastery of the language but who come from other walks of life. Within this context, the institution sees mentoring as serving a powerful, highly practical process for teacher development.

At the Instituto Cultural Peruano Norteamericano (ICPNA) in Lima, Peru, mentoring is embedded within a comprehensive, multimodal learning model called *IMMERSE*. Seasoned teachers and academic supervisors are called upon to act as mentors with each group fulfilling its own clearly defined role. This model is designed to meet the demands of the Peruvian context where teachers often enter the field without previous education, knowledge and credentials (Mercado, 2013). There is a pragmatic real-world balance to be struck. On the one hand, the *IMMERSE* programme needs to ensure quality teachers, and evaluation is instrumental in decisions about which teachers are hired and eventually asked to stay after their trial period. On the other hand, it needs to encourage collaboration and reflection. There is an inevitable tension between a mentor's roles as concerned with collaborative development and 'enlightenment', and an approach where *'the mentoring initiative is based on meeting standards'* (Ingleby, 2011, p. 428). Mentors need to negotiate this difficult balance.

Mentoring is a key aspect of ongoing teacher evaluation at ICPNA because it provides language programme administrators (LPAs) with insights and information related to a teacher's performance, level of progress, needs, degree of professionalism and motivation to continue with her or his development. At the pre-service stage, ICPNA's mentoring programme offers prospective teachers the opportunity to teach real students, under the guidance of the mentor teacher and on the condition that she/he is doing well in the pre-service training seminar.

ICPNA's pre-service seminars are forty-five hours long and complemented by twenty-seven hours of class observation with a mentor; experienced ICPNA teachers who will accompany a prospective teaching candidate over a minimum period of ten days. During the course of the training and development, with a new seminar being held every month, prospective teachers are expected to work with their mentors by observing their classes each day, taking notes and interacting with the mentor whenever questions arise or if assistance is needed with a particular activity she/he is going to eventually teach. In addition, they are expected to plan lessons according to what the mentor will be teaching the next day as well as devise questions in relation to what is being observed. The seminar process consists of the following elements as summarized in Table 2.1:

Table 2.1 Professional development activities at ICPNA new teachers' seminar.

Practice	Purpose	Teacher's role
Lesson planning/ decision making chart	Thinking about decisions we make. Mentees are asked to develop lesson plans as if they were to teach their mentors' lessons and subsequently analyse the decisions made in class. This is reviewed with the mentor to determine the reasons behind the decisions that were made and the degree to which they agree on what the critical incidents were during the lesson.	Planner/Assessor/ Self learner
Presentations on content (e.g. teaching the language skills, assessment, corrective feedback) and demos	Conceptual understanding of 'what' and 'how' to teach. The mentee compares this information to what actually takes place in a real classroom during the observation process. Mentees must report on how the theories, principles and concepts that were discussed the day before at the seminar were actually applied in the mentor's class.	Learner

(Continued)

Table 2.1 Professional development activities at ICPNA new teachers' seminar. (*Continued*)

Practice	Purpose	Teacher's role
Microteaching	Hands on, experiential learning. Teacher candidates must perform at the seminar in front of their peers. This is used for both formative and evaluative purposes, depending on the class that is being taught. The fact that teacher candidates are also mentees provides them with an invaluable source of ideas and scaffolding.	Co-learner
Mentoring: class observation /practice teaching	Learning by example. This is perhaps the most crucial component of the *New Teachers' Seminar*. It connects the formal training they receive to the 'real world' of teaching from the very beginning. When certain conditions are met, teacher candidates actually get to teach real students.	Apprentice/ Mentee
Trainee handbook	Knowledge enrichment. They are assigned a methodology book (e.g. Harmer, 2010) to read during the seminar so they can expand on the topics that are presented by the trainers, find ideas on how to teach their own demo classes, and better understand the events and actions taking place in their mentors' classes.	Learner
Discussion circles	Exchanging ideas. These serve as an opportunity to discuss a variety of topics, including questions that may arise as a result of observing a mentor's class.	Peer
Reflective writing	Exploring practices, beliefs and previous experiences. Among the various reflections teacher candidates must make, they are also asked to reflect on their mentors' classes as well as their desire to become ESL/EFL teachers.	Thinker/ Self-learner

During the pre-service stage, there are two critical evaluations that determine whether the teacher candidate will actually be hired or not. The first is given as a grade which is comprised of a variety of scores and judgements that are based on the teacher candidate's overall performance (e.g. evaluative demo classes) and professional disposition as determined by criteria such as reflection papers, level of participation and attitude towards peers and trainers. The second and most decisive factor is the report that is submitted by the mentor teacher. The mentor provides information on the mentee's attitude, degree of collaboration, willingness to carry out responsibilities, rapport with students, completion of goals and objectives, student participation, and overall desire to commit to the profession. Teachers who pass the *New Teachers' Seminar* and successfully complete the class observation/pre-service mentoring stage will be hired for work the following month.

At the beginning of their first month of formal employment, new ICPNA teachers are given an overview of their responsibilities, general information about workplace policies and an introduction to the official six-month in-service mentoring programme. This includes an overview of their new mentors, goals and details related to the mentoring programme, and details of expectations regarding their participation.

In addition to observing classes and partaking in collaborative, professional relationships with their mentors, mentees engage in ongoing reflection throughout their participation in the mentoring process. The purpose is to foster in mentees the ability to develop inner frames of reference that will help them identify the instructional practices and situations that are most conducive to successful learning. At the same time, reflection can help them come to understand their complex roles as facilitators of their students' learning as well as internalize their successes in the classroom in order to increase their level of confidence, motivation and sense of professionalism (Farrell, 2008). Table 2.2 illustrates some examples of the reflection themes and actual questions ICPNA teachers are asked to contemplate and respond to during their six months in the mentoring programme:

Table 2.2 Reflection themes and sample questions for ICPNA mentoring programme.

Theme	Purpose	Sample questions
Morale	Focusing on those aspects of their teaching experiences that are most conducive to building their confidence and motivation.	What would be four indicators to me that I am in the process of becoming a confident and competent English teaching professional? At this point, do I feel like this is something I enjoy doing and may continue to do for some time?

(Continued)

Table 2.2 Reflection themes and sample questions for ICPNA mentoring programme. (*Continued*)

Theme	Purpose	Sample questions
Professionalism	Increasing awareness of their growth as ELT practitioners.	Of all of the tools and resources that *IMMERSE* provides, which ones have been the most helpful so far? How? How am I different today as I conclude my participation in the mentoring programme as opposed to when I first began?
Development	Considering needs, progress and level of improvement during the first six months.	What are my three greatest needs as a new ICPNA teacher? (straight after passing the *New Teachers' Seminar* and before the first day of class) Have I improved in the area I identified as a target need for this month? How? What is the evidence (e.g. student surveys, own metrics, class videos, supervisor feedback)?
Community	Evaluating their new relationships with their mentors and mentor supervisors as 'significant others' in the ICPNA community.	How did it make me feel? What did I learn from the discussion? How has the mentor helped me so far? What else would I like to learn from her/him?

Novice teachers are provided with guiding questions throughout the six months of their participation in the mentoring programme. The aim is for them to have a better understanding of the reflection and development process as they transition towards becoming fully fledged ICPNA teaching professionals. They are encouraged to share their reflections with their mentor teachers.

An important aspect of the mentoring programme is self-evaluation through video recordings which has the potential of enabling mentees/novice teachers to self-generate alternatives to teaching practices and professional improvement as well as form beliefs about the relationship between teaching behaviour and student learning (Bailey et al., 2001; Gebhard and Oprandy, 1999). Novice teachers are required to have at least one of their lessons video recorded each month and are then asked to use the following checklist (Table 2.3) in order to self-evaluate:

Table 2.3 Self-assessment checklist for self-observation for novice teachers.

ICPNA: Self-assessment checklist			
Teaching practice	**Strong**	**Satisfactory**	**Needs improvement**
1 Classroom management (i.e. grouping, pacing etc.)			
2 Promotes student language production			
3 Praise and positive reinforcement			
4 Use of the board for examples and explanations			
5 Student talk time vs. teacher talk time			
6 T's level of English			
7 Explanations: clear, supported and participatory (S's)			
8 Error correction techniques			
9 Instructions: verbal, modelling, comprehension check			
10 Student engagement: voluntary participation/on-task time			
Critical incidents	**Why was it important?**		
1			
2			
Key decisions	**How did it have an impact on the outcome of the lesson?**		
1			
2			
3			
Action plan:			

The goal of this self-evaluation instrument is to empower teachers with a tool to reflect on their actions as well as events in the classroom so they can create paths to their own development under the guidance of their mentors. In order to support peer evaluation, teachers are encouraged to exchange videos once they have become members of an academic focus group within the ICPNA teaching community. This optional sharing is particularly useful when scheduling issues make it difficult for the mentor or a trusted peer to visit a teacher's class.

The first year of employment is the most crucial, as a 'new hire' transitions from accountant, manager, real estate agent, or another line of work to ESL/EFL teaching professional. During this year, the mentoring programme is integrated progressively with other professional development initiatives in order to maximize the effect in terms of knowledge and skills development, among other key areas. Figure 2.1 illustrates the benefits associated with *IMMERSE*, of which mentoring is an essential component:

FIGURE 2.1 *Pillars of IMMERSE, ICPNA's teacher development programme.*

More specifically, in addition to the development of knowledge and skills, the mentoring programme instils in new teachers a heightened sense of awareness regarding the events that generally take place in the classroom. Extracts 1 and 2 are from a reflection paper that was written by a novice teacher, Rosario, who had just watched her video-recorded class:

Extract 1:
It was good that many students were eager to participate. Sometimes I called for volunteers and sometimes I called students who hadn't participated before.

Extract 2:

I gave the instructions clearly, but I didn't model some of the activities. I think that's why some of the students were kind of lost.

Mentoring is perhaps the initiative that contributes much to the increase in morale among new teachers, as the information from a survey (see Table 2.4) shows (administered to a cohort of thirty novice teachers after completing their second month of employment):

Table 2.4 Selected results from a survey administered to novice teachers in their second month of employment.

Question	Response	Comment
How long do you plan to continue working as an English teacher?	1 year or more = 93%	It seems that initial success in the classroom and the supporting environment are convincing them that teaching is something they may want to do for some time.
If you plan to stay more than six months, what would you say is the main reason?	I get the support I need to succeed through the mentoring programme and other professional development initiatives. = 88%	This seems to indicate that professional development in any of its forms can be a powerful motivator.
If you chose (b) as an answer, could you specify which professional development initiative has been the most helpful?	Mentoring = 71%	The mentoring programme seems to be making a strong contribution to potential retention among these teachers. This is consistent with actual retention rates at ICPNA of close to 90% at the end of the first year of employment.

Collaborative action planning

Novice teachers are regularly observed by their mentors in order to ensure that *IMMERSE* is having a positive effect on their level of preparedness and efficacy in teaching. A number of class observations are formative in nature, giving mentors and teachers alike the opportunity to work in a less intimidating, more collaborative and mutually beneficial manner. *Collaborative action planning* begins with a pre-observation discussion to determine the mentee's areas of concern. The teacher is asked to reflect on the class and complete the self-assessment form (see Appendix 1), which is the same form the mentor will use for the post-observation conference. The form includes two self-reflection questions on the back that change every six months with new items that come from a bank.

The nature of the dialogue at this stage is collaborative rather than prescriptive since it is essential for teachers to feel that they are assuming a pro-active role. New teachers are more likely to view any activity or initiative related to professional development with greater enthusiasm and motivation if it is perceived to reflect their needs and concerns and this is perhaps only possible if the new teacher assumes a proactive stance in the action planning process. The sequence for *collaborative action planning* is outlined in Figure 2.2:

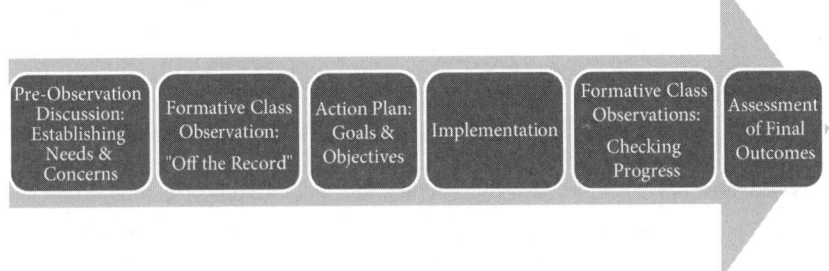

FIGURE 2.2 *Sequence for collaborative action planning process.*

Teachers respond well to this process because formative observations are 'off the record' and not used for formal grading purposes. This helps avoid the limiting features of formal appraisal on reflection (Hobbs, 2007). They do not include negative scoring or a categorization that will be held against teachers in their formal appraisals. Formative class observations can remove much of the pressure on teachers normally associated with observations that are conducted for summative evaluation purposes. The action plan, which guides the mentee as well as the mentor supervisor throughout the process, has the following components:

1 *Focus:* What should the teacher try to enhance or improve? Why?

2 *Measures:* What strategies, procedures or techniques should the teacher try out in class? What is the rationale behind each proposed measure? When should it be done?

3 *Classroom Decision Making:* What important decisions did the teacher make in class and why? How did they affect overall learning outcomes and learner engagement?

4 *Criteria for Progress and Success:* What behaviours, scores or other criteria will serve to mark progress and ultimate success?

5 *Timeline:* When should mentor supervisor and novice teacher get together again? When should the overall goal be achieved?

The role of mentor supervisors

So far in this chapter we have referred to the term *mentor* for the developmental role played in the ICPNA context. However, since mentoring at ICPNA is carried out not only by teachers but also by academic supervisors, there are clearly 'supervisory' elements to consider as well. Thus, there can be some overlap between professional development and teacher evaluation for formal appraisal purposes. Yet, by definition, 'supervisor' often refers to someone in an administrative capacity who has been entrusted with overseeing and helping improve the work of English language teachers (Wallace, 1991), so formative, development work through mentoring on the part of language programme administrators (LPAs) should not represent a contradiction in roles. We use the term 'mentor supervisor' here because it is important to foreground the formative aspects of teacher evaluation. So although the mentor supervisors conduct formal appraisals in order to grade teacher performance (e.g. calling for improvement by prescribing specific measures), they also encourage teachers to engage in self-and peer evaluation, professional reading, online learning, developing portfolios, writing teaching journals and a variety of other professional development alternatives. Despite the distinction that is usually made in the literature between formative and summative teacher evaluation (Popham, 1988; Stiggins and Bridgeford, 1984; White et al., 2008), in practice they represent parameters of evaluation which need to be constantly negotiated. With such high stakes involved, teacher evaluation practices on the part of LPAs have the potential to inadvertently pit teacher against supervisor, which could eventually lead to an antagonistic relationship in which one is seen to exert power over the other (Stoller, 1996; Salas and Mercado, 2010). The challenge is for mentor supervisors to dedicate a significant amount of their time to activities that teachers will recognize and view positively and which value and promote self-evaluation.

At ICPNA, mentor supervisors are expected to spend at least half of the time interacting and working with teachers in formative, developmental and supportive ways (rather than ways that are driven only by quality assurance, compliance with policies and procedures, and performance evaluation). They are *providers* of documentation, tools, resources, information, and, most importantly, encouragement and support. They are *models* who are willing to have their classes observed, either live or by way of recorded videos. They are *evaluators*, offering feedback on classes they observe and encouraging formative self-evaluation (so that any conclusions regarding potential areas of improvement or perceived weaknesses will not affect their formal appraisal scores). Finally, they also act as *advisors*, more experienced others in the profession from whom mentees can receive advice and counselling.

Evaluative perspectives on the mentor scheme

This section of the paper offers an evaluative perspective on the issue of whether mentors have a decisive role in providing support to novice teachers and thus helping them remain in the field. First, mentees are asked to complete a self-assessment questionnaire in their second, fourth and sixth months of employment. This instrument aims to encourage novice teachers to think about their practice from a variety of perspectives from their reflections. Table 2.5 shows data from a survey that was administered to a group of 30 mentees after completing their second month of employment:

Table 2.5 Selected results of survey administered to novice teachers.

Questions		Responses							
		Strongly disagree (1)	Disagree (2)	Uncertain (3)		Agree (4)		Strongly agree (5)	
#	Items	n	n	N	%	n	%	N	%
3	I understand the strategies, techniques and other instructional practices I am expected to apply in the classroom.	0	0	0	0	11	**36.67**	19	**63.33**
5	I have improved according to my expectations.	0	0	1	3.33	15	**50.00**	14	**46.67**

(Continued)

Table 2.5 Selected results of survey administered to novice teachers. (*Continued*)

Questions	Responses				
	Strongly disagree (1)	Disagree (2)	Uncertain (3)	Agree (4)	Strongly agree (5)
6 My reflections on my teaching, my participation in the mentoring programme and other aspects of my work help me develop professionally.	0	0	1 3.33	6 **20.00**	23 **76.67**
7 My mentor's feedback and advice are helpful.	0	0	0 0	1 **3.33**	29 **96.67**
8 My mentor supervisor's feedback and advice are helpful.	0	0	0 0	2 **6.67**	28 **93.33**
9 I enjoy the work I do.	0	0	0 0	1 **3.33**	29 **96.67**

We can see that practically the entire cohort of 30 mentees had positive opinions regarding outcomes they experienced with the mentoring programme. Even though they are only beginning their third month as ESL/EFL instructors, they already feel they understand what is expected of them. They are also content with their gradual improvement, feedback from mentors and the work they do in general. Most importantly, they are aware of the fact that their reflections and participation in the mentoring programme help them develop professionally.

Earlier in the chapter, we made a reference to a self-assessment checklist that places the teacher at the heart of the evaluative process and facilitates reflection on practice. Table 2.6 shows the results of three self-evaluations which used the checklist in order to improve on aspects of their teaching as a goal to meet over a period of time:

Table 2.6 Examples of teacher action plan cycles as a result of self-assessments.

Teacher	Instructional practice Critical incident Key decision in class	Action plan	Outcome
Daniel	T turned away from a student while he was answering her question to attend to another student behind him.	T decided to allot specific time to Q and A and commit to leaving no student question unanswered.	Teacher ensures that 100% of student questions are answered either in T-S or T-C mode.
Cynthia	T chose to correct the student rather than let her try to self correct first, knowing there was a good chance that she could have done. T wanted to 'play it safe' and save time.	T decided to give students more time to respond and use lesson planning more effectively in order to anticipate potential situations in which using corrective feedback to promote self correction might be applicable.	Students produce more language, increasing STT, while the teacher is gradually moving away from habit of correcting students directly before they have a chance to reflect on their responses and succeed on their own.
Milagros	S's arrived late during a group work activity. T decided to give the activity more time in order to orient these S's and let them do the activity. The risk was that other students would get bored because of the excessive time allotment.	Keep a log for all unexpected critical incidents and key decisions in order to anticipate them with effective measures the next time they occur.	Teacher is more resourceful, allowing her to respond to unexpected situations more effectively. Activities will not only be more catered to student needs, but levels of engagement and on-task time are higher.

Novice teachers are also asked to collect feedback from their students at the end of the course. Students 'free write' about their experience by describing what they liked and what could have been done differently. Such texts help the mentees develop an area for reflective focus.

Extract 1: Student feedback on a class at the end of the course

As with other aspects of the ICPNA mentoring programme, reflection is an essential step when processing student feedback. The following extract from a testimonial is an example of how reflection can help teachers become aware of their strengths and arrive at important conclusions about their work:

Extract 2: Testimonial

1. Once I collected the information and I started to read their feedback, it was very rewarding to see what they wrote. I did not expect to receive such good feedback. As I go over each of the students' opinions, I see that they are happy with the job I do. Many of them said that I am very fun and dynamic. These things are so important for a class in my opinion. Especially with a class of young people, it is key that they have fun while learning the language and also have a lot of dynamic interaction.

Daniel, ICPNA Miraflores

So far, we have discussed and seen the benefits of mentoring from the point of view of the mentee. Yet, there is also a clear need for mentors to profit from the experience. Some studies, for example, have found that mentors may sometimes feel there is only one main beneficiary in the process, the mentee (Delaney, 2012). However, the essence of successful mentoring is that both mentor and mentee feel they have gained as they engage in a mutual learning and development process. In a recent institutional survey on the mentoring programme at ICPNA, 63 mentor teachers and supervisors all felt they gained from the experience. Certainly, invaluable opportunities for learning are created when mentors contemplate their own professional development, the challenges they face and whether they are making an impact on their mentees' learning. Here are some examples of such reflections from ICPNA mentor teachers and mentor supervisors:

Extract 3: Mentor reflections

As a mentor, I am responsible for giving proper guidance to the novice teacher; in order to do that I must reflect on what I do in class and why I do it. It is during this reflecting process that I can auto evaluate my own teaching practices and think of ways to improve them, which in the end will benefit my students and myself.

As mentors we guide teachers through a self-discovery process in which progress – with or without adjustment – is evidenced. When I coach mentees, I aim at reflection mostly. If that stage is not observed, change will not take place and it would be just compliance with procedures or following somebody else's ideas without conviction.

A challenge is to be able to give teachers the necessary support they need within the time constraints we have.

I sense that my work is having impact on them when they come and share that they put into practice my suggestion and felt happy with the outcome.

The testimonials above illustrate that mentoring can result in personal and professional growth for mentors. In fact, they are likely to find themselves drawn into self evaluation and reflection as they consider aspects of their own practice.

Conclusion

This chapter describes how mentoring can empower teachers to assume responsibility for their own learning and professional development. Rather than rely on a prescriptive, sometimes antagonizing intervention on the part of a so-called 'expert', mentoring creates the conditions under which mentee, mentor teacher and mentor supervisor can thrive together as a result of a dialogic, mutually beneficial relationship. When implemented as part of a systematic, institutional approach to formative teacher evaluation and development, teachers are more likely to enjoy their work, meet their students' needs and expectations, and ultimately stay in the field. This is crucial to institutions like ICPNA, which may find it particularly difficult to hire qualified ESL/EFL teaching professionals because they are simply not available on the job market in adequate numbers.

We have seen examples of how teachers have taken action in response to the reflections that have been part of the mentoring process. By placing the teacher at the centre of the evaluative process, it is possible to achieve the goal of improving instruction and serving students' needs and expectations. From all perspectives, ICPNA has benefitted from employing mentoring within a multidimensional approach to teacher evaluation and development.

References

Bailey, K., Curtis, A. and Nunan, D. (2001), *Pursuing Professional Development: The Self as Source*. Boston, MA: Heinle and Heinle.

Burns, A. (2010), *Doing Action Research in English Language Teaching. A Guide for Practitioners*. New York: Routledge.

Colley, H. (2002), 'A "rough guide" to the history of mentoring from a Marxist feminist perspective'. *Journal of Education for Teaching*, 28, (3), 257–273.

Delaney, Y. A. (2012), 'Research on mentoring language teachers: Its role in language Education'. *Foreign Language Annals*, 45, (1), 184–202.

Dewey, John. (1933), *How We Think: A Re-statement of The Relation of Reflective Thinking to the Education Process*. Boston: DC Heath and Co.

Farrell, T. S. C. (2008), *Reflective Language Teaching: From Research to Practice*. London: Continuum Press.

Freeman, D. (2004), 'Knowledge architectures: some orienting references'. TESOL Italy Plenary Address. October 2004.

Ganzer, T. (1996), 'Preparing mentors of beginning teachers: An overview for staff developers'. *Journal of Staff Development*, 17, (4), 8–11.

Gebhard J. and Oprandy, R. (1999), 'Exploring our teaching', in J. Gebhard and R. Oprandy (eds), *Language Teaching Awareness: A Guide to Exploring Beliefs and Practices*. Cambridge: Cambridge University Press.

Graddol, D. (2006), *English Next*. London: British Council.

Harmer, J. (2010), *How to Teach*. London: Pearson.

Hobbs, V. (2007), 'Faking it or hating it: Can reflective practice be forced?'. *Reflective Practice*, 8, (3), 405–417.

Hobson, A. J., Ashby, P., Malderez, A. and Tomlinson, P. D. (2009), 'Mentoring beginning teachers: What we know and what we don't'. *Teaching and Teacher Education*, 25, (1), 207–216.

Holliday, A. (1994), *Appropriate Methodology and Social Context*. Cambridge: Cambridge University Press.

Ingersoll, R. and Strong, M. (2011), 'The impact of induction and mentoring programs for beginning teachers: A critical review of the research'. *Review of Education Research*, 81, (2), 201–233.

Ingleby, E. (2011), 'Asclepius or Hippocrates? Differing interpretations of postcompulsory initial teacher training mentoring'. *Journal of Vocational Education and Training*, 63, (1), 15–25.

James, P. (2001), *Teachers in Action: Tasks for In–service Language Teacher Education and Development*. Cambridge: Cambridge University Press.

Kwan, T. and López-Real, F. (2010), 'Identity formation of teacher-mentors: An analysis of contrasting experiences using a Wengerian matrix framework'. *Teaching and Teacher Education*, 26, (3), 722–731.

Malderez, A. (2001), 'New ELT professionals? The role and status of mentors'. *English Teaching Professional*, 19, 57–58.

Mann, S. (2004), 'Evaluation', In H. Harnisch and P. Swanton (eds), *Adults Learning Languages: A CILT Guide to Good Practice*. London: CILT, the National Centre for Languages, pp. 113–129.

———. (2005), 'State-of-the-art: The language teacher's development'. *Language Teaching*, 38, (3), 103–118.

——— and Tang, H. H. (2012), 'The role of mentoring in supporting novice English teachers in Hong Kong'. *TESOL Quarterly*, 46, (3), 472–495.

Mercado, L. (2013), 'IMMERSE: An institutional approach to pre- and early-service teacher development', in J. Edge and S. Mann (eds), *Innovations in Pre-service Education and Training for English Language Teachers*. British Council, pp. 47–62.

Naidu, B., Neeraja, K., Ramani, E., Shivakumar, J. and Viswanatha, V. (1992), Researching heterogeneity: An account of teacher-initiated research into large classes. *ELT Journal*, 46 (3): 252–263.

Popham, W. J. (1988), 'The dysfunctional marriage of formative and summative teacher evaluation'. *The Journal of Personnel Evaluation in Education*, 1, 269–273.

Prabhu, N. S. (1990), 'There is no best method-why?'. *TESOL Quarterly*, 24, 161–176.

Richards, J. C. and Farrell, T. (2005), *Professional Development for Language Teachers: Strategies for Teacher Learning*. Cambridge: Cambridge University Press.

Roberts, J. (1998), *Language Teacher Education*. London: Arnold.

Salas, S. and Mercado, L. (2010), 'Looking for the big picture: Macrostrategies for L2 teacher observation and feedback'. *English Teaching Forum*, 48, (4), 18–23.

Schwille, J., Dembele, M. and Schubert, J. (2007), *Global Perspectives on Teacher Learning: Improving Policy and Practice*. Paris: UNESCO: IIEP.

Stiggins, R. J. and Bridgeford, N. J. (1984), 'Performance assessment for teacher development'. *Educational Evaluation and Policy Analysis*, 7, (1), 85–97.

Stoller, F. (1996), 'Teacher supervision: 'Moving towards and interactive approach'. *English Language Teaching Forum*, 34, 2.

Wallace, M. (1991), *Training Foreign Language Teachers: A Reflective Approach*. Cambridge: Cambridge University Press.

White, R., Hockley, A., ver der Horst Jansen, J. and Laughner, M. S. (2008), *From Teacher to Manager*. Cambridge: Cambridge University Press.

Appendix 1: Reflection questions on back of self-assessment/class observation form

ICPNA
INSTITUTO CULTURAL PERUANO NORTEAMERICANO

Dear Fernando:

1) Please, elaborate on at least two features of your observed class that went according to your expectations.

2) Now elaborate on at least one thing that you would do differently in order to enhance your students' learning in the future.

CHAPTER THREE

Observing for Feedback: A Counselling Perspective

Mick Randall

Introduction

This chapter looks at observation within a teacher training context. It surveys the current views of observation which largely draw on the two fields of research and management. It argues for a different perspective, that of the counsellor–client relationship, and examines current practice in the light of a counselling framework.

Observation plays a central role in teacher training. Maldarez (2003) identifies four areas in which observation is used in education: professional development, training, evaluation and research (Maldarez, 2003, p. 180). This chapter will concentrate on the use of observation in what is perhaps the most common procedure in TESOL training, the *Teaching Practice Cycle* or *Teaching Practicum* consisting of a *Pre-Observation Conference*, *Observation* and *Feedback*. This is a basic feedback loop and exists in nearly all processes in which critical friends, trainers and managers interact with teachers. Although managerial use of such a cycle may concentrate on evaluation as its principal function, I shall concentrate on the training and professional development use of the cycle in which the main purpose is to help the teacher. Thus, the purpose of the observation is to provide the base on which a mentor or trainer can conduct a discussion with the teacher in order to move the teacher on to new understandings and thus influence their professional practice. This process of development will be analysed within the general humanistic counselling framework first proposed in education by Stones (1980) and then developed in TESOL by the likes of

Freeman (1982), Gebhard (1984) and Edge (1992) and can be argued to be the central philosophical approach used by trainers in TESOL (see Randall with Thornton, 2001).

Given the ubiquity of observation, it is surprising that observation procedures have received little theoretical attention. Much of the literature consists of descriptions of large numbers of instruments and checklists and their efficacy in different contexts. This chapter examines the influence of different fields on the development of observation procedures in TESOL and then provides a critical analysis of observation within a general helping process as that proposed by Egan (1994).

Of the three fields in which observation is involved (research, management and training), research can be argued to have had the strongest initial influence on the development of observation processes. The primary aim of research is to produce an objective record of a natural situation, the classroom, through a process of recording and coding. Thus, the principal influence of research on the process of classroom observation is that of making a systematic and therefore 'objective' record of the lesson. This involves the careful categorization of behaviour and provision of categories which can be counted and quantified. This belief in providing an objective record of classroom behaviour through measurement, coding and counting is a major legacy of the research agenda on the way observation is conducted in training.

This emphasis on measurement is reinforced by the other common use of observation as a tool within management. Teacher appraisal and assessment are major uses of observation. From the purely assessment function in teacher certification, both in pre-service and in-service contexts, to the annual appraisal systems demanded of school managers and system inspection, observation is a crucial element. In fact, the growth of managerialism in TESOL has replaced the earlier emphases on training and development; appraisal and assessment have become the principal functions of managers. Within these functions, the purpose of assessment through measuring teacher behaviour in the classroom is a central concern and the development of a plethora of observation instruments and checklists has been a major consequence of this use of observation. These instruments and checklists, in addition to coding behaviours, aim to produce 'objective' judgements through the description and codification of teaching competencies.

Both these contexts have strongly influenced the way observation is conducted in the third field, that of teacher training and development. Although objectification and measurement can be seen as important aspects of observing teachers in that they can arguably lessen prescription, when viewed from the point of view of the feedback conference and counselling, these aspects may also be dysfunctional for providing effective advice. I argue that the concentration on these aspects in the observation phase of the practice cycle is less than optimal for providing a facilitative atmosphere in which effective help can be undertaken.

The recording of the classroom and the promotion of teacher development: The research legacy

During the 1960s and 1970s there was a shift in psychological and educational research towards the collection and examination of naturally occurring data, especially in language. In linguistics and language acquisition the ideas of Chomsky led to the collection of primary data of interaction with children (e.g. Brown, 1973). In line with this new research approach, there were a number of instruments developed for systematically examining the classroom. Flanders developed a series of categories of interaction: the *Flanders Interaction Analysis Categories* (Flanders, 1970). This was followed by *FOCUS* (Fanselow, 1977), an instrument which enabled teacher action and student response categories to be recorded by timed sampling of observations (say every three seconds). It also segmented the lesson into sections by using boundary markers such as '*OK*', drawing on the classroom discourse research of Sinclair and Coulthard (1975). Other instruments such as *Flint, COLT, SCORE* and TALOS followed (for a detailed description, see Allwright, 1988), all involving codification, recording and counting to provide a picture of the lesson. In language teaching, Bowers (1980) developed an instrument and applied it to a series of ELT and FL lessons as a piece of research to investigate, among other things, the balance between teacher talking time (TTT) and student talking time (STT) in different contexts.

Bowers (1980) is an example of the use of codification and measurement with a research agenda but there was a strong movement in teacher education which suggested that by accurately recording what was taking place in the classroom, the trainee could be led to discover, or could discover by themselves, important aspects of their behaviour, both good and bad, through the examination of this systematic record. This technique is routinely used on teacher training programmes to raise awareness of different issues, especially that of TTT/STT.

Systematic recordings of lessons can be used as an effective teacher development tool for raising awareness. Ruth Wajnryb's excellent *Classroom Observation Tasks* (Wajnryb, 1992) provides over twenty instruments to enable the observer to examine different crucial aspects of teacher behaviour. Examples of the areas examined are analysis of TTT/STT, teacher meta-language and questioning, managing error, methods of negotiating meaning, elicitation and checking learning. These instruments can be either used by third party observers such as trainers and critical friends or they can also be used for self-development based on video and audio recordings.

The most complete record of a classroom is obviously video and audio recording. The use of such a detailed record as the basis for a feedback conference was suggested by the early seminal description of the teaching practice cycle in Turney et al. (1982). He suggests recording lessons, editing the recordings and then playing the objective evidence to the trainee for discussion in the feedback conference. However, this process, although in an obvious sense highly 'objective', is somewhat impractical to implement, given the crowded schedule of teacher trainers. On the other hand, audio or visual recording is often suggested as a process which can be undertaken by the teacher as a diagnostic tool for self-examination of their own performance. This can be done by the use of self-critical diaries, but it is often accompanied by the use of coding procedures as described above.

Assessment, appraisal and judgement: the managerial legacy

As noted earlier, teacher appraisal is a major issue in the management of ELT institutions and one of the most important roles educational administrators perform. Observation is a common thread utilized as part of system inspections such as *Ofsted*, annual departmental performance reviews and the assessment of teacher performance within appraisal systems. Many managers complain about the emphasis placed by institution managements on the production of an annual report which perforce includes a judgement of the way teachers have performed. Whilst appraisal systems obviously contain more than lesson observation, lesson observation of some sort is nearly always involved in these processes. Even 'democratic' appraisal systems, such as those employed in some HE institutions, usually involve, at least at the minimum, peer observation. Similarly, all teacher certification programmes such as pre-service degrees and diplomas and, in TESOL, programmes like the CELTA, DELTA and the Trinity Cert TESOL contain an element of assessed teaching practice. These assessments may be moderated by different elements of self-assessment and work portfolios, but they all contain some lesson observation and judgement based on that lesson. As with education in general, assessment often seems to dominate teaching, so many managers complain that assessment plays a much greater role than development in their relationship with teachers.

This institutional demand for assessment produces a large number of different instruments, checklists and protocols as any cursory search of the web will indicate and these are only those in the public domain. There are probably an equal number of different institution-specific instruments. All of these instruments can trace their genesis from the research legacy of measurement identified above.

Observation and teacher learning

Teaching is clearly a practical subject and one of the most important aspects of modern approaches to teacher learning is to recognize this fact and to move from theoretically driven approaches towards practice-driven approaches to learning. One of the principal theories in this field is that of Experiential Learning (Kolb, 1984). Kolb re-aligned the learning process from that of moving from an emphasis on theoretical discussion leading to practice, which had been the traditional 'scholarly' approach to learning in higher education, to one which starts from practice. Kolb proposed instead a process which started from Concrete Experience, followed by Critical Reflection on this experience which then leads to Abstract Conceptualization, followed by Active Experimentation. This experiential learning process provides a powerful theoretical framework for the Teaching Practice Cycle. Along with this learning cycle, which Kolb saw as a general cycle of adult learning and one which would be undertaken by the individual, Schön (1983) re-emphasized the importance of critical reflection in professional development and added the idea that such critical reflection could be aided by a coach.

Another highly influential approach to teacher training and education, developed in the United States, is that of Clinical Supervision (Sergiovanni, 1977). Despite its rather austere title, the movement encapsulates many of the ideas which have become orthodox thinking in teacher training. Its principles are that:

1   Teaching is a complex set of activities that requires careful analysis.
2   Teachers are responsible and competent professionals who desire help if it is offered in a collegial way.
3   The purpose of clinical supervision is to assist teachers to modify existing patterns of teaching.

Guernsey, (2013)

It should be noted that the approach has, as its starting point, the careful analysis of classroom data.

These principles are developed into what Wallace (1991) describes as the classic collaborative approach which he distinguishes from the classic prescriptive approach. The collaborative approach involves looking at the classroom, the learner and the teacher, bringing back data to the feedback conference for discussion and then using counselling skills to explore the situation and facilitate learning.

All of these approaches emphasize the learning aspect of teacher training and within such a context the use of the sorts of instruments I have been discussing have definite advantages. All instruments focus on understanding the classroom, which is a central principle of these approaches to learning, and they are practice-driven rather than theory-driven. Instruments allow the mentor and the teacher to focus on micro-activities in order for patterns to emerge from the data rather than be imposed from outside prescriptions. They can also be used by the individual as a basis for critical reflection, a common factor in all of the approaches. The *Teaching Practice Cycle or Practicum* as a feedback–learning cycle can be diagrammatically represented as a feedback (Figure 3.1) loop:

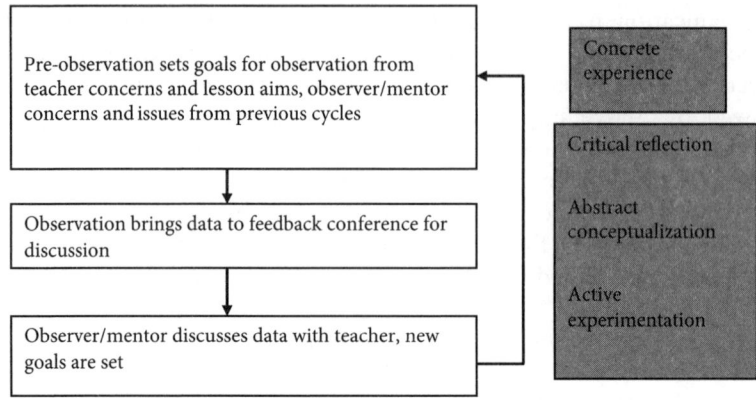

FIGURE 3.1 *Practice cycle and learning cycle.*

The focus on recording classroom data is a crucial phase within the learning cycle with its emphasis on analysis, problem solving and active experimentation as the way for teachers to learn and develop. In addition, the codification of specific competencies and the examination of classroom data to see if such competencies have been acquired can also be seen as beneficial to the learning process. By isolating and concentrating on competencies and gathering information on their attainment, advisors/trainers/mentors can work with teachers effectively to learn about ways of teaching, especially in pre service contexts.

Thus, within a rationalistic/intellectual framework, the influences of research and management on observation can be seen as facilitative. However, in the next section I want to examine observation within a counselling framework.

Observation and giving feedback: The counselling perspective

The discussion above focuses on the theoretical foundations for learning from the rational/intellectual perspective. However, as indicated in most of the models, such learning is most often a dialogic process between an advisor/mentor and a teacher/trainee. This dialogic context involves an examination of interpersonal dynamics and for this I turn to counselling frameworks and examine observation from within them.

There can be said to be three broad approaches to counselling/helping: the Behavioural, the Cognitive/Behavioural and the Humanistic/Person Centred (see Randall with Thornton, 2001).

The Behavioural approach is associated with training and the control of behaviour through positive reinforcement and shaping. Such approaches underpin micro-teaching, a common technique used in pre-service education. This approach is also common in training and inspection contexts and can often be highly prescriptive. Although prescriptive and authoritative interventions are often seen in a pejorative light, as Heron (1990) points out, they are part of the overall armoury of the mentor and may be highly effective in certain contexts.

The Cognitive/Behavioural approach is best illustrated by Egan's three-stage model (Figure 3.2) of helping (Egan, 1994):

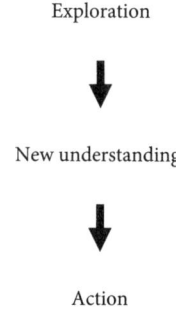

Exploration

New understanding

Action

FIGURE 3.2 *Egan's three-stage model of helping.*

Source: See also Exploration, Discovery and Action in Edge, 1992.

The Cognitive/Behavioural approach is one of the underlying counselling principles behind the classic collaborative approach (Wallace, 1991). It involves the examination and change of beliefs as well as behaviours. In this, the mentor and mentee look at the lesson and use it as a springboard to explore not only how things could have been done better, but derive principles for effective teaching as well. They attempt to shed new light on the teaching process, '*the deep structures of learning*' (Stones, 1984), and from this to jointly discover both what has happened and guidelines for future practice. The objective record of the classroom from observation is often heralded as a useful tool for the start of this process provided the record does not contain any hidden agenda on the part of the observer, that is, it is an open record without any pre-formed judgements as to a preconceived 'best' way to teach. In fact, Heron's very useful Informative Intervention (from within his authoritative interventions) is an example of this within a counselling framework (Heron, 1990). However, from the Cognitive/Behavioural perspective, competency checklists are less easy to use in collaborative approaches than records of what actually happened as they provide less opportunity for the teacher and advisor to explore the situation and discover new insights.

The third approach to counselling, the Humanistic/Person Centred approach, prioritizes the role of the client in solving their problems. Thus, the feedback session provides a platform for the teacher to work through the experience and to arrive at a new understanding. The role of the mentor/counsellor is to act as a catalyst to stimulate the teacher/client to be aware of their problems and to suggest how they can be resolved. This involves the use of three crucial concepts of humanistic counselling to create an atmosphere in which such self-discovery can take (Table 3.1) place:

Table 3.1 The three central concepts of humanistic counselling.

Non-judgemental	Advice should be non-judgemental.
Empathy	The advisor should empathize with and value the teacher as a person.
Active listening	The advisor will need to actively listen to the teacher.

Perhaps the most difficult concept to understand and the one which causes most controversy is that of non-judgemental. On the face of it, the objective observation which brings in a record of the classroom clearly fulfils this criterion. By providing a record, uncontaminated by any pre-set agenda, it is possible for the discussion to proceed from a non-judgemental platform. However, counsellors are keen to point out that non-judgemental does not mean having no view of the lesson. Egan (1994) talks about '*tough minded listening*' which means that the advisor is not judging the teacher as a person (they should be at pains to demonstrate that they value the teacher as a person), but they still have a view on the behaviour which is being discussed. Thus, creating empathy is a vital ingredient of effective humanistic counselling. It is important that the advisor is sensitive to and deeply understands the teacher's perspective on teaching.

This deep empathy is achieved through active listening. It is achieved by attending closely to what the teacher says or believes to be true. For effective counselling to take place, the advisor needs to get much closer to the teacher than the standard, often purely phatic, opener to the feedback session '*Tell me how it went*'. Even paying close attention when the teacher talks through what they thought of the lesson, as important as this is, is only part of active listening.

Getting to understand the teacher and the way the teacher thinks is a function of effective observation which is much more than the advisor acting as a surrogate tape recorder, generating a faithful record of the lesson for later discussion. It is an opportunity for the advisor to 'get inside the skin' of the teacher, to genuinely attempt to understand and empathize with the teacher. All the instruments I have examined and the legacy of research and management are focused on providing an accurate record of behaviour. They involve 'looking **at** the teacher' rather than 'looking **with** the teacher' which is a crucial element in creating empathy with the mentee.

The role of the advisor within the Practice Cycle can then be diagrammatically represented in Figure 3.3:

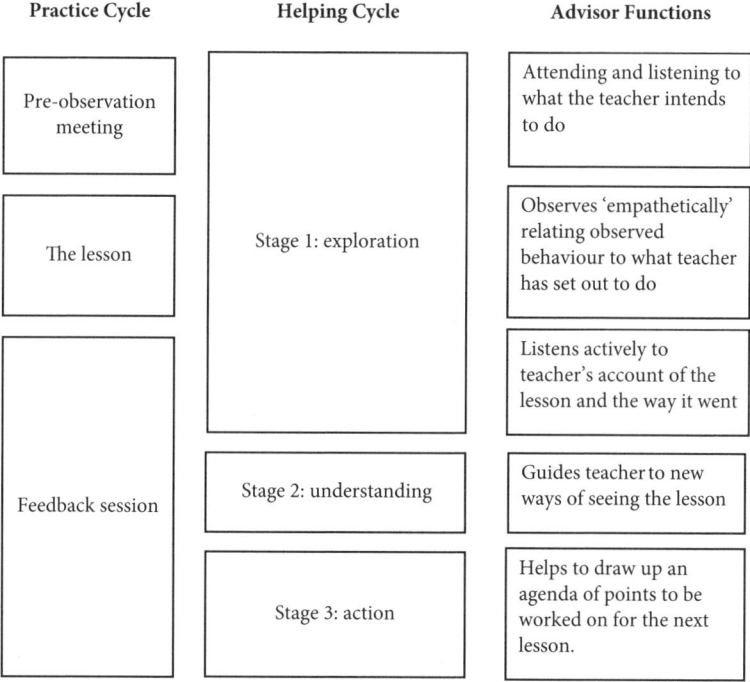

FIGURE 3.3 *The teaching practice cycle viewed as a helping cycle.*
Source: Randall with Thornton, 2001, p. 72

It is not suggested that the three counselling approaches are mutually exclusive and are the sole approaches used within any particular approach to training. Rather it is suggested that the different approaches emphasize one counselling approach over the other. I argue here that the third approach, that of humanistic/person-centred counselling, is crucial for effective helping and that it needs to be taken into account when examining observation within a teaching practice cycle.

When viewed from the perspective of a counselling/helping process, 'objective' observation, as important as it is in contrast with judgemental assessment, is only part of the picture. Problem-solving and humanistic approaches to counselling/helping emphasize the importance of starting from the situation as perceived by the client. That is why such sessions routinely start by asking the client to explain the situation as they see it in order to raise awareness and move to self-evaluation and solution. Through actively listening to the client, the helper tries to 'divine' the problem from the client's point of view and empathize with it. In teaching we are privileged in having access to the problem in context, in that we see the situation under discussion, a privileged access which is denied to the social counsellor. From the point of view of creating empathy and active listening, the behaviour of the advisor in the lesson can send significant signals to the teacher. If the advisor spends their time making notes, filling out observation instruments, even with the agreement of the teacher under observation, the signals to the teacher are those of the detached scrutinizer, not the involved helper eager to understand the lesson from the teacher's point of view. Thus, eye contact, signalling empathy and engagement and sharing the experience on a deep level, even participation with the teacher, are more important than providing objective data for later discussion.

It has always surprised me that, with so many observation instruments, most of my colleagues, along with myself, prefer the blank sheet of paper for observing lessons. I believe that is because good counsellor/helpers are doing more than simply recording data in observation, but are beginning to build an empathetic relationship with the teacher. Observation notes erect barriers between the observer and the observed which are dysfunctional for effectively providing feedback from a humanistic perspective.

Conclusion

This examination of observation within the context of the *Teaching Practice Cycle or Practicum* and from a counselling perspective has added a new perspective on lesson observation. Although the prevailing view of observation has been that the observer should, where possible, strive to provide an objective, unbiased record to bring to the feedback conference, this examination has highlighted the need to take interpersonal factors into consideration during lesson observation when the purpose of the observation is to help the teacher to develop.

References

Allwright, D. (1988), *Observation in the Language Classroom*. London: Longman.
Bowers, R. (1980), *Verbal Behaviour in the Language Teaching Classroom*, PhD Thesis. University of Reading.
Brown, R. (1973), *A First Language: The Early Stages*. Cambridge, MA: Harvard University Press.

Edge, J. (1992), *Cooperative Development: Professional Self-development through Cooperation with Colleagues*. Harlow, Essex: Longman.

Egan, G. (1994), *The Skilled Helper*, 5th Ed. Pacific Grove California: Brooks/Cole Publishing Co.

Fanselow, J. F. (1977), 'The treatment of error in oral work'. *Foreign Language Annals*, 10, (5), 583–593.

Flanders, N. A. (1970), *Analysing Teacher Behavior*. Reading, MA: Addison-Wesley.

Freeman, D. (1982), 'Observing teachers: Three approaches to in-service training and development'. *TESOL Quarterly*, 16, (1), 21–28.

Gebhard, J. (1984), 'Models of supervision: Choices'. *TESOL Quarterly*, 18, (3), 501–514.

Guernsey, D. (2013), Clinical Supervision. NAPCIS http://www.napcis.org/resources.html accessed 17 July 2013.

Heron, J. (1990), *Helping the Client: A Creative Practical Guide*. London: Sage Publications.

Kolb. (1984), *Experiential Learning: Experience as a Source of Learning and Development*. New Jersey: Prentice Hall.

Maldarez, A. (2003), 'Observation'. *ELT Journal*, 57, (2), 179–181.

Randall, M. with Thornton, B. (2001), *Advising and Supporting Teachers*. Cambridge: Cambridge University Press.

Schön, D. A. (1983), *The Reflective Practitioner: How Professionals Think in Action*. London: Temple Smith.

Sergiovanni, T. J. (1977), 'Reforming teacher evaluation: Naturalistic alternatives'. *Education Leadership*, 34, (8), 602–607.

Sinclair, J. and Coulthard, R. M. (1975), *Towards an Analysis of Discourse*. Oxford: Oxford University Press.

Stones, E. (1980) *Supervision in Teacher Education*. London: Routledge

———. (1984), *Supervision in Teacher Education: A Counselling and Pedagogical Approach*. London: Methuen.

Turney, C., Cairns, L., Eltis, K., Hatton, N., Thew, D., Towler, J. and Wright, R. (1982), *Supervisor Development Programmes*. Sydney: Sydney University Press.

Wajnryb, R. (1992), *Classroom Observation*. Cambridge: Cambridge University Press.

Wallace, M. (1991), *Training Foreign Language Teachers*. Cambridge: Cambridge University Press.

PART TWO

Tools for Investigation and Collaboration

CHAPTER FOUR

From Bit to Whole: Reframing Feedback Dialogue through Critical Incidents

Radhika Iyer-O'Sullivan

Introduction

In most teacher education and teacher training contexts, observations of teaching and feedback are seen as necessary and imperative tools towards producing effective teachers. This is usually coupled with reflective practice where student teachers are expected to reflect on their practices and harness those reflections towards identifying strategies for self-improvement. At feedback sessions it is assumed that the verbal reflections shared during the feedback process will be incorporated into written reflections which in turn will lead to improved teaching practices and teacher development. Observing teachers, providing feedback and encouraging them to engage in reflective practice are not a recent phenomenon as in the 1960s Shutz (1967) mooted the idea that deconstructing the meaning of their experiences through observation and feedback processes can help teachers to construct some form of reality about their practices.

Observation, feedback and reflection

The rise of clinical supervision in the 1950s, which aimed to inject a more democratic approach to teacher supervisory methods, concentrated mainly on the cycle of pre-observation, observation and post-observation feedback (Goldhammer, 1969). The major advantage of clinical supervision is that it aspires to encourage dialogue between teachers and supervisors about actual teaching experiences. It also facilitates enquiry on tacit, perhaps even treasured assumptions and practices (Smyth, 1984). However, since clinical supervision was developed for the basic relationship between supervisors and supervisees, the fundamental top-down relationship has remained ingrained in many contexts and has thus somewhat disrupted the ideal clinical supervision cycle, which is meant to sustain dignity and autonomy towards teacher empowerment. As this cycle relies mainly on feedback dialogues for continuation, it has to be construed that feedback dialogues are pivotal in sustaining observation and feedback cycles. Smyth (1989, cited in Moon, 1999, p. 59), while being a strong proponent of clinical supervision, does admit that sometimes dialogue can become '*unempowering*' when it is reduced to '*prescribing what teachers ought to teach within tight guidelines, while co-opting one another into policing the implementation of predetermined goals*'.

What has persistently emerged from research in the field of teacher education is the value of reflection (Hoover, 1994; Spilkova, 2001). The newly qualified teacher is expected to be more than a technician who fulfils a range of standardized competencies and to develop as a reflective practitioner. Teachers' own reflections have been perceived as invaluable in instigating change and action within themselves in learning environments and learners and in the wider context of institutions and legislation (Parsons and Stephenson, 2005). Reflective teachers' professional development is rooted in a range of works and ideas that have explored the link between reflection and learning. Some of these include Schön (1983) who divided reflection into reflection-in-action and reflection-on-action, Dewey (1933) who described the process of reflection as beginning from '*perplexity*' and Kolb (1984) who considered this within the cycle of experiential learning. Although none of these works on reflection may have explicitly explored the value of discourse and language in depth, the processes described involve deliberate expression and sharing of thoughts, which inevitably would involve language. Moon (1999) asserts that for learning towards professional development, reflection is mandatory, identifying a set of guidelines for developing reflective practices in various scenarios. These guidelines do not identify language as an inherent tool in reflection but many of her suggested tasks can only be successful if they are based on a clear framework of agreed discourse.

It has been widely acknowledged that teaching is a personal, emotional and highly complex activity and is '*primarily a personal or emotional act*' (Mills and Satterthwait, 2000, p. 30). Bolitho (1986) argues that reflection is only meaningful when teachers are allowed to include past and present experiences and emotions so that they can challenge their own personal and professional beliefs to create new understandings of teaching and learning. He then proceeds to claim that the affective domain is sometimes neglected in teacher training courses because personalities are seen to '*represent an unwelcome variable*' (p. 2). Cochran-Smith (2003, p. 374) further encapsulates the inseparable notion of emotion and teaching through her claim that '*teaching and learning are matters of both head and heart, both reason and passion*'. Zembylas (2007) supports this notion by describing this link as an intersection of the personal and pedagogical. Shoffner (2009) also recommends that the affective domain must be embraced when encouraging reflection among teachers if meaningful learning is to take place. The challenge then lies in devising ways of exploring how the affective domain can be an integral part of reflective learning so that teachers can be reflective practitioners. The key tool to achieve the latter would be development of discourse. If reflection is a key component of teacher education, then teacher educators will need to focus on building language and feedback discourse that allows teachers to express their reflections, share fears, thoughts and ideas and identify paths of change and empowerment. Engaging in reflective practice through a coherent and agreed discourse framework enables integration of '*various aspects of teaching and learning and supports pre-service teachers' considerations of emotional and personal as well as the managerial and pedagogical*' (Shoffner, 2009, p. 784).

In light of the above, the process of observation and feedback has been found to be rather problematic. Holly (1987, p. 14) laments that observation may fail to reveal the '*entire story of the classroom*' and in the same vein, feedback sessions with mentor teachers can also limit reflective exploration of the lesson, teacher beliefs and practices, sometimes disregarding the affective domain. Due to time and workload constraints, feedback dialogues can sometimes focus heavily on teaching skills and planning without including teacher beliefs, motivation and affective and cognitive knowledge. Standard observation and feedback procedures call for situations where teachers may find themselves describing and reflecting on a lesson in chronological order. They feel compelled to comment on every aspect of the lesson and this can put undue pressure on teachers as they then hesitate to be positive about their own teaching. While exploring every aspect of the lesson can be useful, it can also cause discomfort and tension in the mentor–mentee relationship as observed teachers will feel that they are expected to say more or they will be held 'in contempt' for failing to see something blatant. The feedback session could then end up focusing on what the observer thinks rather than what the teacher thinks.

In this chapter, mentor–mentee feedback dialogue will be explored and some limitations will be identified. Two extracts from recorded feedback dialogues between a mentor and mentee will be analysed and an alternative strategy using critical incidents will be suggested in reconstructing feedback discourse. For purposes of consistency, the term *mentor* will be used to refer to teacher trainers or observers and the term *mentee* will be used to refer to student teachers or observed teachers.

Deconstructing feedback dialogue

Generally, in teacher education institutions, student teachers are responsible for maintaining some sort of reflective log of self-evaluations where they are expected to demonstrate depth of reflection. The problem arises with the concept of being reflective itself. Reflection is a challenging activity and students who have not grasped the basics of how to reflect usually end up describing what went right and wrong. In many teacher self-evaluations, the entire lesson is described in chronological order with accompanying judgements of their own teaching or the learners' (in the class) progress, which remain shallow and descriptive.

The following are standard or common questions that are often posed at the pre-observation stage to teachers/trainee teachers:

- This is an interesting resource. How are you going to use it?
- Do you think pupils might find the activity too easy/difficult?
- Why did you arrange the exercises in this order?
- Do you think pupils will have enough time to complete this activity?
- Why did you choose these activities?
- What steps will you take if this class is not able to do this activity?
- What strategies have you planned for the difficult pupils?

Many teachers would have either posed the above questions as observers, or been asked the questions by an observer and consequently these questions may have become acceptable in observation–feedback cycles in various institutions. However, when these questions are spoken out loud, each could have different connotations depending on the tone, volume or intonation and the context of the observation. For example an observer could ask the fifth question, '*Why did you choose these activities?*' simply because they are curious and interested but if articulated in a different tone with accompanying facial expression and body language, this 'innocent' question could be misinterpreted by the teacher that the choice of activities was not appropriate. Intonation, tone of voice and use of non-verbal communication can have varying levels of interpretation depending on the context, the participants and their culture (Randall with Thornton, 2001). Thus, it is important that the intention of the observer is always transparent and shared with the mentee so that questions or comments are not misinterpreted and misunderstood. In a pre-observation meeting scenario, the mentee is usually anxious to discover the observer's expectations and standards so the discussion at this stage is crucial in establishing trust, transparency and collegiality so that both observer and observee can survive the observation, which can be potentially rewarding or equally debilitating for both parties.

Below is a list of standard or common post-observation questions. These questions could be just as problematic as the pre-observation questions presented earlier:

- So…how do you think that went?

- What do you think went well?

- What would you do again?

- What did not work so well? Why do you think that?

- What would you do differently?

- What were you most anxious about?

- Are you still confident and anxious about the same issues? Why? Why not?

- What targets would you like to set for your next lesson?

Post-observation feedback can be even more challenging as both the mentor and mentee would have experienced a range of emotions and thoughts during the observation, which would be explicitly or implicitly evident in the post-observation feedback. Thus, it is even more crucial to pay attention to how post-observation feedback is initiated and conducted. The first question itself can be extremely problematic as it forces the mentee to express what she thought about all aspects of her lesson when she has no knowledge as to whether the mentor agrees with what the former has identified as her strengths. Although this question appears to allow the mentee to take the lead in the post-observation dialogue, it can also be a very precarious situation for the mentor to be in. If the mentee chooses to talk about a part of the lesson that went well, she risks the possibility of that aspect being the very segment that the observer feels did not go so well. If the mentee begins with what did not go so well, then the entire dialogue could be focused on the flaws of the lesson rather than the positive elements. In the context of experienced teachers, Montgomery (1999) encapsulates three basic systems of appraisal derived from various previous studies. These are essentially the *Tell and Sell* method, the *Tell and Listen* method and the *Problem-solving* system. In the first method, the observer tells the teacher her evaluation and then attempts to persuade the teacher to change, adopt or implement strategies or measures. This type of appraisal is 'top down' and can be demotivating. In a top-down approach, the feedback is usually controlled and directed by the observing teacher or supervisor who is seen to hold a higher position than the observee. In the second method, the evaluation is still 'told' to the teacher but in this method, the latter is allowed to respond, disagree and ask for clarification. This remains a top-down approach too because the observer initiates the discussion. In the final method, there is room for negotiation and for both parties to discuss problems and issues, but as the emphasis is on problem solving this can restrict the dialogue to negative issues and some problems may remain unresolved.

The following extracts are from two recorded post-observation feedback dialogues between a teacher trainer (Mentor) and student teacher (Mentee). In both extracts, the student teachers are training to teach English as a Foreign Language (EFL) in secondary schools in the United Arab Emirates. In Extract 1, the initial question from the mentor compelled the mentee to immediately evaluate her entire lesson and then proceed to focus on negative aspects.

Extract 1:

Mentor:	So how do you think that went?
Mentee:	First … it went well … the interaction between students was very good
Mentor:	Okay
Mentee:	I liked the introduction … hmmmm … what did not go well was giving instructions. It was my personal focus for this lesson but I need to focus more on it.
Mentor:	At which stage do you think your instructions were not so good? What do you think you left out?
Mentee:	The example
Mentor:	Yes, okay. Good! Good! Okay let's focus on what went well first, okay? I would agree with you about the instructions at the first stage. Is there anything else that went well? What do you think about the brainstorming, the reading or the other stages in your lesson?
Mentee:	Actually, I did a mistake by asking them to open their books before they brainstormed although it was not in my lesson plan. So I tried to ask questions….
Mentor:	So what do you think worked well and you would definitely do again?
Mentee:	The first stage
Mentor:	The first stage, okay … good.

It is evident from Extract 1 that the mentor tried very hard to encourage the mentee to focus on positive aspects of the lesson first. The mentor tried to frame the question on positive facets of the lesson in three different ways but still the mentee would only briefly touch on the positive and then quickly reverted to the negative. This kind of attitude from mentees where they tend to want to discuss what did not go so well is confirmed by several experts who assert that most student teachers and even experienced teachers tend to focus on the negative elements of the lesson and thus feel they can avoid further criticism from the mentor (Beyer, 1989; Nias, 1987; Harmer, 2007; Malderez and Bodoczky, 1999; Smyth, 1984).

Extract 2 below presents another feedback dialogue between the same mentor as Extract 1 with a different mentee. In this extract too, the mentee also immediately focuses on the negative aspects, but interestingly further probing helps him identify some positive outcomes from that negative start.

Extract 2:

Mentor:	Okay, what did you think?
Mentee:	I think my starting instructions need to be clearer.
Mentor:	Yeah
Mentee:	Because it's a new activity for them … the first time they ask questions … but I need them to know how to ask because it's useful for daily life … for
Mentor:	Mmmmm.
Mentee:	Okay … also it's for link with other lessons – future here also …. for the crossword they did all these words before and match it. Okay. They were read [sic] the word and understanding but here just definition and more … more difficult for them even if they did crossword at [sic] their books. I see …. this crossword is simple, so easy … I think primary schools can do it but here more difficult but if they do it again they will do it better I think.
Mentor:	Okay …. yeah. Yeah, I think it's a good idea for you to try the crossword but I think they are not used to such a challenging one … I think because the ones in the book are quite easy. How do you think you could have made it easier? Do you have any ideas?
Mentee:	Yes, to limit the words
Mentor:	Yes, limit the words, yeah. I think you had too many words and maybe too many definitions.
Mentee:	Yes, 16 words … if it was 10 words … it could be better
Mentor:	Yeah, ten words would have been better plus you can give them some letter clues once you have printed it out, write in some letter clues and then photocopy it.
Mentee:	I thought of this idea in the morning but I didn't have time
Mentor:	You didn't have time to do the copies
Mentee:	I have to do it by hand for each one.
Mentor:	Yeah, before photocopying … but you learn … if you ever do a crossword again, you can reduce the number of definitions and give more letter clues, maybe the beginnings or endings or in the middle or something like that, you know. That would help. But how did they do when you walked around? I saw some of them were doing okay but some of them were struggling.

Mentee:	Uh…most of the good students were absent, they didn't come. Four students…good students didn't come to school. Another few students are okay but the rest are very weak so I must try but some of them, the weaker student they worked if you noticed – Tariq. Salam who came late is very, very weak.
Mentor:	I could see that.
Mentee:	He can't even write his own name in English yet.
Mentor:	Oh my God.
Mentee:	Yes, Isa also is weak but other students were doing.
Mentor:	But when you walked around, was there any pair that had completed it?
Mentee:	Yeah.
Mentor:	So there were pupils who managed to….
Mentee:	Nasser, on the right…Marwan…also he didn't take my answer sheets because he wanted to complete it himself.
Mentor:	That's a good sign.

Just like the mentee in Extract 1, the mentee in Extract 2 very quickly began to focus on the negative component; in this case being the crossword activity. In this dialogue, not only did the mentee acknowledge that the activity had been too challenging but also critically reflected on what he could have done prior to the lesson as he had realized the possibility of the problem earlier. However, through deconstruction of the event, the mentee was surprised to discover that some of his pupils were able to complete the crossword, as he had assumed that most of the pupils were very weak in English based on information given to him by his school mentor teacher.

Reconstructing feedback dialogue

Although Extracts 1 and 2 only give snapshots of the first few minutes of the feedback dialogue, it is quite apparent that in both cases the mentees had immediate concerns about the lesson that they wanted to share and discuss. Thus, even with the mentor initiating and leading the dialogue, both mentees also showed some control in the way they were steering the feedback. While the feedback scenarios above may have benefitted the concerned mentees to a certain extent, it is also equally clear that much more could have been achieved if the feedback had been approached in a different way. The above extracts are taken from feedback dialogues with student teachers but they are also indicators of how post-observation feedback dialogues can unfold when an experienced teacher has been observed. While reflective practice is expected from student teachers as part of their practicum evaluation, in-service teachers are expected to continue reflecting on their practice throughout their career as part of their professional development. The onus then is on the teacher to chart his or her own reflective mode and sustain it.

Although teachers as 'reflective practitioners' is a well-touted idea, in reality, this rarely happens. Large classes, examination pressures, workloads and other issues can seriously limit an in-service teacher from embarking on a progressive, sustained and continuous cycle of reflective practice that can promote learning and development. Many long serving teachers resent the observation procedure because the classroom has become their territory and comfort zone. It is then vital for observers to demonstrate both non-judgemental attitude and behaviour (Head and Taylor, 1997). Accordingly, language can be a powerful instrument and needs to be facilitative so that a non-threatening observation and feedback scenario can be achieved.

Moon (1999) contends that while reflective practice among experienced teachers is viewed as desirable, many studies have mainly explored reflection only within the area of teacher training. Wildman and Niles (1987) further argue that experienced teachers are inhibited from being reflective practitioners by limitations of time, immense workloads and lack of institutional and administrative support. In addition, many teachers find it difficult to actually return to the reflective process after a period of hiatus. It is important then to recognize that reflection needs a structured condition for it to happen successfully.

Reflective dialogue through critical incidents

One such structured method, which has been successfully applied in ESL/EFL teacher training contexts to enable students to reflect and talk about their practice, is the use of critical incidents. By helping teachers identify and probe one event from a delivered lesson, they are encouraged to break down and deconstruct that event which usually leads to reflecting on the entire lesson, prior beliefs and post-lesson strategies.

Critical incidents are defined as:

> straightforward accounts of very commonplace events that occur in routine professional practice which are critical in the rather different sense that they are indicative of underlying trends, motives and structures. These incidents appear to be 'typical' rather than 'critical' at first sight, but are rendered critical through analysis. (Tripp, 2012, pp. 24–25)

Teachers are encouraged to focus on one event in the lesson and use this as a springboard for reflection. In this way, reflection becomes accessible to novice teachers as they can choose and justify the critical incident, and then deconstruct it using some guided questions to help students initiate self-reflection. This is a technique that can be used to elicit teachers' contextualized knowledge. When asked to reflect on a particular incident, the dialogue will usually reveal a rich, episodic knowledge resource which is readily related to classroom situations (Calderhead, 1990). This has been found to be successful within the realm of teacher training for English language teachers. Through systematic questioning and scaffolding, teachers can be challenged on the premise of their comments, highlighting their underlying beliefs and perhaps modifying them in light of their general professional learning. When feedback dialogue is founded on critical incidents, the questions employed will tend to be practical, diagnostic, critical and reflective in nature (Farrell, 2008).

Using critical incidents becomes meaningful to teachers as they identify the incident and analyse it. The involvement of a mentor means that assumptions that an individual may be unaware of can be explored and that the teacher can be brought to relate his incident to aspects of 'public' (as opposed to their personal) theory. The systematic nature of the questioning ensures that analysis of an event does not remain superficial, or insignificant, taking the teacher through a cycle of description of the event, an explanation of it in its immediate context and interpretation in a wider context (James, 2001). Moreover, the dialogue will also depart from a chronological and descriptive recount of events to one that focuses on deep analysis, possibly leading to deep and meaningful learning. While critical incidents have been used in social sciences and education for many years (Brookfield, 1987), Randall (with Thornton, 2001) suggests that the technique can also be used informally in a post-observation dialogue. The mentee can be asked to describe what they felt was the most important part of the lesson, and then this can be explored and probed in depth. In this way, critical incidents can be used as catalytic interventions where the mentee can take control of their own learning and development and 'own' their solutions, which will give them a sense of empowerment.

In both the extracts of feedback dialogue above, it is evident that there were several critical incidents that could be identified, such as the crossword puzzle (in Extract 2), which was deemed too challenging for students. It is already apparent that while the crossword incident appears on the surface to be negative, the fact that some students wanted to complete it on their own and that some were able to complete it provides a positive aspect to the incident. Deeper analysis of why the mentee decided to adapt the crossword puzzle and his opinion on why some students were able to complete it would have facilitated insight into his personal-professional beliefs and practices. In Extract 1, it is clear that the mentee's instructions could be analysed as a critical incident and would have potentially revealed the mentee's anxiety, which perhaps caused her to forget what she had planned to do. As the mentee had already been concerned about the effectiveness of her instructions, some deeper scrutiny was necessary to identify the mentee's challenges concerning planning and giving instructions during a lesson.

While the value of using critical incidents with student teachers to promote reflective practice is immediately apparent, it has not been so widely used in the area of professional development for experienced teachers. In many contexts, professional development for in-service teachers tends to be predetermined by heads of departments or heads of schools. Getting in-service teachers to use critical incidents means requiring them to take charge of their own development, which ultimately means granting teachers autonomy and trusting them to get on with it. Studies by Little (1982) and Holly (1983) found that teachers talk to each other continuously about classroom events so development of shared language is grounded on the belief that teachers are willing to discuss their practices. This implies that teachers can be equal and powerful participants in deciding, determining and directing feedback discourse. The role of dialogue in learning how to teach and reflect upon teaching is salient in teacher education and teacher development. Teachers need to develop not only the techniques but also the ability to recognize deep structures of learning through rationalizing the use of particular techniques, matching them to pedagogic purposes and relating them to theoretical models of learning (Randall with Thornton, 2001). Tilstone (1998) believes that teachers should be given the opportunity to 'own' the process and observers need to create opportunities that allow teachers to 'examine critically the values and practices which determine practice' (p. 66).

Brockbank and McGill (2006) argue that while reflection as an individual activity has innate value, it is insufficient in terms of enhancing 'transformatory' and evolutionary learning. They contend that the latter two stages of development can be best achieved through dialogue. Dialogue is repeatedly identified as integral to learning and development especially in mentoring or collaborative contexts. These include educational contexts, such as teacher training, peer observation and teacher supervision (Nias, 1987; Wallace, 1991; Randall and Thornton, 2001) and also corporate settings like mentoring new staff or helping staff members acquire added skills or responsibilities (Goleman, 2000; Harrison, 2009; Turnbull, 2009; Armstrong, 2012). Intentional dialogue that aims to promote reflective thought and action needs to be properly structured through appropriate discourse so it can acknowledge and deal with any uncertainty or emotions that the participant may bring to the dialogue. These requirements are hard to achieve in any professional dialogue situation and thus critical incidents can play a vital role in setting the ball rolling for a professional dialogue situation. In conditions where experienced teachers feel that they are doing well and are satisfied with their own self-developmental strategies (if any), using critical incidents can further encourage them to revisit and deconstruct some of their practices that they deem effective.

In comparison with other reflective methods, critical incidents can be more effective as they immediately require interpretation. Interpretation is exercised in identifying an incident and analysing it. According to Tripp (2012), critical incidents are not just what teachers observe; they are actually 'created'. What a teacher chooses as an incident in itself is an interpretive exercise and then further justification, description and analysis are all steps that require sustained interpretation. Tripp believes that diagnosing critical incidents ensures that teachers' reflections and evaluations are *'grounded in actuality'* (p. 31) and further asserts *'interpretation is essential to professional practice because it always comes between observation and action'* (p. 30). Using critical incidents towards self-reflection and development may be more inspirational because teachers will have the power to focus on an event of their choice, demonstrate intimate knowledge of the learners and learner behaviour and be able to reflect on the incident and its surrounding events on their own terms. These opportunities will then hopefully enable teacher empowerment and effective teacher development.

Fundamentally, using critical incidents is actually *'reflection on action'*. However, instead of describing the entire lesson or reflecting on the entire lesson, which is impossible, it allows one to select one instance and reflect on not only the event but also any *'reflection in action'* that may have happened. Thus, while Schön (1983) may have differentiated between the two types of reflection, using critical incidents could enable a combination of both *'reflection in action'* and *'reflection on action'* as, during the lesson, the teacher may already start to identify critical events. According to Tripp (2012), every single thing that happens in the classroom has the potential to be a critical incident so teachers can reflect during action to make a note of events and then reflect later to select the one that would be considered as the most crucial.

Generally, feedback dialogues tend to go through the entire lesson step by step, often focusing on what the mentor has deemed as pertinent and sometimes including what went into the planning stage as well. Consequently, they are usually initiated, led and controlled by the mentor. However, when critical incidents are consciously and explicitly identified during and after the lesson and form the crux of the feedback discourse, they can change the course of the feedback dialogue. With both trainees and experienced teachers, post-observation dialogue can then be initiated and led by the mentee and not necessarily by the mentor. The mentee can propel the dialogue by choosing to talk about any part of her lesson or, if the mentee is reluctant, the mentor could begin by asking this question:

What would you like to talk about? OR
Which part of your lesson would you like to talk about?

A question could also be avoided altogether and the teacher could be just invited to speak using the following prompt:

Please tell me about your lesson OR
Please feel free to talk about any aspect of your lesson.

Of course, the above statements may frighten a trainee or an experienced teacher. In teacher training situations, ideally the mentee would have had some practice in identifying and analysing critical incidents and would be aware that the feedback dialogue is expected to begin with the mentee's account of a critical incident. Similarly, if partnerships are formed among teaching peers, then the concept of critical incidents could be shared and established so that by the time of post-observational meetings, critical incidents will most likely form the crux of the dialogue. Additionally, in many post-observation feedback scenarios, the meeting happens immediately after the observation so the mentee is actually bursting with emotion and needs an opportunity to 'vent' or be able to express feelings openly before embarking on a constructive dialogue about the lesson.

There are some drawbacks in using *critical incidents*. The term itself can be seen as unfortunate because of each word. The word 'critical' is most likely to be associated with the word 'criticize' and 'incident' also has negative connotations. Thus, several studies have found that student teachers especially tend to focus on negative critical incidents (Francis, 1995; Farrell, 2008). Although a critical incident can be both positive and negative, the term 'critical' can have a negative connotation. Thus, mentors will have to make an extra effort to ensure that even if a mentee identifies a negative critical incident, he or she is guided through appropriate discourse to explore events and reach a positive outcome in terms of learning.

Conclusion

As the extracts indicate, most teachers find it hard to recall and talk about the positive aspects of their practice. Feedback that is carried out immediately after the lesson will most probably invite a focus on the negative because the teacher has just taught the lesson and would be anxious to know how they performed so the tendency to remember and concentrate on what did not go so well is likely. Feedback that is perhaps slightly delayed may help teachers to relax, reflect and recall incidents so they can weigh up events and choose what they want to talk about. The idea is not to think of what went wrong or right, but to select an event that is significant according to the teacher and then probe it. With deeper probing, both negative and positive aspects should emerge. For instance, in Extract 1, the critical incident based on the difficulty of the crossword puzzle allowed the mentee not only to analyse why he had adapted the existing crossword already available in the textbook, but also enabled him to judge the abilities of the students for himself rather than rely solely on the judgements of other teachers or exam scores. He was able to discern that students will have both strengths and weaknesses across the spectrum of language skills. For example, he was able to see that although one of his students, N, was always quiet and non-participatory, he was able to complete the crossword with little help. Thus, the mentee discovered that the child was not necessarily being passive because of weak language.

In addressing problematic terminology, Farrell (2007, p. 49) recommends adopting Thiel's (1999) terminology: *teaching highs* and *teaching lows*. A positive critical incident can also be referred to as a *magic moment* (Harmer, 2007, p. 157). In this way, perhaps the negative connotations of the term *critical incidents* can be avoided and teachers can identify, talk about and analyse events without labelling them as positive or negative. When teachers are given this comfort, the process of observation and feedback becomes meaningful and consequently, teachers will gain a sense of empowerment.

Hence, pre-observational preparation is imperative in using critical incidents as a platform for reflection. Teachers and observers alike need to understand, try and test critical incidents so that both parties are also aware of the issues and challenges of using critical incidents before arriving at the post-observational feedback dialogue stage. The basic construct of feedback dialogue is professional judgement which is usually shaped by theories of practice. However, these theories are dichotomized by various conceptual and social barriers; so it becomes more significant for teachers to develop their own theories of work (Tripp, 2012). The latter can be achieved through the use of critical incidents which can help teachers explore and understand how personal views and experiences can influence teaching. The added collaboration with a peer or mentor within the cycle of observation and feedback will further enhance the value of this process of ongoing reflection.

References

Armstrong, H. (2012), 'Coaching as dialogue: Creating spaces for (mis) understandings'. *International Journal of Evidence Based Coaching and Mentoring*, 10 (1), 33–46.

Beyer, L. E. (1989), *Critical Reflection and the Culture of Schooling: Empowering Teachers*. Victoria: Deakin University Press.

Bolitho, R. (1986), 'Teacher Development – a personal perspective'. *Teacher Development Newsletter*, 1, 2.

Brockbank, A. and McGill, I. (2006), *Facilitating Reflective Learning Through Mentoring and Coaching*. London: Kogan Page.

Brookfield, S. (1987), *Developing Critical Thinkers: Challenging Adults to Explore Alternative Ways*. Milton Keynes: Open University Press.

Calderhead, J. (1990), 'Conceptualising and evaluating teachers' professional learning'. *European Journal of Teacher Education*, 13 (3), 153–160.

Cochran-Smith, M. (2003), 'Sometimes it's not about the money: Teaching and heart'. *Journal of Teacher Education*, 54 (5), 371–375.

Dewey, J. (1933), *How We Think*. Boston: D C Heath and Co.

Farrell, T. S. C. (2007), *Reflective Language Teaching*. London: Continuum.

———. (2008), 'Critical incidents in ELT initial teacher training'. *ELT Journal*, 62 (1), 3–10.

Francis, D. (1995), 'The reflective journal: A window to pre-service teachers' practical knowledge'. *Teaching and Teacher Education*, 11 (3), 229–241.

Goldhammer, R. (1969), *Clinical Supervision; Special Methods for the Supervision of Teachers*. New York: Holt, Rinehart and Winston.

Goleman, D. (2000), 'Leadership that gets results'. *Harvard Business Review*, March–April.

Harmer, J. (2007), *How to teach English*, new ed. Essex: Pearson-Longman Publishers.

Harrison, R. (2009), *Learning and Development*, 5th ed. London: Chartered Institute of Personnel and Development.

Head, K. and Taylor, P. (1997), *Readings in Teacher Development*. Oxford: Heinemann.

Holly, M. L. (1983), 'Teacher reflections on classroom life: Collaboration and Professional Development'. *Australian Administrator*, 4 (4), 1–4.

———. (1987), *Keeping a Personal-Professional Journal*. Victoria: Deakin University Press.

Hoover, L. A. (1994), 'Reflective writing as a window on pre-service teachers' thought processes'. *Teaching and Teacher Education*, 10 (1), 83–93.

James, P. (2001), *Teachers in Action: Tasks for In-service Language Teacher Education and Development*. Cambridge: CUP.

Kolb, D. (1984), *Experiential Learning as the Science of Learning and Development*. New Jersey: Prentice Hall.

Little, J. W. (1982), 'Norms of collegiality and experimentation: Workplace conditions of school success'. *American Educational Research Journal*, 19 (3), 325–340.

Malderez, A. and Bodoczky, C. (1999), *Mentor Courses: A Resource Book for Trainer-Trainers*. Cambridge: Cambridge University Press.

Mills, M. and Satterthwait, D. (2000), 'The disciplining of pre-service teachers: Reflections on the teaching of reflective teaching'. *Asia-Pacific Journal of Teacher Education*, 28 (1), 29–38.

Montgomery, D. (1999), *Helping Teachers Develop through Classroom Observation*, 2nd edn. London: David Fultan Publishers.

Moon, J. (1999), *Reflection in Learning and Professional Development: Theory and Practice*. London: RoutledgeFalmer.

Nias, J. (1987), *Seeing Anew: Teachers' Theories of Action*. Victoria: Deakin University Press.

Parsons, M. and Stephenson, M. (2005), 'Developing reflective practice in student teachers: Collaboration and critical partnerships'. *Teachers and Teaching*, 11 (1), 95–116.

Randall, M. with Thornton, B. (2001), *Advising and Supporting Teachers*. Cambridge: CUP.

Schön, D. (1983), *The Reflective Practitioner*. San Francisco: Jossey-Bass.

Shoffner, M. (2009), 'The place of the personal: Exploring the affective domain through reflection in teacher preparation'. *Teaching and Teacher Education*, 25 (6), 783–789.

Shutz, A. (1967), 'On multiple realities', in M. Natanson (ed.), *The Problem of Social Reality, Collected Papers I*. The Hague: Martinus Nijhoff, pp. 209–212.

Smyth, W. J. (1984), *Clinical Supervison – Collaborative Learning about Teaching*. Victoria: Deakin University Press.

Spilkova, V. (2001), 'Professional development of teachers and student teachers through reflection on practice'. *European Journal of Teacher Education*, 24 (1), 59–65.

Thiel, T. (1999), 'Reflections on critical incidents'. *Prospect*, 14, 44–52.

Tilstone, C. (1998), *Observing Teaching and Learning: Principles and Practice*. London: David Fulton Publishers.

Tripp, D. (2012), *Critical Incidents in Teaching: Developing Professional Judgement*, classic ed. Abingdon: Routledge Publishers.

Turnbull, J. (2009), *Coaching for Learning*. London: Continuum International Publishing Group.

Wallace, M. J. (1991), *Training Foreign Language Teachers: A Reflective Approach*. Cambridge: Cambridge University Press.

Wildman, T. and Niles, J. (1987), 'Reflective teachers: Tensions between abstractions and realities'. *Journal of Teacher Education*, 3, 25–31.

Zembylas, M. (2007), 'Emotional ecology: The intersection of emotional knowledge and pedagogical content knowledge in teaching'. *Teaching and Teacher Education*, 23 (4), 355–367.

CHAPTER FIVE

Artefacts in Scaffolding the Construction of Teaching Knowledge

Marion Engin

Introduction

Teacher training is a highly social and interactional activity. Much of the learning and construction of teaching knowledge takes place through constructive and pedagogic dialogue. The main tool in these dialogues is talk, or language, which is a psychological tool (Vygotsky, 1986). Considerable research has been carried out into the role and function of talk as a tool and scaffold in the learning process, both in a school environment (Mercer, 1995, 2000; Mercer and Littleton, 2007; Myhill, 2004, 2006; Myhill and Warren, 2005) and in a teacher training context (Engin, 2011, 2013; Freeman, 1996; Golombek and Johnson, 2004; Randall with Thornton, 2001). However, little has been researched and written about another primary tool in the learning process: the use of material and physical artefacts.

Artefacts may be described as '*a technological device which, in combination with labor use, transforms the consciousness of those who use it and the society in which it is used*' (McDonald et al., 2005, p. 114). In an educational context, this means that particular use of an artefact in an activity can contribute to the development and learning of those using it. The discussion in this chapter revolves around written documents as artefacts and their materiality and meditation in interaction. As Wertsch (1998) points out, a material artefact is created by the user and also creates meaning in its use. Thus, an artefact is meaningless unless used for a specific purpose by participants in the interaction.

Learning environments may contain many artefacts. As McDonald et al. (2005) state, '*classrooms are not only full of material artifacts, they are dependent on them*' (p. 116). In the same way that a classroom is full of physical artefacts such as board, projector, stationery, books and computers, a teacher training context is rich in written material artefacts such as teaching transcripts, lesson plans, running commentaries, self-evaluation forms, as well as many other forms and reports required as part of the professional and training goals. The tendency in the literature on learning has been to *refer* to the artefact in the interaction, rather than *examine* and *describe* its use and role in learning (McDonald et al., 2005). It is important to note that these artefacts are not neutral; they are formed within a certain social, cultural and educational culture. The artefacts have also been shaped by prior practice and they exist in a particular discourse. This chapter takes a view of learning as sociocultural in that learning takes place through mediation with a more competent other. At the centre of this study is a Vygotskian conceptual framework based on sociocultural theory (Vygotsky, 1986). The role of artefacts in the construction of knowledge is a significant one in a sociocultural theory of learning as the artefact takes on the role of a meditational means. This chapter is an attempt to analyse and examine certain written material artefacts in the construction of teaching knowledge and discuss possible implications for pre-service teacher training.

A sociocultural theory of learning

Vygotsky and other researchers in sociocultural theory postulate that learning is mediated by cultural tools (Daniels, 2001; Lantolf and Thorne, 2006). Sociocultural theory (SCT) is a '*theory of mediated mental development and it is most compatible with theories of language which focus on communication, cognition, and meaning rather than on formalist positions that privilege structure*' (Lantolf and Thorne, 2006, p. 4).

SCT emphasizes the social and interactive nature of learning. Vygotsky (1986) proposed that there are two stages to constructing knowledge. First, we understand on a social level, between people: the dialogic nature of understanding. Second, we understand individually, the understanding that happens inside ourselves (Vygotsky, 1986). In order to get to this stage of internalization, the new topic has to be mediated. This interactional experience is also known as '*interthinking*' (Mercer and Littleton, 2007) and the basic premise is that thinking and higher cognitive development occur through social interaction (Lantolf and Appel, 1994). Such a notion is vital to teacher training contexts since most teacher training activities are highly social and interactive. Much of this interaction in a training context involves scaffolding the learning and development of the novice teacher.

Scaffolding as a metaphor to describe the assistance a teacher or more knowledgeable peer can give in a learning context is derived from the work of Wood et al. (1976). The term *scaffolding* was introduced in the context of tutorials and refers to the help given by a teacher or more able peer in an educational setting. The goal of research in the area of scaffolding has been to explore the nature of the support that the more competent other provides in the learning context (Wood and Wood, 1996). Bruner (1978, cited by Mercer, 1995) writes of scaffolding thus, '*(it) refers to the steps taken to reduce the degrees of freedom in carrying out some task so that the child can concentrate on the difficult skill she is in the process of acquiring*' (p. 73).

Most studies on scaffolding in a second language teacher training context focus on the scaffolding techniques trainers use. In a teaching practice context, examples of trainer scaffolding techniques might be modelling, contingency management and feedback on lessons, instructions, questioning and cognitive structuring (Eun, 2008), mentoring techniques (Randall with Thornton, 2001), and questioning techniques (Engin, 2013). However, there has been little examination of the artefacts around which much of the scaffolding talk takes place. Carroll (2005) examines the role of artefacts or tools such as plans and videos in mediating talk with teachers. It is significant that the interaction and talk were stimulated by artefacts from the mentoring practice the teachers were engaged in. He concludes that construction of teaching knowledge took place '*by fostering interactive talk around artifacts of mentoring practice*' (p. 472). This emphasizes the central role of the artefact, as well as the fact that the artefact should be part of the practice the teachers are engaged in.

Mediating artefacts

Artefacts in education have been referred to as '*tools for thinking and acting*' (Fors, 2003, p. 2) and as either scaffolds themselves (Orlikowski, 2005; Sherin et al., 2004) or as part of the scaffolding process (Hammond and Gibbons, 2005). Wartofsky (1979) points out that there are three types of artefacts. Primary artefacts are the material equipment and secondary artefacts are the mental models of artefacts. It is these which mediate human interaction. The third type of artefact is the tertiary artefact which creates possibilities for further activity. In terms of semantics, McDonald et al. (2005) note that there is considerable overlap between the terms *tool* and *artefact*, with some writers suggesting that tool is a subcategory of artefact (Cole and Wertsch, 1996). For the purposes of this chapter, I shall refer to artefacts as material, concrete, physical objects which are permanent documents.

Artefacts are created for a specific purpose. They are not random objects in the learning environment. Wartofsky's (1980) distinction is highly applicable in the educational context. '*Artifacts need to be made, in some manner of deliberate, even self-conscious creation, then in order to be artifacts at all, rather than accidental or natural objects'* (p. 239). Thus, artefacts in a teacher training context are specifically created documents or other artefacts for the purposes of teacher learning. The artefact has been shaped by the trainer or more able peer. The artefact also shapes the thinking of the user, thus highlighting the transformational function of an artefact (Cole and Wertsch, 1996). Such uses and functions will be culturally, historically and institutionally situated and context specific (Cole and Wertsch, 1996, p. 252).

Wertsch (1998) refers to artefacts as material mediational means which are cultural tools, powerless unless manipulated and used by an agent. This definition most closely suits the concept of documents which are used to guide thinking in a teacher training context. Such a definition brings into the equation a user, or agent, who may or may not have power and authority to determine how the artefact will be used. As a result, there may be conflicts as to the intended uses of the artefact, and the actual use or interpretation of the artefact. Wertsch (2000) describes written texts as *thinking* devices (p. 24) as a material mediational means, and it is such written texts which are at the centre of this chapter. According to Wertsch (1998), in an analysis of written artefacts, one must consider their affordances, their constraints, their use for action and the power and authority that designate how they are to be used. These considerations form a possible framework in which to examine artefacts in a second language teacher education context.

In their research into scaffolding in the classroom, Hammond and Gibbons (2005) view meditational texts as being central to the learning and pedagogic talk. Although their research focus was the interaction rather than the artefact, they found there was *'significant talk occurring around them'* (p. 17) which pointed to the central and pivotal role of the artefact in the conversation. The artefact (written text) was found in conversations across a sequence of lessons, thus highlighting the permanent quality of an artefact and its affordances of continuing to guide across interactions and time.

In this study, the artefacts played a scaffolding role in the interaction between the trainer and the trainee. The educational artefacts were found to prompt, or create, *'an impediment or disturbance in an automatic activity'* (Vygotsky, 1986, p. 30) and guide thinking in a post-observation feedback conversation. The artefact alone does not scaffold; it is the talk which occurs around the artefact which also scaffolds since learning conversations involve a task, actions and talk (Askew, 2004) as well as an artefact. However, this is not to deny the significant role of the artefact in guiding the conversation. As McDonald et al. (2005) point out, *'Without denying the value of discourse as evidence for successful communication and shared understanding, classrooms are not only full of material artifacts, they are dependent on them'* (p. 116). Carroll (2005) notes that in a teacher education context, artefacts such as lesson plans and transcripts guided conversations about teaching as the artefacts were grounded in the professional work of teachers. In his study, the lesson plans and transcripts not only mirrored the work of the teachers, but they also stimulated thinking and acted as catalysts for investigation, comparison and learning about teaching.

Research context

This chapter reports on part of a larger research which examined scaffolding in the construction of teaching knowledge in a pre-service teacher training course in an English-medium university in Turkey. The participants were all Turkish trainee teachers of English on an MA course which led to qualified teacher status. The group was composed of twenty-seven teacher trainees in their final year of the teacher education programme. The main focus of the research was the role of talk in scaffolding the construction of teaching knowledge, but it became clear that the various artefacts which were used in the interactional talk, as well as in the self-evaluation and reflections, were catalysts for guiding thinking and ultimately construction of knowledge.

Artefacts

The artefacts which will be examined in this chapter are running commentaries, lesson plans and transcripts of feedback sessions. The first two were institutional documents which were used by all trainers working with the trainees. They were *'explicit'* mediational means (Wertsch, 2007, p. 188), or *'material genres'* (Edwards, 2010, p. 8) in that the document being used *'involves the intentional introduction of what is to be learnt into a learning activity, which is managed by someone who is designated as "teacher", and therefore reflects what is common in formal education settings'* (p. 8). In other words, these documents were designed by the instructors/trainers of the course to specifically guide the reflection and thinking of the trainees. The transcripts of the feedback sessions were from sessions carried out, recorded and transcribed by the researcher as part of a doctoral study.

The running commentary was used by the trainer to comment on the teaching practice (see Appendix 1). As can be seen, the trainer describes the activities in the lesson, to be used as an aide mémoire, as well as noting down questions or comments to bring up in the post-observation feedback session. This artefact was produced by the trainer, but referred to in the feedback session; thus it played a pivotal role as an artefact in the interaction. The lesson plan was an institutional document which had to be filled in before the lesson by the trainee, often in consultation with the trainer. Trainees were required to include information on aims of the lesson, resources to be used, stages of the lesson and times for each stage. This was given to the trainer before the teaching practice lesson and was referred to in the post-observation feedback session. The transcripts of the feedback sessions were made from audio recordings of the feedback sessions. The audio recording was then transcribed *verbatim* (Rapley, 2007, p. 122) and typed up. At the end of the course, the participants received the transcripts and audio recordings of their feedback sessions.

Data collection

As mentioned above, transcripts of feedback sessions were the main artefacts in the research. These transcripts were also an essential part of the data since they provided evidence of the talk between the trainer and trainee in the feedback session and they served as the main data in the research. Data was also collected from the respondent validations. Participants were given a copy of the transcripts of their feedback sessions and asked to respond to the transcript in any way they wanted. The final data collection instrument was a reflection that trainees were asked to write as part of their school experience final exam. Trainees were asked to reflect on their observations of school culture, ethos, students and teaching methodology. They also reflected on their teaching experiences and areas where they still needed to make progress.

Results: Artefacts in action

In this section, the role of artefacts in the scaffolding process will be presented and examined through short vignettes of the feedback sessions, excerpts from respondents' validations and trainee reflections.

Extract 1: Running commentary

In Extract 1, an excerpt from a feedback session, the trainer is describing a particular part of a lesson using the running commentary as a prompt. She starts by pointing out how the teacher could give more specific instructions for an activity. The trainer shares her running commentary with the student teacher. The trainer had made a note of incorrect pronunciation of the word '*tarpaulin*'. In the feedback session, the trainer and trainee were sitting next to each other with the running commentary placed on the desk between them. The commentary was fully visible to the trainee as well as the trainer:

Extract 1: Transcript

T: Well, you can stop everybody *'please stop'*, *'look at me a minute here are the questions, I want to see the answers written on your paper'* or *'I want you to underline where you found the information'*. You can stop the activity Ok, you nominated, you're encouraging very nicely.

ST: What word is that? (points to running commentary)

T: Ah yes, the pronunciation.

ST: Yes, I was not sure. I checked the online dictionary.

T: Yes, you said?

ST: Tarpaylin.

T: Yes, like trampoline. Tarpaulin.

ST: Tarpaulin. Ok.

The trainer starts the conversation by pointing out certain teaching points. However, the student teacher changes the direction of the conversation by picking up on a note the trainer had made in the running commentary. The running commentary and the notes in it serve as an artefact to stimulate a pedagogic conversation about the teaching. The student teacher is a non-native speaker of English so it is therefore important that she learn the correct pronunciation of a word that she is teaching. The shared understanding of the use of the artefact here is also important. The intended purpose of the artefact is as an aide mémoire and a jumping board for instructional dialogue. The student teacher also understands this function of the document and similarly uses it as an aide mémoire. Thus the artefact is institutionally specific and is used with its explicit purpose to prompt discussion. In terms of authority, the trainer has forced the conversation by intentionally noting down the learning point, but it is the trainee who chooses to bring up the point in the discussion.

Extract 2: Running commentary

In Extract 2, taken from a school experience report, a student teacher describes how the running commentary served as a constant reminder of priorities in teaching:

Extract 2: School experience reflection

Getting this feedback was one of the most useful experiences for me because after this I always remembered sticking to the main aim of the lesson maybe because I still can see the question on the feedback paper *'Is it a reading or a vocabulary lesson?'* which had a striking effect on me. That learning experience also helped me to improve not gradually but immediately as the previous case. After this experience, I kept my main aim in mind and taught accordingly, not shifting from the main point.

The artefact is clearly permanent. The document as a written genre plays the role of aide mémoire. As it is a physical object, the notes the trainer had written were a constant reminder to the trainee. Although again the document is institutionally specific and both student teacher and trainer share expectations of its use, the fact that the student teacher continues to look at it is surprising. Most student teachers refer to the running commentary for their feedback session and then file them away. The trainer holds the power in the words she has written on the document, thus establishing the authority. However, the unanticipated result here is that the trainee continues to refer to the document. The artefact does not only play a role in one conversation about the lesson, but clearly extends to further conversations and reflections on the lesson.

Extract 3: Lesson plans

In Extract 3, from a feedback session, the trainer and student teacher are discussing the lesson. The trainer refers to the lesson plan that the student teacher prepared beforehand and which they have in front of them on the desk.

Extract 3: Transcript

T: No, Ok, well let's have a look at your aims then. So, Ok, so in terms of your aims, how do you feel your lesson was, could you manage to achieve your aims, did the students do what you've written here? (Trainer refers to lesson plan).

ST: That's actually I planned my lesson in accordance with the aim in accordance with the sentence itself, by means of recognizing first I used paragraphs, where students could see them in context and, recognize, underline them and guess their meanings and practising with exercises, and matching and fill in the blanks, and using them in a story, using in creative skills.

T: Ok, so you are saying you, they did this, they did this, they did this, and they did this? (T pointing to the aims on the lesson plan).

ST: That's the last one, story completion that's that was not finished, but I will collect them next week and, I'll give feedback, and probably grade, let's see.

The trainer wants the student teacher to reflect on whether she achieved her aims or not. It seems that the trainer thinks the student teacher did not, and so uses the lesson plan as a reference point and to guide the reflection. By seeing the written form of the lesson aims, the student teacher can more easily compare what she had planned with what she actually did. This conversation is an example of what Hammond and Gibbons (2005) refer to when they point out the importance of the talk which occurs around the artefact. In this case, the talk is stimulated and constrained by the artefact. The student teacher cannot go off topic as the artefact is physical, concrete, specifically referred to and plays a major role in the conversation. The trainer refers to the lesson plan '*here*' at the beginning of the conversation, but when the student teacher describes what she did rather than whether she achieved her aims, the trainer more specifically refers to each lesson aim and asks '*they did this? they did this?*'. It is at this point the student teacher realizes she had not finished all her activities. The lesson plan thus serves as a physical reminder of what she did, rather than what she thinks she did.

Extract 4: Lesson plans

In Extract 4, the student teacher reports on her experience of the lesson plan and how useful it was to her learning. She reflects on this in her school experience reflection paper:

Extract 4: School experience reflection

Through following the lesson plan, reflecting on my lesson became easier as I remembered every stage that I taught in my lesson. I remembered what I did and I realized what I should have done according to the lesson plan. Furthermore, I also recognized the drawbacks of the lesson plan when I compared it with my lesson.

The artefact of a lesson plan is clearly used as an aide mémoire as the student teacher uses the word '*remember*' twice. The artefact also serves as a tool for reflection, seen in the use of the words '*realized*', '*recognized*' and '*compared*'. The lesson plan as an institutional document in the training course is being used in unanticipated ways. The artefact is manipulated by the student teacher to play a pivotal role in her reflection. This was not necessarily expected by the trainer, however, it is a positive spin-off. The affordance of the lesson plan as a preparation tool has far exceeded that, moving into the realms of a reflection tool. As Askew (2004) points out, the artefact does not stand alone and requires task, talk and actions. In this case, the student teacher has created her own task for the artefact, that of a reflection tool. The purpose of the lesson plan has transcended its original purpose and has undergone a transformation.

Extract 5: Transcriptions of feedback session

In Extract 5, the student teacher has read the transcript of her feedback session. In response to the open question '*Please comment on the transcript*', she writes:

Extract 5: Respondent validation

By the way, after reading the script, I remembered once again what I should do before giving instructions. I realized that I need to check students' knowledge about the phrasal verb that I'll teach...thanks to this script, I have both the points that I need to consider and the points that I am good at. It's a written document that will stay forever and from time to time, I'll read it to check whether I am on the right track or no.

The artefact of a transcript of a feedback session is interesting in that it is a permanent record of a conversation which would normally be ephemeral and temporary, thus easily forgotten. For the purposes of the wider research, the researcher had asked the student teachers to read through the transcript of a feedback session some three months earlier and comment on them in any way they chose. The student teacher here comments on the permanent nature of the artefact and the materiality of it, thus its function as an aide mémoire and guide for future teaching practice (Wartofsky, 1979). Reading through transcripts of teaching can help to raise awareness of what teachers actually do compared to what they think they do (Thornbury, 1996). Similarly in this case, the student teacher is able to reflect both on the conversation and the lesson she taught through the transcript. The student teacher emphasizes the permanent nature of the document. She also takes ownership of the artefact by establishing the purpose for which she will use it. The function of the transcript as a permanent guide to good teaching is an example of a tool for thinking and learning (Fors, 2003) as well as an example of how an artefact has been shaped by the trainer and shapes the thinking of the student teacher.

Extract 6: Transcriptions of feedback sessions: Spin-offs

As discussed earlier, the function of the artefact may change from its original purpose. Respondent validation was sought by giving the student teachers the transcripts of their feedback sessions and they were asked to comment on the conversation. Most student teachers responded by noticing how much they had developed in terms of teaching knowledge. However, in Extract 6, the student teacher wrote only about her language in her respondent validation. She in fact writes a detailed language analysis of her talk in the feedback session. This is from the beginning of her response:

Extract 6: Respondent validation

First of all, before I had read my conversations, I suppose that I just made pronunciation mistakes while speaking. However, I became aware that I had also grammar mistakes. For example, when you asked your questions to me in past simple tense, I answered in present simple of future tense. So there is no tense agreement in my speech.

This response was totally unexpected. Rather than commenting, as other student teachers did, on the learning experience of the feedback session, she commented only on her own language use. This shows a preoccupation with her accuracy as an English language user and teacher. This particular student teacher had received some negative feedback about her own language use in her practice lessons. This was clearly a concern of hers. The interesting and unanticipated spin-off from this artefact was the fact that the student teacher was able to analyse her own language mistakes with such clarity and accuracy, confirming what her supervisors had been telling her throughout the course. This cultural tool was appropriated by the student teacher for her own benefit and manipulated to suit her own concerns. This is what Wertsch (1998) refers to when he describes the spin-offs from the conflict between the goals of the agent, in this case the student teacher, and the embedded goals of the tool, which was to reflect on teaching.

Discussion

This chapter has been an attempt to respond to McDonald et al.'s (2005) call for the need to 'describe', rather than 'refer' to artefacts. This specific study examines material artefacts, in the shape of documents, in the construction of teaching knowledge in a second language teacher education context. The aim of this chapter was not to evaluate the effectiveness of artefacts, but to examine their potential role in the scaffolding of teaching knowledge. While the main focus of this chapter has been the artefacts, and their uses, it has become clear that they cannot be examined in isolation. As Askew (2004) points out, the artefact must be studied with regard to the talk, action and tasks surrounding the artefact. Artefacts, both the real and ideal (Askew, 2004), need also to be examined within the cultural and educational context in which they are being used. From the data, a few conclusions may be made which bring together some of the theoretical concepts from SCT, those of social interaction and scaffolding, as well as a possible theoretical framework for description suggested by Wertsch (1998) which includes notions of affordances, constraints and power/authority.

There is no right or wrong way to use a material artefact in a teacher training context. From the extracts we can see that there is a symbiotic relationship between the artefact and the talk. This has been pointed out by Hammond and Gibbons (2005), who refer to the artefacts as meditational texts in the social interaction between teacher and learner. However, it is clear from the extracts that the talk mediates the text as well as the text mediating the talk. If we consider some of the main tenets of SCT, learning takes place through the mediation of a more able peer, as well as through mediating artefacts. The social interaction is crucial to create a space for interthinking and thus construction of knowledge. With regard to the artefact, it plays an important role in being the catalyst for stimulating the thinking and the talk about teaching. The artefact can act as a scaffold itself, as a physical, material object. The artefact can also create scaffolding opportunities through the nature of the text.

A material artefact such as those which have been presented in this chapter can have many affordances. One is that it provides a catalyst for thinking (Carroll, 2005; Fors, 2003; Thornbury, 1996). The physicality of the artefact as well as the fact it is a written text can encourage questioning, justification and explaining, which are all cognitive thinking skills. As can be seen in the extracts, not only the trainer, but also the trainee can refer to the artefact and use the text to create a pedagogic dialogue. The artefact may also afford unexpected spin-offs which may give the trainer insight into alternative uses and purposes of an artefact. In short, the artefact helps to create a space for talking about teaching.

In terms of possible constraints, the artefact may also act as a straightjacket rather than a scaffold (Myhill and Warren, 2005). This may come about for several reasons. If there is not a shared understanding of the purpose of the artefact, or a shared understanding of its meaning, divergent conversations may result. Although artefacts are usually institutionally specific (Cole and Wertsch, 1996), a misunderstanding may take place. Similarly, the implicit mediation of the text (Wertsch, 2007) may cause confusion or restrict the dialogue and resultant learning. In other words, the discourse embedded in the artefact, or the specific discourse around the artefact may force learners to think and talk in a particular way. A trainer's use of very specialized vocabulary related to teaching or high-level terminology may in fact exclude the student teacher from the conversation. The artefact then becomes a restriction rather than a guide and is a manifestation of the unequal power and authority vested in learning artefacts.

The reality in a teacher training context is that student teachers have to become qualified teachers in a short space of time. As a result, trainers may impose their authority over the artefact in their choice of language or choice of task. Although trainees expect their trainer to guide them (Bailey, 2006), the authority of the trainer may be obviously present in the way the artefact is used, the way it is presented and, of course, the way it has been shaped.

Nevertheless, the affordances of a material artefact in a second language teacher education context are many. It can be a useful exercise to explicitly discuss with trainees the role and purposes of the different artefacts. This may encourage more shared understanding. However, this is not to suggest that trainees should be restricted in their interpretations. They may be very creative in manipulating the artefact for other purposes. This should also be encouraged. As long as the institutional aims are clear, trainees should be able to create their own space for thinking around the written artefact.

Conclusion

Thus, it can be seen that material artefacts, in the shape of written institutionally specific documents, can be powerful scaffolding tools in the interaction between trainer and trainee, as well as catalysts for thinking and talking about teaching. It is also clear that artefacts must be examined in their very specific educational context, with regard to the aims and purposes of the artefact. One artefact may create opportunities for learning in one context, but not another, or with one trainee, but not another. The social interactional context is also significant, and the talk which surrounds the artefact also needs to be examined. It is only through the talk that we can understand how the trainer and trainee are making meaning: '*While we cannot directly observe such sense making, we can take teachers' and pupils' particular response and uses of mediational means as indicators of how they are interpreting their experience*' (Askew, 2004, p. 78). Therefore, there needs to be more examination and description of different material artefacts, such as books, videos, DVDs, pictures and other educational tools through short classroom excerpts or vignettes (McDonald et al., 2005). By studying the artefact in action through the actions and the talk (Askew, 2004) we can then build a better picture of how the artefact contributes to the scaffolding of teaching knowledge. In a second language teacher training context it is also relevant and timely to examine not only the explicit mediation in the form of text and documents, but also the implicit mediation in the form of the discourse which promotes the artefact and the discourse which the artefact promotes (Wertsch, 2007).

References

Askew, M. (2004), 'Mediation and interpretation: Exploring the interpersonal and the intrapersonal in primary mathematics lessons'. *Proceedings of the 28th Conference of the International Group for the Psychology of Mathematics Education*. 2, 71–78.

Bailey, K. M. (2006), *Language Teacher Supervision*. Cambridge: Cambridge University Press.

Carroll, D. (2005), 'Learning through interactive talk: A school-based mentor teacher study group as a context for professional learning'. *Teaching and Teacher Education*, 21, 457–473.

Cole, M. and Wertsch, J. V. (1996), 'Beyond the individual-social antimony in discussions of Piaget and Vygotsky'. *Human Development*, 39, 250–256.

Daniels, H. (2001), *Vygotsky and Pedagogy*. New York: Routledge.

Edwards, A. (2010), *Being an Expert Professional Practitioner: The Relational Turn in Expertise*. Dordrecht: Springer.

Engin, M. (2011), 'Scaffolding the construction of teaching knowledge in a pre-service teacher training context: Language Teacher Education in a Turkish University'. EdD. Diss. Bath University.

———. (2013), 'Questioning to scaffold: An exploration of questions in pre-service teacher training feedback sessions'. *European Journal of Teacher Education*, 36, 39–54.

Eun, B. (2008), 'Making connections: Grounding professional development in the developmental theories of Vygotsky'. *The Teacher Educator*, 43, 134–155.

Fors, V. (2003), 'Artefacts and learning'. 34th Annual Conference ASERA, Melbourne, Australia, 9–12 July 2003.

Freeman, D. (1996), 'The "unstudied problem": Research on teacher learning in language teaching', in D. Freeman and J. C. Richards (eds), *Teacher Learning in Language Teaching*. Cambridge: Cambridge University Press, pp. 397–417.

Golombek, P. R. and Johnson, K. E. (2004), 'Narrative inquiry as a mediational space: Examining emotional and cognitive dissonance in second language teachers' development'. *Teachers and Teaching, Theory and Practice*, 10, 307–327.

Hammond, J. and Gibbons, P. (2005), 'Putting scaffolding to work: The contribution of scaffolding in articulating ESL education'. *Prospect*, 20, 6–30.

Lantolf, J. P. and Appel, G. (eds) (1994), *Vygotskian Approaches to Second Language Research*. New Jersey: Ablex Publishing Corporation.

——— and Thorne, S. L. (2006), *Sociocultural Theory and the Genesis of Second Language Development*. Oxford: Oxford University Press.

McDonald, G., Le, H., Higgins, J. and Podmore, V. (2005), 'Artifacts, tools and classrooms'. *Mind, Culture and Activity*, 12, 113–127.

Mercer, N. (1995), *The Guided Construction of Knowledge: Talk amongst Teachers and Learners*. Clevedon: Multilingual Matters Ltd.

———. (2000), *Words and Minds: How we use Language to Think Together*. London: Routledge.

——— and Littleton, K. (2007), *Dialogue and the Development of Children's Thinking*. London: Routledge.

Myhill, D. (2004), 'Making connections: Teachers' use of children's prior knowledge in whole-class discussion'. *British Journal of Education Studies*, 52, 263–275.

———. (2006), 'Talk, talk, talk: Teaching and learning in whole-class discussion'. *Research Papers in Education*, 21, 19–41.

——— and Warren, P. (2005), 'Scaffolds or straitjackets? Critical moments in classroom discourse'. *Educational Review*, 57, 55–69.

Orlikowski, W. J. (2005), 'Material knowing: The scaffolding of human knowledgeability'. Sixth European Conference on Organisational Knowledge, Learning and Capabilities, Cambridge, MA.

Randall, M. with Thornton, B. (2001), *Advising and Supporting Teachers*. Cambridge: Cambridge University Press.

Rapley, T. (2007), *Doing Conversation and Document Analysis*. London: Sage.

Sherin, B., Reiser, B. J. and Edelson, D. (2004), 'Scaffolding analysis: Extending the scaffolding metaphor to learning artifacts'. *Journal of the Learning Sciences*, 13, 387–421.

Thornbury, S. (1996), 'Teachers research teacher talk'. *English Language Teaching Journal*, 50, 279–289.

Vygotsky, L. S. (1986), *Thought and Language*. Cambridge, MA: MIT Press.

Wartofsky, M. W. (1979), *Models: Representation and the Scientific Understanding*. Dordrecht, The Netherlands: D. Reidel.

———. (1980), 'Art, artworlds, and ideology'. *The Journal of Aesthetics and Art Criticism*, 38, 239–247.

Wertsch, J.V. (1998), *Mind as Action*. Oxford: Oxford University Press.

———. (2000), 'Intersubjectivity and alterity in human communication', in N. Budwig, I. C. Uzgiris and J. V. Wertsch (eds), *Communication: An Arena of Development*. Connecticut: Ablex Publishing Corporation, pp. 17–32.

———. (2007), 'Mediation', in H. Daniels, M. Cole and J. V. Wertsch (eds), *The Cambridge Companion to Vygotsky*. Cambridge: Cambridge University Press, pp. 178–192.

Wood, D., Bruner, J. S. and Ross, G. (1976), 'The role of tutoring and problem solving'. *Journal of Child Psychology and Psychiatry*, 17, 89–100.

——— and Wood, H. (1996), 'Vygotsky, tutoring and learning'. *Oxford Review of Education*, 22, 5–16.

Appendix 1: Running commentary sheet used by trainers

TEACHER: DATE:

OBSERVER:

LEVEL OF CLASS: TIME:

MAIN AIMS OF LESSON:

STAGE OF LESSON/ DESCRIPTION	TIME	COMMENTS/QUESTIONS

CHAPTER SIX

A System for Teacher Evaluation

Phil Quirke

Introduction

This chapter outlines a seven-stage teacher appraisal programme, developed by an institutional committee involving teachers, chairs, managers and human resources personnel. It is claimed that the resulting programme is effective because it is standard and coherent, adheres to best practice and principles, focuses on appraisal and professional development as opposed to evaluation and aims to enhance teacher practice through reflection in a structured framework. Since the focus is on quality, the approach is a qualitative one that relies on the guided interpretation of feedback from all those involved in the day-to-day work of the teacher, presented in a portfolio format.

Many researchers believe that teacher evaluation practices are in need of change (Bouchamma et al., 2008; Campbell et al., 2004; Danielson and McGreal, 2000; Thaine, 2004), including Peterson who suggests that '*poor practice in teacher evaluation is quietly accepted*' (2000, p. ix). This view is hardly surprising when you consider that most current practice is based on a supervisory report which in turn is based on a classroom visit or a checklist of what good teaching should involve (Good and Mulryan, 1990). The appraisal approach suggested here advocates a guided discussion framework between the teacher and supervisor. By outlining seven key stages with practical examples, this chapter aims to present an appraisal programme that merges formative and summative principles into a powerful professional development resource which is driven by the individual being appraised.

Principles of an effective appraisal system

The principles outlined in this section have been drawn from an extensive review of the surprisingly sparse literature on the evaluation and appraisal of teachers although this has been growing over the last couple of years. Peterson (2000) suggested that teacher evaluation requires twelve new directions and these form the foundation of eight principles that our committee considered essential for an effective teacher evaluation scheme (see Table 6.1).

Table 6.1 Teacher evaluation principles.

Number	Principle	Reference
1.	Be fair to all and respect diversity through transparency of process and protection from political influences	Peterson, 2000, p. 84
2.	Ensure the process is teacher centred and driven, so the criteria for judging teacher quality reflect that teaching is a complex activity dependent on a specific context and delivered to a specific audience, determined with the input of those teachers whose quality is being judged.	Quirke, 2007, pp. 89–105
3.	Link the process to teachers' professional development by providing a clear definition of quality teaching that is not based on a minimum competency, but which determines outstanding practice and aims to enhance teaching throughout the institution by tying appraisal to ongoing professional development.	Burns, 2010
4.	Include processes that allow for the early detection of problems with teacher involvement in every stage of the process, including ongoing cyclical review of competencies and standards.	Kyriacou, 2009
5.	Ensure that the teacher appraisal programme is one that is both summative and formative with consideration given to the multiple roles of teachers, so is a scheme which demonstrably and pointedly looks beyond the classroom walls.	Quirke, 2007, pp. 89–105
6.	Assure that the teacher appraisal programme is consistent, valid and reliable with a transparent process to continually demonstrate this consistency, validity and reliability.	Scriven, 1981 Peterson, 2000 Quirke, 2007
7.	Use multiple data sources.	Peterson et al., 1998
8.	Have clear and transparent documentation, which begins with clear purposes transparently communicated to all parties including teachers, students, supervisors, chairs, administrators, human resources departments, institutional management and parents.	Owens, 1991; Lawrence et al., 1993

A balanced and effective teacher evaluation scheme should allow teachers to collect data from multiple sources in the form of portfolios or dossiers. As well as clarity on what to include in the teacher-compiled portfolio or dossier, there should also be clear guidelines on the form and length of the compilations and, most importantly, detail on how they are to be reviewed. A short portfolio extract summary of three to six pages is my preference although the literature tends towards a larger fifteen pages of documentation (Bird, 1990; Peterson, 2000; Ponzio et al., 1994; Wolf and Dietz, 1998). How these compilations are then evaluated has been widely discussed, with most recommending a teacher evaluation board or review panel using guidelines for review (Peterson, 2000, pp. 257–266). A guided discussion framework between the teacher and supervisor with the pair summarizing the year's work, as captured in the teacher's portfolio and extract, is the approach that most teachers prefer in my experience.

ASPIRA: The annual cycle

An example of an approach to teacher appraisal that meets these criteria is *ASPIRA* (Annual, Strategic, Professional Improvement Roadmap and Appraisal), which has been implemented at a tertiary institution in the United Arab Emirates over the last few years. Figure 6.1 shows the seven stages of this teacher appraisal programme.

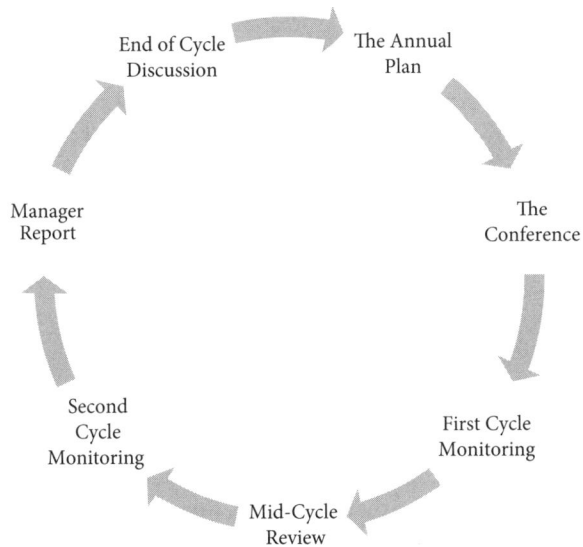

FIGURE 6.1 *The annual ASPIRA cycle.*

To start the process and the annual cycle, teachers reflect on their professional standing against sixteen teacher competencies. The teachers set their goals for the coming year covering the full array of their workload and submit this to their supervisor. Once the supervisor has reviewed this *Annual Plan*, teacher and supervisor will hold a *Conference*, the first meeting of the year, during which the teacher's reflection against competencies and the goals set are reviewed and amended, where required and agreed. Should teachers have no previous experience on which to base this reflection and goal setting they would be assigned an experienced teacher mentor to guide them through this first stage before they meet with the supervisor.

The next stage of the process is the *First Cycle Monitoring*, which is the collection of data to support the goal attainment of the teacher during the first semester. At the end of this semester, teacher and supervisor meet for a *Mid-Cycle Review* to discuss the progress in goal attainment and the effectiveness of the data collected during the first semester. The next stage of the process is the *Second Cycle Monitoring*, which is the collection of data to support goal attainment during the second semester. At the end of the second semester and teaching year, the supervisor will write a subjective, summative *End of Cycle Report* about the teacher's work over the year. The acknowledgement of the subjectivity of this report by all parties within the institution is a key feature of this approach and its adherence to the principles laid out above. Finally, the teacher and supervisor will meet for the *End of Cycle Discussion, Appraisal and Future Planning* when both review the teacher's portfolio extract summarizing the work of the past two semesters. The two agree on the final appraisal by signing off the discussion document and outlining the goals for the next year. This setting of goals for the coming year ensures the cyclical nature of the *ASPIRA* approach, as it links stages one and seven tightly together.

Stage one: Goals and reflection

Teachers first reflect on their teaching against the sixteen teacher competencies, which are divided into three domains, covering:

1 Content, Pedagogy and the Learning Process
2 Developing Professional Practice
3 The Teaching and Learning Context.

Each competency is associated with a set of four behavioural descriptors which aim to express a continuum of performance from Novice to Expert (Levels 1–4). Teachers place themselves on this continuum for each of the competencies as they reflect on their current professional standing. Based upon this reflection, teachers draw up goals to cover seven areas that mirror the different tasks teachers are required to undertake both inside and outside the classroom (see Table 6.2).

Table 6.2 The seven areas of teacher work.

1.	*Classroom Teaching* covering the courses and classes to be taught and the teacher's reflection against the competencies.
2.	*Professional Development* covering the teacher's reflection against the competencies and the key focal points for the research area below.
3.	*Research* covering the teacher's professional development goals above and their reflection against the competencies with a focus on action research in the classes they are teaching. The aim is to present and hopefully even publish the results of their local research.
4.	*Departmental Duties* covering tasks and roles such team leadership, coordination, materials and assessment writing duties.
5.	*College Duties* covering extra curricula activities such as clubs and contributions to college events.
6.	*System Duties beyond the College*, if applicable, covering tasks and activities such as curricula design, system coordination duties and international field trips with students.
7.	*Other Duties and Tasks* covering any goal that is not neatly subsumed in any of the above six areas.

Stage two: The first meeting

This is probably the most important stage of the whole process especially if it is the first time that the teacher is taking part in the *ASPIRA* process. This is the point when supervisors must demonstrate the principles that underlie the appraisal approach and throughout the meeting ensure that they sell *ASPIRA* as an evaluation system. The supervisor can do this by ensuring that the process is fully explained and teachers understand their central role in the appraisal. By adhering to the principles and by giving the teacher choices at every stage of the meeting supervisors demonstrate that they understand that the teacher may well have a better understanding of the context and more experience than the supervisor. The meeting starts with a *Competency Review* where the supervisor and teacher share their reflections on the teacher's current professional standing against each of the sixteen competencies. The two agree on each and flag the competencies that the teacher wants to strengthen and focus on during the academic year. Next is the *Goal Review* where teacher and supervisor discuss the goals in the *Annual Plan* and the most appropriate outcome measures for each. The third stage involves the discussion and decision on the best data the teacher should collect during the semester. This is undoubtedly the area that teachers unfamiliar with a teacher centred approach will find to be unique and possibly difficult, because observation becomes just one potential data source rather than the central lynchpin it is in so many appraisal programmes. A review of the literature suggests a wealth of possible data sources that teachers can collect for use in their portfolio and teacher portfolio extract (TPE) and I use the table in Stage Three below to discuss what data would be best for each teacher to explore in the first semester. This approach is particularly helpful for teachers new to the *ASPIRA* process.

The next stage of the first meeting should cover the format of the *Teaching Portfolio* and the final summary *Teaching Portfolio Extract (TPE)*. I personally do not insist on any format as I find the choice the teacher makes as revealing and interesting as the content. The Teaching Portfolio could simply be all the teacher's work of the year or could be selected highlights carefully bound or stored electronically. The *TPE*, on the other hand, must include a teacher's reflection on goal achievement and the competencies worked on during the year and it must refer to student, peer and supervisor feedback. Finally, it needs to state goals for the coming year and be a specified length. In the *ASPIRA* approach we recommend six pages maximum, as the focus of teachers' work and reflection should be the portfolio. The *TPE* should simply summarize the portfolio in a format that can inform all other parties. The final stage of this first essential meeting is an open and frank discussion about the supervisor's role and attitude in the *ASPIRA* process.

Stage three: Semester one data collection

As discussed in the first meeting, teachers have an endless wealth of data they can draw on, record and save simply to their portfolio. The required elements, as noted above, include observations, student evaluations, professional development and peer and supervisor feedback. In each of these cases, the *TPE* should refer to these elements without necessarily including them in full but they should be drawn upon to help the teacher develop professionally.

Scriven (1981) is correct in emphasizing that we should not use classroom visits because the observer alters the classroom dynamics, cannot visit enough classes to be representative, cannot avoid their personal prejudices, cannot observe as a student and teaching styles cannot be linked to student achievement. However, I believe that observation can be one of the most powerful developmental tools at our disposal as long as it focuses on the formative growth of the teacher rather than the summative evaluation of a 'performance'. Therefore I include within the source of data a wide variety of self-, peer, student, team and supervisor observations in formats such as audio, video, blitz, twenty-minute, full lesson, and unseen (where the observer does not go into the classroom but observes through the teacher's eyes and reflection after the class). I also suggest teachers observe both peers and supervisors. Above all, the most important feature of *ASPIRA* is that teachers have the choice about how they wish to build observation into their portfolio and appraisal.

Student Evaluations should be discussed with colleagues teaching the same class of students and supervisors' records of these discussions should be drawn upon for the teacher's reflection on their year's performance. I also encourage teachers to gather feedback from students on a continual basis as an excellent classroom technique to involve students more deeply in their learning. There are a myriad of ways to do this which cannot be covered in this chapter but which I have outlined previously in some detail (Quirke, 2001).

The importance of professional development (PD) is a central aspect of all appraisals and the *Teaching Portfolio Extract* should include reference to all the professional development activities that the teacher has undertaken throughout the year.

Table 6.3 summarizes information teachers have included in their portfolios with me over the past ten years and I often use it when brainstorming ideas for data to collect with teachers in the first meeting.

Table 6.3 Possible data sources for portfolios.

Videotaped classes	Materials created	Peer reviews (Bird, 1990)	Research reports
Student reports (Scriven, 1994)	Sample lesson plans	Letters of recommendation	Parent reports (Morgan, 1988)
Professional development plan	Reflective journal or statements	Samples of students' work/ projects	Future career or personal goals
Self-evaluations	Documentation on professional organization memberships	Testimonials from students/ other teachers/ others...	Teacher tests e.g. TKT (Strike, 1990; Haertel, 1990)
Documentation of professional development activity (Peterson, 1988)	Systematic observation (Evertson and Burry, 1989; Allwright, 1988; McGreal, 1983; Good, 1980)	Observation reports: self, peer and supervisory (Quirke, 1996)	Supervisor reports (Lawrence et al., 1993)
Pictures of student activities and events	Student achievement data (Berk, 1988)	Any other data unique to a teacher's situation (Danielson, 1996, Webster and Mendro, 1995; Peterson, 2000; Thaine, 2004)	

Stage four: The mid-cycle review

This mid-year review is another essential stage of the process, especially for those teachers experiencing this kind of appraisal approach for the first time, so that they feel fully supported through the year long process. The meeting would usually cover a review of goals and competencies selected and give the teacher the opportunity to adapt their goals based upon the first semester's work and experience. During the meeting, the supervisor and teacher would also review the data collected and decide what is required in the second semester. There should also be an extensive review and discussion of student evaluations from semester one, which is the key element of this mid-year meeting and is often the most stressful element of the whole process. The supervisor will approach the review of student evaluations positively and demonstrate to the teacher that student evaluations are key indicators of potential professional development opportunities and not the sole indicator of effective teacher performance. Above all, teachers must understand that their opinion counts and that the institution values their insights into their students' responses, positive and negative, as it is the teachers who know their students best. Teachers should have access to the student evaluation summary forms from each of the classes they have taught during the first semester prior to the mid-cycle review meeting so that they can reference them in their *Teaching Portfolio* along with their comments and feedback on the student evaluations, all of which will be discussed in full at the meeting.

During the student evaluation review, I find it useful to highlight a main teaching strength and an area that the teacher could work on based upon the student feedback. This section of the meeting often begins with these two points and teachers are asked if they consider this to be a fair interpretation of the student evaluations and what two points they would extract from the feedback. Once agreed upon, these two points are then included as new teaching goals for the second semester and the teacher and supervisor decide on how these impact the choice of competencies to be focused on for the second half of the year.

It is important that there is a process in place that is transparent to both students and teachers when student evaluations come back which are mainly negative (Quirke, 2007). The process used in *ASPIRA* encourages an open discussion with the teacher and an initial observation of the class who have given the negative feedback. The supervisor or observer then brings students and teacher together in an open discussion: 95% of the time, in our experience, this results in miscommunication and misunderstandings being clarified. In the 5% of cases where students and/or teacher are still dissatisfied, a third party such as the student counsellor is involved. They work with the students and teacher to draw up an action plan that addresses the student grievances and this becomes part of the teacher's new classroom goals. In my twenty years' experience using this method to deal with student dissatisfaction about teaching, I have found that this collaborative, open approach involving both students and teachers in reaching a consensus never fails and almost always leads to an improvement in both teaching and learning. Moreover, it reduces the fear factor so often associated with student evaluations. This approach is by no means the only way of gathering student feedback and the literature has suggested a range of approaches such as focus groups, representative committees, student-led feedback, reflective writing and discussion forums (Cohen and Manion, 1985; Harvey, 2003; Williams and Wessel, 2004). The key is that feedback should be a regular part of students' learning experiences (Swan, 2008), especially as most agree that students have a major contribution to make in the quality of education (Watson, 2003). One of the most effective and unique methods I have witnessed is a modular training approach to student feedback where they are taught how to give constructively critical feedback over a period of weeks and only when they have completed this training is their student evaluation feedback considered. The advantage of this approach is that both teachers and students begin to feel a real sense of ownership, which is one key factor in effective student feedback (Richardson, 2005). The need for the transparent publication of feedback results and clear institutional action to demonstrate that feedback is being taken seriously cannot be overstated. If this does not happen, the whole process becomes a rather futile exercise in historical routine rather than a drive to improve our teaching and student learning (Harvey, 2003). New technologies have allowed many institutions and teachers to experiment with a range of different online feedback methods and forms such as podcasting and embedded surveys within online course material (Brew, 2008; Jara and Mellar, 2010) and it has been suggested that the quantity and quality of student comments is improved in this online medium (Donovan et al., 2010). Whatever the medium and method may be, there should always be a teacher and supervisor discussion around the student feedback and where issues arise that need further student input they should be involved in the process as well. The key will always be the personal follow up and open and transparent communication in an atmosphere of honesty and trust. If that does not exist then it is extremely unlikely that student evaluations will have an impact on classroom teaching and learning quality.

Stage five: Semester two data collection

At *Second Cycle Monitoring* stage, the teacher collects data throughout the second semester as agreed in the mid-year cycle review meeting and will normally use different methods from those employed in the first semester. I also often ask teachers to consider the difference between the data collected in the first semester and the data being gathered in the second semester and the rationale behind the change and include this in their reflective statement in the *Teaching Portfolio Extract*.

Stage six: The manager's summative report

The manager/supervisor's report has proven to be, in my experience, an indispensable element of the *ASPIRA* process for most teachers, especially when they are developing professional development teaching portfolios for the first time. This summative write-up is the supervisor's personal subjective summary of the teacher's work during the year, and the supervisor should include a paragraph on each objective. This summative report is essential to the appraisal process because it allows supervisors to demonstrate that they really know the work the teacher has done over the year and their contribution to the institute. It is a real motivational tool for teachers as they realize that their supervisor knows their work so well and, most importantly, it gives teachers a framework for their portfolio extract. The supervisor's summative report should support the teacher's professional development, provide input against each of the teacher's goals and objectives and should be phrased in a way that allows teachers to respond to it easily and build upon it in their *TPE*. Finally, all parties must acknowledge that the report is a subjective view of the teacher's work over the year.

Stage seven: The end of cycle discussion

The power of the *End of Cycle Discussion* meeting is that it looks back and reviews the previous year, drawing on that review to look forward and set goals for the coming year, which ensures a truly cyclical process. Before the meeting, the supervisor should review the four-to-six-page *TPE*, the teacher's summary of their portfolio which includes a self-evaluation with reflection on teaching, reference to student evaluations and reference to the supervisor's summative report, all supported by documentation. Table 6.4 outlines a six-page model:

Table 6.4 A model for the teaching portfolio extract (TPE).

Page 1:	Pages 2–3:
The teacher's objectives and competencies focused on and already written and updated during the year.	The teacher's self-evaluation based on their objectives. This needs to be written by the teacher, but by using the objectives as the framework and by following the guide of the supervisor's summative report this should not take more than a couple of hours.
Pages 4–5:	**Page 6:**
The supervisor's summative report.	The student evaluation summary table.

This model is given to teachers as a guide for them to draw upon, but I give teachers no set format and encourage them to develop their own. Teachers I have worked with over the years have produced *TPEs* which follow the above to the letter and others which read like a six-page narrative that meets all the requirements by taking quotes from supervisor emails, write-ups and other documents, student feedback both official and informal and everything in between. When the teacher submits their *TPE* the supervisor should ensure that it meets all the requirements, and, if it fails to do so, should return it for re-submission. I have often needed to send a *TPE* back as it has missed, for example, reference to student evaluations.

The final meeting should be led by the teacher talking the supervisor through the extract, while focusing on the coming year. The supervisor should guide the discussion and ensure the meeting covers the following:

1 The objectives for the year and the competencies focused on.

2 The evidence in the portfolio that meets the requirements of reference to student evaluations, reference to supervisory comments and self-reflection. The teacher should also be required to demonstrate their adherence to the honesty principle by producing documents from their portfolio, which they have referred to in their *TPE*.

3 How the objectives and *TPE* match departmental and college goals.

4 Supervisory comments for the year.

5 Teacher comments for the year.

6 Teacher goals and priorities for the coming year. This is the most important part of the meeting as it provides a continuation from one year to the next and ensures that the *ASPIRA* process is truly cyclical. The goals for the coming year should be written up by the teacher after the meeting and used as the basis of the next year's first meeting.

7 The support that the teacher will require to meet these future goals focusing on professional development.

During the meeting the supervisor should complete the *Final Discussion Record* form, which covers each of these seven areas, and, once completed, both supervisor and teacher should sign. The signed *Final Discussion Record* form is then attached to the *TPE* and submitted for final signature by the director before filing in the personnel records, with a copy given to the teacher. This ensures that teachers know exactly what is going into their personnel files and the transparency of the programme is assured.

Conclusion

I would argue that the *ASPIRA* process outlined in this chapter is not especially innovative, but it is significantly distinctive as it is the only appraisal programme I have encountered in over twenty years of teaching that meets all the best practice principles of teacher appraisal. The advantage of the *ASPIRA* approach to teacher appraisal is that it meets all eight of the principles considered essential for an effective teacher appraisal system, as outlined in Figure 6.1 at the beginning of this chapter. It is an appraisal approach that contains both a personnel evaluation aspect and a professional development focus, as it is concerned with the teacher's personal and professional well-being. Many experts argue that formative and summative evaluation processes should be separated, but the success of the *ASPIRA* process would suggest that a truly effective appraisal scheme must bring the two together.

The process is not one set in stone and is continually evaluated by those being appraised. Feedback on the *ASPIRA* programme is encouraged and it is always exciting to see how teachers, students and managers suggest improvements. One factor that cannot be changed is the time that the process takes for supervisors, but surely, if we are focused on quality education, then our primary concern should be for our teachers, the quality of their teaching and the learning opportunities they provide to their students. It is the teachers who have the most interaction with our primary clients, the students, and if we can assure teacher satisfaction through fair and rigorous appraisal, then we can also ensure we meet student needs and institutional excellence. If we do not have the time for these, then I would suggest we have our priorities seriously misplaced as educational managers and leaders of learning.

References

Allwright, D. (1988), *Observation in the Language Classroom*. London: Longman.

Berk, R. A. (1988), 'Fifty reasons why student achievement gain does not mean teacher effectiveness'. *Journal of Personnel Evaluation in Education*, 1, 345–363.

Bird, T. (1990), 'The Schoolteachers' portfolio: An essay on possibilities', In J. Millman and L. Darling-Hammond (eds), *The New Handbook of Teacher Evaluation: Assessing Elementary and Secondary School Teachers*. Newbury Park, CA: Sage, pp. 241–256.

Bouchamma, Y., Godin, M. and Godin, C. J. (2008), *A Guide to Teacher Evaluation: Structured Observations for all Evaluators*. Plymouth: Rowman and Littlefield Education.

Brew, L. S. (2008), 'The role of student feedback in evaluating and revising a blended learning course'. *The Internet and Higher Education*, 11 (2), 98–105.

Burns, A. (2010), *Doing Action Research in English Language Teaching: A Guide for Practitioners*. London: Routledge.

Campbell, J., Kyriakides, L., Muijs, D. and Robinson, W. (2004), *Assessing Teacher Effectiveness: Developing a Differentiated Model*. London: RoutledgeFalmer.

Cohen, L. and Manion, L. (1985), *Research Methods in Education*. London: Croom Helm.

Danielson, C. (1996), *Enhancing Professional Practice: A Framework for Teaching*. Alexandria, VA: Association for Supervision and Curriculum Development.

—— and McGreal, T. L. (2000), *Teacher Evaluation to Enhance Professional Practice*. Alexandria, VA: Educational Testing Service.

Donovan, J., Mader, C. E. and Shinsky, J. (2010), 'Constructive student feedback: Online vs. traditional course evaluations'. *Journal of Interactive Online Learning*, 9 (3), 283–296.

Evertson, C. M. and Burry, J. A. (1989), 'Capturing classroom context: The observation system as lens for assessment'. *Journal of Personnel Evaluation in Education*, 2, 297–320.

Good, T. L. (1980), 'Classroom observations: Potential and problems', in W. R. Duckett (ed.), *Observation and the Evaluation of Teaching*. Bloomington: Phi Delta Kappa, pp. 2–44.

—— and Mulryan, C. (1990), 'Teacher ratings: A call for teacher control and self evaluation', in J. Millman and L. Darling-Hammond (eds), *The New Handbook of Teacher Evaluation: Assessing Elementary and Secondary School Teachers*. Newbury Park, CA: Sage, pp. 191–215.

Haertel, E. H. (1990), 'Performance tests, simulations and other methods', in J. Millman and L. Darling-Hammond (eds), *The New Handbook of Teacher Evaluation: Assessing Elementary and Secondary School teachers*. Newbury Park, CA: Sage, pp. 278–294.

Harvey, L. (2003), 'Student feedback'. *Quality in Higher Education*, 9 (1), 3–20.

Jara, M. and Mellar, H. (2010), 'Quality enhancement for e-learning courses: The role of student feedback'. *Computers & Education*, 54 (3), 709–714.

Kyriacou, C. (2009), *Effective Teaching in Schools: Theory and Practice*. Cheltenham: Nelson Thornes.

Lawrence, C. E., Vachon, M. K., Leake, D. O. and Leake, B. H. (1993), *The Marginal Teacher*. Newbury Park, CA: Corwin.

McGreal, T. L. (1983), *Successful Teacher Evaluation*. Alexandria, VA: Association for Supervision and Curriculum Development.

Morgan, D. L. (1988), *Focus Groups as Qualitative Research*. Newbury Park, CA: Sage.

Owens, R. G. (1991), *Organisational Behaviour in Education*. Englewood Cliffs, NJ: Prentice Hall.

Peterson, K. D. (1988), 'Reliability of panel judgments for promotion in a school teacher career ladder system'. *Journal of Research and Development in Education*, 21 (4), 95–99.

——. (2000), *Teacher Evaluation: A Comprehensive Guide to New Directions and Practices*. Thousand Oaks, CA: Corwin Press.

——, Stevens, D. and Ponzio, R. C. (1998), 'Variable data sources in teacher evaluation'. *Journal of Research and Development in Education*, 31 (3), 123–132.

Ponzio, R. C., Peterson, K. D., Miller, J. P. and Kinney, M. B. (1994), 'A program portfolio/panel review evaluation of 4-H sponsored community-based, social action projects for at-risk youth'. *Journal of Research and Development in Education*, 28 (1), 55–65.

Quirke, P. (1996), 'Using unseen observations for an IST development programme'. *The Teacher Trainer*, 10 (1), 18–19.

——. (2001), 'Hearing voices: A reliable and flexible framework for gathering and using student feedback', in J. Edge (ed.), *Action Research: Case Studies in TESOL Practices Series*. Alexandria, VA: TESOL, pp. 81–91.

———. (2007), 'A coherent approach to faculty appraisal', in C. Coombe, M. Al-Hamly and P. Davidson (eds), *Evaluating Teaching Effectiveness in EFL/ ESL Contexts*. Ann Arbor, MI: University of Michigan Press, pp. 89–105.

Richardson, J. T. E. (2005), 'Instruments for obtaining student feedback: A review of the literature'. *Assessment & Evaluation in Higher Education*, 30 (4), 387–415.

Scriven, M. (1981), 'Summative teacher evaluation', in J. Millman and L. Darling-Hammond (eds), *The New Handbook of Teacher Evaluation: Assessing Elementary and Secondary School Teachers*. Newbury Park, CA: Sage, pp. 244–271.

———. (1994), 'Using student ratings in teacher evaluation'. *Evaluation Perspectives*, 4 (1), 1–6.

Strike, K. A. (1990), 'The ethics of educational evaluation', in J. Millman and L. Darling-Hammond (eds), *The New Handbook of Teacher Evaluation: Assessing Elementary and Secondary School Teachers*. Newbury Park, CA: Sage, pp. 356–373.

Swan, H. (2008), 'Student feedback'. *Times Higher Education*, 14 February.

Thaine, C. (2004), 'The assessment of second language teaching'. *ELT Journal*, 58 (4), 336–345.

Watson, S. (2003), 'Closing the feedback loop: Ensuring effective action from student feedback'. *Tertiary Education and Management*, 9 (2), 145–157.

Webster, W. and Mendro, R. (1995), 'An accountability system featuring both "value-added" and product measures of schooling', in J. Shinkfield and D. Stufflebeam (eds), *Teacher Evaluation: Guide to Effective Practice*. Boston: Kluwer, pp. 350–376.

Williams, R. M. and Wessel, J. (2004), 'Reflective journal writing to obtain student feedback about their learning during the study of chronic musculoskeletal conditions'. *Journal of Allied Health*, 33 (1), 17–23.

Wolf, K. and Dietz, M. (1998), 'Teaching portfolios: Purposes and possibilities'. *Teacher Education Quarterly*, 25, 9–22.

PART THREE

Focus on Discourse

CHAPTER SEVEN

Differences between Supervisors' Espoused Feedback Styles and Their Discourse in Post-Observation Meetings

Helen Donaghue

Introduction

Teacher training, development or evaluation often involves an observed lesson followed by a feedback meeting in which the teacher and observer discuss the lesson and plan how the teacher can improve the teaching and learning in his/her class. Kilbourn et al. (2005) compare this to feedback in other professional fields such as drama (directing), sport (coaching) and literature (editing), identifying feedback as an important aspect of learning, induction and improvement. As an opportunity for teachers and observers to share experience and discuss teaching practice, the post-observation meeting has the potential to stimulate reflection and professional growth. However, despite the prevalence and potential affordances of the observation and feedback process in educational settings, Kilbourn et al. (2005) claim that teaching falls short in comparison to other professions as teachers typically find that not enough quality feedback is provided. The authors state that supervision models have potential but:

> Learning how to engage these models of feedback in a sensitive and productive way – how to give genuinely constructive feedback – is not easy and can be a stumbling block to the realization of its potential (Kilbourn et al., 2005, p. 299)

Within English language teaching (ELT) much has been written about different models of supervision (Freeman, 1982; Gebhard, 1990; Wallace, 1991) but these models, whether prescriptive or collaborative (Wallace, 1991), tend to be discussed theoretically with little focus on the language used to construct a particular model (Knox, 2008, p.13). However, any supervisory model must be realized through talk. Supervisors construct a collaborative or directive identity via talk and feedback is realized through the interaction between supervisors and teachers. Supervisors' talk, therefore, deserves attention.

This chapter reports on analysis of both audio recordings of post-observation meetings and interviews with supervisors. The focus of analysis is whether supervisors' espoused style of supervision was realized in their discourse. Post-observation feedback meetings can be *'difficult discoursal events'* (Copland, 2008, p. 67) especially if evaluative. There can be much at stake, both for the teacher whose lesson is being observed and who can risk failure or even loss of job, and the observer whose dual (and often conflicting (Brandt, 2008)) role of supporter/advisor and evaluator are a considerable responsibility. Documenting and understanding participants' use of language may help to support both observers and teachers in dealing with the event as analysis can inform supervisors/tutors and help them reflect on their own practice (Farr, 2011). For example, after studying the discourse of feedback meeting, Copland (2008) gained a greater awareness of the organization of feedback, how much space trainees had to talk and the trainer's use of *'loaded, "probing" questions'* (p. 291) and Vásquez and Reppen (2007) gained insight into their own interaction patterns as trainers which led them to initiate changes in their feedback, resulting in more balanced levels of interaction (i.e. the supervisors were less dominant). By looking at real data, the reality that supervisors and teachers present can be uncovered, especially as there may be contradictions between a supervisor's espoused approach and what they actually do during feedback (Farr, 2011; Hyland and Lo, 2006; Waite, 1992).

Supervisory styles in ELT

In this volume, Mick Randall gives a comprehensive overview of different styles of supervision used in ELT (see also Farr, 2011 for an excellent discussion of the advantages and disadvantages of different styles). At opposite ends of a continuum lie prescriptive and collaborative styles (Wallace, 1991). In a prescriptive (or directive) approach, the supervisor is an authority and will offer opinions and prescribe suggestions for the teacher to adopt. A prescriptive supervisor's job can be difficult as this model relies on him or her being able to identify and describe good teaching as well as take into account contextual features which will influence this (Farr, 2011, p. 19). Although this model may discourage teacher reflection, experimentation and independence, some teachers appreciate direction: '*Although prescriptive and authoritative interventions are often seen in a pejorative light ... they are part of the overall armoury of the mentor and may be highly effective in certain context*' (Randall, this volume). It has been suggested that a prescriptive style may be better appreciated by novice (rather than experienced) teachers (Copeland, 1982; Freeman, 1982).

At the other end of the spectrum is a collaborative style of supervision which involves the teacher and observer working together to solve problematic classroom issues in a process of observation and discussion, exploration and resolution followed by possible change in practice: '*the mentor and mentee look at the lesson and use it as a springboard to explore not only how things could have been done better, but derive principles for effective teaching*' (Randall, this volume). Within the collaborative model, the observer and teacher are viewed as equals. This style often involves the supervisor asking questions to elicit opinions and suggestions and the teacher taking responsibility for making and evaluating teaching decisions (Copeland, 1982). Teachers may thus have more ownership of their teaching practice and the social, collaborative nature of this model may encourage reflection. However, a collaborative style can be viewed as less appropriate for novice teachers who may lack the theoretical or experiential knowledge needed to make instructional decisions (Farr, 2011).

Participants, setting, data

As part of a wider study on the discourse of post-observation meetings, I recorded data from two sources at a tertiary institution in the United Arab Emirates. The first source was one to one post-observation meetings between experienced in-service ELT teachers and their supervisors over a four year period. The second source was group feedback meetings with trainees and their tutors on a Certificate in Teaching English to Speakers of Other Languages (CELTA) course over a period of four years. I also interviewed supervisors and CELTA trainers about their experience as observers.

This chapter focuses specifically on one supervisor and one tutor from the larger data set. Over a three year period, I recorded nine feedback meetings with Tom, an in-service supervisor whose one-to-one feedback meetings followed an annual observation carried out as part of an institutional appraisal process. Lena, a CELTA tutor, had weekly group feedback meetings with six trainees following their teaching practice. I recorded eight of her feedback meetings from three CELTA courses over a three year period. Recordings were analysed to see if supervisors' espoused style was realized in their discourse.

Supervisors' beliefs about their style of feedback

I interviewed Tom and Lena separately and asked them about their supervisory styles. Tom, who supervised and observed the in-service teachers, identified the purpose of the observation and feedback process thus:

Extract 1 (Tom: Interview)

To tell the teachers what they're doing really well and what they need to improve on if anything and to let them know what the students are experiencing because that's how I always like to go as I'm a s- I'm actually a student

His use of '*tell*' is interesting as this seems to suggest a more directive or prescriptive approach. However, when asked about his supervisory style, Tom was certain that it was not prescriptive or directive:

Extract 2 (Tom: Interview)

I'm definitely not directive...here our teachers are so experienced that I don't think I need to be cos they do know how to act.... I give alternatives more with their teaching method and style and content...my collaborative [style] is more with the behaviour and classroom management

Tom claims that he draws on two models of supervision in his feedback meetings: giving teachers alternative suggestions to explore and collaborating with them over classroom management issues.

Lena, the CELTA tutor, believes that there is a conflict between the theoretical purpose of observation and feedback and what actually happens in practice. She believes that in theory the process is educational for both parties:

Extract 3 (Lena: Interview)

it's supposed to be educational and a way to improve and it's also in theory for the person giving feedback it's a learning experience as well because you're discussing as an equal em you should be discussing what you saw and how things could be improved, what the person who actually performed thought they did etc etc

Lena's view concurs with CELTA trainers in Copland's (2011) study who saw the purpose of feedback as encouraging trainees to reflect on and evaluate their lessons, helping trainees to develop and supporting them in their discovery of teaching. That Lena's theoretical scenario involves '*discussing as an equal*' and eliciting the observed teacher's perspective and opinion seems to suggest that she leans towards a more collaborative style. However, she thinks that the evaluative nature of a CELTA course can interfere with the educational aim of the process:

Extract 4 (Lena: Interview)

in practice it's high stakes so … it can be very defensive it can be felt to be a personal attack and it's not always on equal footing because you are still an assessor and you're seen to go in there as inspecting as opposed to let's have a sort of peer feedback evaluation

Thus we see a conflict in how Lena believes the meeting should be conducted and her role as assessor which introduces both an asymmetric relationship between her and the trainees and trainee anxiety about being assessed (Brandt, 2008; Shah, 2014). Lena therefore believes that because of her role as assessor, her supervisory style has to be prescriptive:

Extract 5 (Lena: Interview)

there are certain criteria that you're evaluating the person against so to a certain extent em that's the bar that needs to be met so i- it's quite prescriptive and we're both aware of what needs to be done in the classroom even before the lesson takes place to a certain extent

What supervisors actually do

This section reports on aspects of talk recorded in feedback meetings with the two supervisors in this study. It examines first the beginning of post-observation meetings and the identity supervisors establish and, second, ways in which supervisors construct a more collaborative or prescriptive style through talk.

Establishing a supervisory identity

The beginning of a feedback meeting is illuminating, particularly the way that supervisors present and construct an identity. In this data set, Tom and Lena almost always start their meetings in the same way. Tom typically begins by making immediate reference to the institutional observation instrument which has various criteria and a scoring system of 1–4:

Extract 6 (Tom: Feedback meeting 4)

1	*Tom*	so Eric the way I do this () is I'm gonna call up the hard copy I mean the soft
2		copy you have the hard copy in front of you () we just kind of go through the
3		observation em before we do it a three is what I give myself when I teach so 3
4		is **good** anything that's a 3 is normal acce- accep- you know accepted expected
5	*Eric*	ok expected
6	*Tom*	in the classroom if there's anything above that it's something that stood out
7		or that you do very **well** or maybe I'll share with other teachers anything below
8		that is something you might want to look at em I know this is your first year
9		so I don't know if you've taken any of the special courses from Alice or had
10		her come into the classroom or even videotape your class which a lot of new
11		teachers do so you might want to just think about it just to get some ideas it's
12		always good to see yourself teaching on video even though you don't like the
13	*Eric*	yeah yeah yeah
14	*Tom*	way you look but em this is a **living** document so we can change things clarify
15		things you can argue sometimes I'll change sometimes I won't it depends on
16		the your point but I can type the stuff in the comments in the bottom so we'll
17		start on the first page which is mostly about the class and the s- em says and
18		student behaviour and management everything here was good the only one
19		was the first one 4.1.1. the teacher made good use of available resources I think
20		you could do **more** but I understand you only have lab access once a week

In Extract 6, Tom constructs a clear identity through his discourse. He is authoritative: he controls what happens in the meeting. He is also powerful: he states explicitly that he is an assessor and the person who decides what is '*normal,*' '*acceptable*' or '*expected*'. He allows that there is room for negotiation in scoring (lines 14–15), but makes it clear that the scores will ultimately be his decision. He also refers to sharing Eric's ideas or good practice with other teachers (lines 7–8) but does not ask Eric's permission to do this.

Tom's role as supervisor and institutional representative is very evident in this extract as he refers to both the institutional document and to institutional services, that is, the teacher support centre (lines 9–11). He is focused on the job at hand and there is no pre-amble or social small talk. Tom also positions himself as an experienced teacher (lines 3–4) and he seems to imply that he is a standard to be measured against. In contrast, he refers to Eric as a teacher new to the institution (line 8) who may need help from the teaching support centre ('*Alice*' line 9), even though Eric has many years of teaching experience. Thus, Tom appears to be constructing an identity which manifests expertise, authority, power and control, in contrast with his espoused style of collaboration and his belief that a prescriptive style is not appropriate with in-service teachers.

Lena typically starts her meeting by asking trainees whose lesson the group is discussing to share their thoughts about the lesson they taught. She then nominates one other trainee to give feedback and then she opens the floor to all trainees to add anything if they wish:

Extract 7 (Lena: Feedback meeting 7)

1	*Lena*	so as usual the person who taught gets to go first because it's only fair that
2		they should tell us how they felt about their lesson () I'll nominate just one
3		person to comment -
4	*Trainee*	Ok
5	*Lena*	- on the person who taught () then if there's anything we've left out fine we
6		can add if not let's just gently move on

Like Tom, Lena is in control of the structure and proceedings of the feedback meetings – she decides on the structure and who will speak. However, she seems to be trying to project a more collaborative identity than Tom in the form of a facilitator who will ensure fairness ('*it's only fair*') by giving trainees the opportunity to discuss their lesson before others (including herself). By using the plural pronoun '*we*'/'*we've*' (line 5) she positions herself as a group member and collaborator. Giving trainees voice and attempting to create equality both match her theoretical stance that feedback should be collaborative. However, despite this apparent collaboration, the relationship between herself and her trainees is still asymmetrical as she controls turns and contributions.

Supervisory style in general: Lena

Lena's attempt at a collaborative orientation is generally maintained throughout her meetings. Unlike Tom, Lena makes no reference to criteria or assessment and she tends to add comment rather than initiate. She frequently invites trainees to talk first and in most of the meetings her turns are shorter than those of the trainees. Trainees in Lena's feedback meetings spend much time talking to each other and there are long stretches where Lena is silent. She uses questions to elicit reflection and evaluation from trainees (see Copland, this volume) and also asks trainees to answer their own and each other's questions. For example, in extract 8 below, Lena asks trainee 3 to elaborate on an evaluation she has made on the beginning of a lesson where she had tried and failed during a pre-reading activity to get students to speak.

Extract 8 (Lena: Feedback meeting 3)

1	Lena	you said you thought you should plan the questions () what were you
2		thinking there?
3	Trainee 3	em () at the beginning I think I might've got a bit more (xx) of a
4		response if a- if the questions were actually planned
5	Lena	mm all right yeah any any questions that you could think of that you would ask
6	Trainee 3	em
7	Lena	say you had to do this again
8	Trainee 3	probably elicit the information better and () I think if I had elicited better they
9		would've eh responded better and I would've got more feedback and I
10		would've been able to exploit the pictures more and () I panicked
11	Lena	you panicked a bit from the start yeah that kind of threw you ok but as we

12		said hat off to you at least you didn't **seem** to be panicking on the outside
13	*Trainee 3*	yeah I tried my best just get them to
14		speak laughs
15	*Lena*	laughs all right well there were other good things about the lesson what else
16		do the others have to say good things that you saw in the lesson
17	*Trainee 5*	I thought it was a good idea that you moved the students around (xx)
18	*Trainee 3*	yeah
19	*Trainee 5*	I mean that was really good what you did at the beginning I think you wanted
20		to put the weaker and the stronger together
21	*Trainee 3*	yeah and not have the girls together and
22		even I think that the girls spoke more when they were with -
23	*Lena*	they certainly did yeah
24	*Trainee 5*	em very good drilling really really good em () you moved around a lot and
25		you were able to catch a few students who were not pronouncing words em in
26		the correct way
27	*Trainee 3*	yeah

Lena picks up on a comment the trainee has made about planning questions to ask students in advance of the lesson and asks Trainee 3 to explain what she means (lines 1–2). This question seems to prompt Trainee 3 to consolidate her thinking about the value of pre-planning questions to elicit ideas and information from students. Lena then invites other trainees to comment on the lesson, making sure (lines 15–16) that they focus on positive aspects in order to balance Trainee 3's negative evaluation. The shared laughter in the middle of this extract (lines 14–15) is also interesting as Lena and the trainees often laugh and joke in the feedback meetings and this seems to build affiliation and contribute to group solidarity (Thonus, 2008).

However, not all Lena's attempts at elicitation are as successful and sometimes she chooses to be directive. The following episode (Extract 9) is fairly typical with Lena asking questions and trying to prompt reflection:

Extract 9 (Lena: Feedback meeting 9)

1	*Lena*	with hindsight now that you went through it () what do you think the
2		focus should've been in fact what-
3	*Trainee 6*	well I could've chosen either or just cut out the other if I want to make
4		it a writ- and they're too low for integrated skills content based lesson
5		unless you **do** have 2 hours
6	*Lena*	Mm
7	*Trainee 6*	ah so I it I after teaching it if I was gonna do it again I would concentrate
8		on writing and I probably wouldn't even bring that reading out and use
9		the forty minutes to try and get some writing out of them
10	*Lena*	writing out of them?
11	*Trainee 6*	yeah if I had to re-plan it and teach it again that's would I do
12	*Lena*	if if you wanted to use the reading () could you use it differently?
13	*Trainee 6*	well one sentence I'd do it in if I was gonna use that reading as an
14		integrated topic lesson I would pick out one sentence and put it on the eh
15		board just a sentence and not give them all the rest of the language
16	*Lena*	mm hm
17	*Trainee 6*	because their re- their level's too low
18	*Lena*	what about modifying the text itself?
19	*Trainee 6*	Eh
20	*Lena*	cos the texts were were could've been good and your pictures were
21		excellent as well like they referred to the text what about looking at those
22		texts and just
23	*Trainee 6*	making it simpler simplifying the language
24	*Lena*	absolutely

Lena's purpose in asking questions seems to be aimed at getting the answer she wants, that is, modifying/simplifying the text. She asks three questions but, failing to elicit the answer she wants, then explicitly provides the answer herself, albeit in question form: '*what about modifying the text itself?*' This shift from a collaborative to prescriptive approach is even more explicit in the following episode (Extract 10) which happens after one of the trainees has asked if it is a good idea for students to listen to reading texts read aloud and some of the trainees have talked about doing this at school as learners themselves:

Extract 10 (Lena: Feedback meeting 4)

1	*Lena*	what does it do if you're listening to something as you're reading and the
2		purpose of your activity is reading you're you want them to read for
3		specific information true or false gist listening whatever gist reading
4		whatever it is () would you have them listen to a text then? How would
5		that help them achieve their aims?
6	*Trainee 1*	that's why I'm asking the question to figure out the answer
7	*Lena*	and I'm throwing it back to you
8	*Trainee 1*	I can't small laugh I just can't
9	*Lena*	ok let me give you an answer no
10	*Trainee 1*	yes please
11	*Lena*	No
12	*Trainee 1*	thanks

Lena tries to elicit the answer from trainee 1 (lines 1–5) but trainee 1 wants prescriptive advice because she does not know the answer (line 8). Lena then relents and gives a prescriptive answer which is gratefully received by Trainee 1. Overall, Lena's approach seems to be aimed at a collaborative approach which provides trainees with the opportunity to talk and reflect with recourse to a more directive approach when this is needed.

Supervisory style in general: Tom

The criteria in the institutional observation instrument form the basis and structure of all Tom's feedback meetings – most of the meetings consist of him explaining the scores that he has given, so his talk is predominantly evaluative. He rarely elicits teachers' opinions or explanations and he almost always initiates change of topic, usually in the form of moving to the next criteria. His turns are also significantly longer than the teachers'. Thus, despite his belief that he is collaborative, Tom mostly assumes the role of assessor and seems therefore more directive. The influence of the institutional observation is interesting. Engin (this volume) discusses the benefits that artefacts such as teaching transcripts, lesson plans and self-evaluation forms can afford in the context of teacher training, but in this case the artefact in question seems to constrain Tom and prevent him from giving the more collaborative feedback he believes appropriate with experienced teachers.

Other studies of supervisory discourse show that Tom's interaction patterns are more typical than Lena's. Supervisors in Hyland and Lo's (2006) study expressed the belief that teachers should be active participants but analysis found that teachers tended to take a passive role, mostly contributing information and accepting tutors' comments, whereas tutors spoke for longer and were more likely to initiate topics and to interrupt than teachers. Vásquez (2004) found that supervisors had longer turns, with teachers often uttering a single minimal response and Farr's (2011) study also found that tutors assumed a dominant role evident in the uneven levels of participation and tutor control of talk and evaluation, despite their belief that collaboration and student teacher reflection was important. Similarly, Waite (1992) discussed the ways in which supervisors gain control over feedback meetings by initiating talk and topics and maintaining control of the floor and in Copland's (2008) study, asymmetrical power was also displayed through CELTA trainers' control of the floor.

Constraints

Why, then, is there a discrepancy between the way these supervisors believe they give (or should give) feedback and the way they actually do? One explanation could be that contextual constraints restrict them or force them to behave contrary to their beliefs. A constraint which may influence the way feedback is given is the large number of observations that supervisors have to do and the resulting lack of time. Tom supervised fifty-five teachers in the first two years in his job and Lena said that the lack of time sometimes resulted in her rushing through feedback and not giving it enough attention.

In addition, both supervisors talked about their duty as an evaluator:

Extract 11 (Tom: Interview)

if it's the first year we have to make sure that they're teaching the way that we expect them to teach and then each year it's part of their annual summative so we have to you know make sure they're still maintaining quality in the classroom and their last year of their contract we use their observations to determine if we wanna continue employing them

Extract 12 (Lena: Interview)

Definitely a big responsibility because when on the CELTA course as a tutor [teaching practice is a] very important part of the person's overall performance in the end … it can lead to a certificate or not … it's a big weight on my shoulders and em e- I'm constantly questioning myself when I have to give feedback especially borderline cases

Their institutional responsibility to maintain quality and the importance of their assessment which can determine whether an individual keeps his/her job or is awarded a CELTA certificate may result in one supervisory style featuring more dominantly in the discourse. In Tom's case, the assessor's role is more evident whereas Lena's discourse reflects more a facilitator. Context may explain this difference. Although Lena acts as a gatekeeper to the CELTA qualification, the outcome of an individual observation is less crucial than in Tom's context where one single observation can play a major part in deciding whether or not to extend a teacher's probation or renew their contract. The format of the meeting may also influence feedback. Lena's feedback is conducted through group interaction and she uses this as a means to providing trainees with the opportunity to talk and reflect but also to find out if there is a need to be prescriptive about certain issues. In contrast, the one-to-one interaction in Tom's meetings allows him to direct most of the talk towards explaining the scoring on the observation instrument. The number of teachers and lessons observed may also influence feedback style. In one academic year, Tom conducted single observations of more than 30 teachers whereas Lena worked with six CELTA trainees, observing each trainee teach nine lessons over a period of twelve weeks.

Both supervisors indicate that within their role of evaluator, the observation instrument and its criteria play an important part and actually influence their feedback:

Extract 13 (Tom: Interview)

because of the document we have to adhere to here that's stopped me in giving feedback the way I'd like to because you still have to respond to that criteria … but it really kinds of takes away from the whole purpose of the feedback which is just to try to help the person become a better teacher in the future it just becomes a bit of a negotiating meeting. It's just how many [high marks] can I score because ultimately that … determines whether or not you get your next contract

Extract 14 (Lena: Interview)

you are also aware of the documents that you've completed which then there's a written record of what you're eh using to support the oral feedback then it's got to match somehow so your language is more guarded probably a lot more diplomatic but maybe you're not telling all at that point

However, the influence of the observation instrument is most striking in Tom's talk. Supervisory dominance resulting from the influence of institutional documents was also evident in Waite's (1992) study which found that supervisors' ownership of and presentation of observational data (e.g. from observational records) meant that teachers had little time left for discussion of topics not initiated by supervisors or for reflection: '*Supervisors who take the lead in the presentation and analysis of observational data severely limit the teacher's potential for participation, reflection and growth*' (Waite, 1992, p. 369).

Another interesting issue to emerge from Tom's interview was that the context of the college and its students led him to be more directive because of his belief that the style of teaching that many new teachers brought to the college did not work in that context – he believes that the nature of the students and the considerable use of technology in the college dictate a need for them to be directed to a different way of teaching:

Extract 15 (Tom: Interview)

Some of the new teachers... they're teaching the way they taught in their last jobs and that doesn't work here... because the population you're dealing with is nothing you've ever dealt with before it's not so much you it's the style of teaching that doesn't match what our students need to receive... there's a disconnect

Extract 16 (Tom: Interview)

in just the past couple of years I've seen teachers who came in kind of rocky and then by the second now by the third year they teach the way the veterans teach with our students and so I think they have a fear of I don't know a bad observation as meaning it's oh my god it's the end of the world it's not you know it's just because there's room for improvement

During his feedback meetings, Tom makes frequent reference to '*veteran*' teachers who have been at the institution for a number of years and often relates episodes from their lessons. He almost always discusses technology in his feedback meetings and frequently encourages teachers to use it more. He seems to have a fairly strong sense of the type of teacher the institution requires and a belief that, with direction, they can be guided to '*teach the way our veterans teach with our students*'. His attitude to '*conformist teaching*' may in part be influenced by the observation form's prescriptive checklist (King, this volume) which includes, for example, criteria focusing on use of technology.

Conclusion

The results from this study indicate that it is important to raise supervisors' awareness of different supervisory styles and the way they conduct feedback in order to prompt reflection on which style is best suited to their context. Directing attention to their context, the style(s) of supervision appropriate to that context and an awareness of their own talk may help supervisors progress from the '*prevalent trial and error type approach to feedback*' (Farr, 2011, p. 173) to a more informed one. The data discussed in this chapter show how instrumental context is in shaping how supervisors conduct feedback. Contrary to opinion prevalent in the literature on supervisory styles, in a context where keeping a job can rest on an observation, a collaborative style may not be efficient or effective with experienced teachers. In his context, Tom needs to evaluate teachers and justify this evaluation both to teachers and senior managers. Although the teachers in his institution are all highly experienced, contextual factors seem to force him to be directive in order for him to carry out his duty as institutional representative and perhaps to help his teachers keep their jobs. Lena's interaction patterns also contradict much of the literature on supervisory styles. First, she demonstrates that a more collaborative style can sometimes be appropriate with novice teachers. Second, although the literature seems to suggest that supervisors adopt (consciously or unconsciously) one particular style when conducting feedback, Lena's combination of both a collaborative and directive approach may be a more realistic alternative.

Results also suggest that supervisors, managers and institutions (both local and international, e.g. Cambridge ESOL) should monitor their observation and feedback processes in order to identify if institutional demands are limiting or changing the way that supervisors give feedback. It may be possible to reduce the number of observations, for example, or introduce peer observations with some teachers (Engin and Priest, 2014). It is also recommended that institutions review observation instruments and their use in feedback. As this data shows, these artefacts can influence the way feedback is given, at worst by dominating proceedings, leaving little space for trainees to talk and reflect.

Finally, in order for teachers to reflect and develop, they need the opportunity to talk and interact (O'Connell and Dyment, 2006; Robson and Turner, 2007). Hyland and Lo (2006) interviewed supervisors and teachers about their expectations of the feedback meeting. Most of the teachers expected to be *'full participants, able to express their view and justify their actions'* (Hyland and Lo, 2006, p. 69). Similarly, the tutors expressed the desire for teachers to be active participants. It therefore seems essential that supervisors give conscious attention to providing teachers with opportunities to talk in post-observation meetings, making sure they do not dominate the interaction themselves.

References

Brandt, C. (2008), 'Allowing for practice: A critical issue in TESOL teacher preparation'. *ELT Journal*, 60, 355–364.

Copeland, W. D. (1982), 'Student teachers' preference for supervisory approach'. *Journal of Teacher Education*, 33, 32–36.

Copland, F. (2008), *Feedback in Pre-service English Language Teacher Training: Discourses of Process and Power*, PhD. University of Birmingham.

———. (2011), 'Negotiating face in feedback conferences: A linguistic ethnographic analysis'. *Journal of Pragmatics*, 43, 3832–3843.

Engin, M. and Priest, B. (2014), 'Peer observation as a learning tool', in A. Howard, H. Donaghue and L. Burke (eds), *Participant Voices: Observation in Educational Settings*. Abu Dhabi: HCT Press, pp. 65–78.

Farr, F. (2011), *The Discourse of Teaching Practice Feedback*. London: Routledge.

Freeman, D. (1982), 'Observing teachers: Three approaches to in-service training and development'. *TESOL Quarterly*, 16, 21–28.

Gebhard, J. (1990), 'Models of supervision: Choices', in J. Richards and D. Nunan (eds), *Second Langauge Teacher Education*. Cambridge: Cambridge University Press, pp. 156–166.

Hyland, F. and Lo, M. (2006), 'Examining interaction in the teaching practicum: Issues of language, power and control'. *Mentoring & Tutoring: Partnership in Learning*, 14, 163–186.

Kilbourn, B., Keating, C., Murray, K. and Ross, I. (2005), 'Balancing feedback and inquiry: How novice observers (supervisors) learn from inquiry into their own practice'. *Journal of Curriculum & Supervision*, 20, 298–318.

Knox, L. (2008), *Three-Step Sequences in Trainee Teacher-Supervisor Talk: Mitigation and Ambiguity in Post-Observation Conferences*, MSc. Edinburgh.

O'Connell, T. and Dyment, J. (2006), 'Reflections on using journals in higher education: A focus group discussion with faculty'. *Assessment & Evaluation in Higher Education*, 31, 671–691.

Robson, S. and Turner, Y. (2007), 'Teaching is a co-learning experience: Academics reflecting on learning and teaching in an 'internationalized' faculty'. *Teaching in Higher Education*, 12, 41–54.

Shah, F. (2014), 'The Role of Observation in the Development of ESOL Teachers: The perceptions of ESOL teachers working in an FE college in London', in A. Howard, H. Donaghue and L. Burke (eds), *Participant Voices: Observation in Educational Settings*. Abu Dhabi: HCT Press, pp. 19–33.

Thonus, T. (2008), 'Acquaintanceship, familiarity, and coordinated laughter in writing tutorials'. *Linguistics and Education*, 19, 333–350.

Vasquez, C. (2004), '"Very carefully managed": Advice and suggestions in post-observation meetings'. *Linguistics and Education*, 15, 33–58.

—— and Reppen, R. (2007), 'Transforming practice: Changing patterns of participation in post-observation meetings'. *Language Awareness*, 16, 153–172.

Waite, D. (1992), 'Supervisors' talk: Making sense of conferences from an anthropological linguistic perspective'. *Journal of Curriculum and Supervision*, 7, 349–371.

Wallace, M. (1991), *Training Foreign Language Teachers*. Cambridge: Cambridge University Press.

CHAPTER EIGHT

Evaluative Talk in Feedback Conferences

Fiona Copland

Introduction

Feedback conferences in initial teacher training contexts have recently been under the spotlight. For example, Hooton (2008) has investigated the design of feedback conferences, Howard (2012, 2013) has examined appraisal, Copland has looked at legitimate talk (2010), the negotiation of face (2011) and ethical dilemmas (forthcoming), while Mann and Copland have examined the dialogic features of feedback talk (2010). These researchers recognize the centrality of the feedback conference in teacher training courses as a site for knowledge construction, contestation and change. Nevertheless, there is still much work to be done in understanding the range and nature of talk in the feedback conference, particularly in relation to evaluation. Drawing on a linguistic ethnographic study of feedback conferences on Certificate in English Language Teaching to Adults (CELTA) courses, this chapter introduces a number of approaches used by trainers and trainees to deliver positive and negative evaluation and suggests that questions are a particularly valuable resource for identifying trainees' understandings of weaknesses in their lessons.

Evaluation in feedback conferences

The CELTA is an initial teacher training programme, validated by Cambridge ESOL and accepted by private language institutions globally as a baseline qualification for English language teaching. It can be taken in one intensive month and includes input sessions on methodology and language systems, observations of experienced teachers and a teaching practicum of six hours.

The teaching practice is observed by a trainer and often by other trainees, and is followed by a post-observation feedback conference which generally takes place very soon after (Brandt, 2008). On many CELTA courses teaching practice and feedback are carried out in groups. This means that lessons are divided into sections, with each trainee having responsibility for one section (in a ninety-minute lesson, trainees might each teach for twenty, thirty or forty-five minutes, depending on the number of trainees and the stage of the course).

The conference usually lasts up to an hour and during this time each trainee's lesson is discussed. In line with other training programmes on which teaching is assessed, the trainer fulfils a number of roles simultaneously, from offering support and advice to formally assessing the quality of the teacher's work (Holland, 2005). Supervisors on these programmes, therefore, have a gatekeeping role (Erickson and Schultz, 1982; Roberts and Sarangi, 1999) which puts them in a position of some power with respect to the trainee. Many researchers have commented on the seeming incompatibility of carrying out an assessment role at the same time as a developmental role (Holland, 2005; Farr, 2006; Brandt, 2008), but this is the reality on the CELTA programme, where time pressures are intense.

Participants, setting, data

The research project on which the chapter is based focused on two twenty-day CELTA programmes: one a ten-week semi-intensive programme (twice a week), the other a four-week intensive programme (week days). Fourteen feedback conferences were audio recorded and eleven of the twelve participants (four trainers and eight trainees) were interviewed: the trainers (before and after the courses) and the trainees (in groups, after the courses). The researcher observed the fourteen feedback conferences and made fieldnotes. Ethnographic data and linguistic data were both central to the study, which was broadly situated within linguistic ethnography (see Copland and Creese, forthcoming).

The data were analysed using an ethnographically grounded analytic framework. First of all the audio and interview data were transcribed. These transcriptions and the fieldnotes were then examined to identify themes, which were colour-coded. The transcriptions were then examined on a turn-by-turn basis and cross referenced with the ethnographic data from fieldnotes and interviews. For a full description see Copland (forthcoming).

This chapter focuses on evaluative talk in one feedback conference on the intensive programme, just over half way through the course. Focusing on one conference highlights the pervasiveness of evaluative talk in conferences of this type, something which is more difficult to do when selecting extracts from a range of feedback conferences. I also follow Erickson (2004) in believing that focusing on one extended interactional event enables the researcher to unpack the ecology of the talk as it unfolds over time and space. I have chosen this particular conference because although all the data were analysed, very few extracts have been used to present arguments in other papers.

Phases in feedback conferences

A genre analysis of the complete data set revealed a number of phases to which trainers and trainees oriented (see Copland, 2011 for details). These phases, although present in all feedback conferences, did not follow a particular order, could be revisited and often merged. Each phase is glossed in Table 8.1, but for the purposes of this chapter, only four are relevant: self-evaluation, trainer feedback, peer feedback and questioning.

Table 8.1 Phases in feedback conferences.

Phases	Generic expectations
1. Self-evaluation	Trainee discusses his/her own lesson and highlights strong and weak aspects. Turns are generally short.
2. Trainer feedback	Trainer critiques trainee's lesson with positive and negative evaluation, and provides advice and suggestions.
3. Peer feedback	Trainees provide feedback to their peers on the strengths and weaknesses of the peer's lessons. Turns, if long, tend to provide a lot of descriptive comment.
4. Questioning	Trainers ask trainees a series of questions about particular sections of their lessons.
5. Clarification	Trainers and trainees talk about things not directly relevant to the lesson taught, for example, assignments. This is the only phase that is often trainee-initiated.

As this chapter focuses on one complete feedback conference, it is important to show how these phases unfolded. Table 8.2 shows the phases in order. The table is divided in two to differentiate between the feedback given to two trainees, CAL and SEB. Each taught for 45 minutes. JEN observed but did not teach on that day. The Trainer (Tr) observed both lessons.

Table 8.2 Feedback phases in order.

Analysis of feedback on CAL	C1. Self-evaluation (CAL)
	C2. Peer feedback(by JEN)
	C3. Self-evaluation (by CAL)
	C4. Questioning
	C5. Trainer feedback (by Tr)
	C6. Peer feedback (by SEB)
	C7. Questioning
	C8. Trainer feedback (by Tr)
Analysis of feedback on SEB	S1. Self-evaluation (by SEB)
	S2. Peer feedback (by JEN)
	S3. Clarification
	S4. Trainer evaluation (by Tr)
	S5. Self-evaluation (SEB)
	S6. Peer feedback (by JEN)
	S7. Clarification
	S8. Peer feedback (by JEN)
	S9. Peer feedback (by CAL)
	S10. Clarification
	S11. Peer feedback (by CAL)
	S12. Trainer feedback (by Tr)
	S13. Questioning
	S14. Trainer evaluation (by Tr)

As can be seen, feedback on SEB has more distinct and repeated phases than feedback on CAL. What is more, there is no clarification in CAL's feedback. The analysis in Table 8.2 is supported by my fieldnotes where I write *'SEB took a long turn…there was quite a long discussion'* suggesting that SEB's feedback was marked in comparison to CAL's. It is also noteworthy that in CAL's feedback there are two distinct peer feedback sections while in SEB's feedback there are five (unfortunately the space considerations for this chapter preclude a discussion of why SEB's feedback is more complex and includes more peer evaluation than CAL's). Peer feedback is a conspicuous element of feedback done in groups and it means that a particular set of interactional features comes into play. For example, it means that all evaluative comment is heard by all members of the group, whether they are the recipient of the feedback or not. Their status as ratified hearers (Goffman, 1981) means speakers must take them into account when producing evaluative comment, which has implications for face issues (see Copland, 2011). It also means that there is pressure on those trainees not teaching to observe their peers so they can say something useful in the peer feedback phases, a skill at which some trainees are more adept than others.

Evaluative talk in feedback phases

As Table 8.2 shows, the feedback conference under discussion is dominated by talk which is evaluative. This section will examine this talk in some detail.

Self-evaluation

In the self-evaluation phase, trainees are expected to provide feedback on their own lessons. Although most self-evaluation is both positive and negative, it is negative evaluation that is important (see Copland, 2010, for a discussion of what happens when a trainee fails to self-evaluate appropriately). In Extract 1 (S1) (reduced here because of space considerations), SEB provides a detailed self-evaluation which highlights thirteen negative points and only one positive point (in italics).

Extract 1: S1

1   *S1.* I should have written all those names on the side of the board ... I should have

2   learnt the story, rather than read it ... I should have prepared more material

3   so they didn't have to switch over ... I should have prepared more

4   explanations ... I probably could have done with one with one more clear-cut

5   example of how people exaggerate ... *they all seemed quite happy just*

6   *selecting topics for themselves* ... maybe I could have given them a more

7   definite idea of what the stories could be about ... I thought I was quite vague

8   ... the drilling wasn't particularly lively ... I should have decided in advance

9   which of the ten sentences were most suitable to be drilled...

10   selection aside the drilling still could have been a lot faster ... I don't

11   think it worked having them in pairs ... I probably should have asked them to

12   discuss a little bit about what you could write a story about and then write a

13   story individually ... and then maybe just like a clearer focus for the lesson

14   generally....

15   It was okay.

An argument could be made in this case that the trainee is producing a parody of self-evaluation (as generally turns are short (see Table 8.1) and CAL comments *'Beat that!'* at the end of SEB's turn). The trainer's response is to evaluate the contribution positively (*'Okay. Good'*.) indicating, parody or not, that the trainee has fulfilled the expectations for self-evaluation. CAL also offered a fairly lengthy self-evaluation (CAL1); in her case, however, she provided four positive comments and four negative comments, thus offering a more balanced view.

Peer feedback

Peer feedback also requires trainees to provide positive and negative evaluation of each other's lessons. Here is an example:

Extract 2: S2

1	*JEN*	I wasn't sure about the content I thought it was good that you did that in the
2		beginning because it seemed like it was necessary to have a bit of an
3		introduction again…and the same thing happened as last time they didn't
4		get the object of the game…Erm, the story was funny they liked the
5		story they were laughing, I could see that. Erm er (..) I think he marks
6		the stages really well I think. The way you say, '*okay, stop*' then
7		you're really clear which is something that I don't do very well.

This extract is typical of peer feedback in that it is hedged (using softeners, for example, '*a bit*', and modals, for example, '*seemed*' and '*I think*'), more positive than negative, and often links the evaluation to a weakness in the peer evaluator's own teaching ('*which is something that I don't do very well*'). Hedging and emphasizing the positive can be seen in the next extract where JEN feeds back to CAL:

Extract 3: C2

1	*JEN*	They were definitely really really really enthusiastic about the topic
2		I thought. They were really interested. They erm they had a lot of
3		questions. Erm blah blah yeah I had wrote down about the the the
4		answers cos you were kind of scrambling around to find them

There are examples when peer feedback is deviant (see Copland, forthcoming for an example) but for the most part it displays these features.

Trainer feedback

Trainers display more resources for giving feedback. Positive evaluation is the most straightforward as can be seen in the following extract:

Extract 4: S4

1	*Tr*	I think it worked really well. It was erm very, very clear stages, you know, I
2		think that's that's a real strength really and very clear instructions and you
3		managed the class extremely well … they enjoyed the matching activities
4		and the anecdote … was very clear. It was pitched at the right level as far as
5		speed was concerned.

This approach to positive evaluation is typical of the data in that positive elements tend to be summarized (staging, instructions, classroom management, the matching activities and the pitch of the anecdote are all praised in this short section) and positive adjectives are usually pre-modified ('*very*', '*really*', '*extremely*') in order to intensify the praise. Often praise is given by the tutor at the beginning and at the end of the 'tutor feedback phase' (see Table 8.1), which has been referred to in the literature as a '*shit sandwich*' (Adey et al., 2004) as criticism inevitably makes up the filling, to which I now turn.

Trainers have a range of techniques through which they deliver negative feedback. The first technique is to provide an on-record (Brown and Levinson, 1987) evaluation of the trainee's lesson, as in the following example:

Extract 5: S12

1	*Tr*	All you need there is the pronoun to make sense of to match up the
2		idiom. So you're not actually getting them to remember what the
3		idiom is … so you just need to know a bit of grammar so and here you
4		just need to know the plural … so I would say the usefulness of that
5		activity, probably not, not not the most useful
6	*SEB*	Okay.

In Extract 5, the trainer is critical of the activity (matching idioms). She explains her reasons (the student can do the activity from knowing grammar rather than through remembering the idioms) and provides negative evaluation ('*not the most useful*'). Although there is mitigation in the section of talk ('*I think*', '*probably*', '*not the most*') which reduces the strength of the potential face threat (Brown and Levinson, 1987), the criticism is clearly stated. The trainee accepts the criticism ('*okay*') and although the discussion of the idiom activity continues in the data, the focus is on how to improve the activity rather than whether it was useful or not.

Another technique used by trainers is to offer an alternative approach or activity to the one the trainee has carried out, as in the following example:

Extract 6: C5

1	*Tr*	You had a very helpful student in the orange t-shirt…he seemed to know
2		something about geishas and he started to sort of tell the whole class,
3		and I felt you could have exploited his input quite a lot more
4		rather than cutting him off cos he was actually doing your job for you.
5		And that would have been a point then to sort of let him sort of inform the
6		class really.
7	*CAL*	Yeah yeah.

In this extract the trainer suggests that instead of the trainee providing the 'input' to the class, she should have let the student continue his turn. This advice is most probably derived from communicative approaches to language teaching in which students are encouraged to talk as much as possible and in which they are seen as bringing with them to class repositories of knowledge and information which can be shared with classmates (see Edge and Garton, 2009). Again, the advice is hedged to reduce the imposition on the trainee ('*I felt*', '*sort of*', '*really*') but the advice is nevertheless straightforward (don't stop students from speaking). CAL accepts the advice ('*yeah yeah*') and later goes on to agree with the trainer ('*I could have exploited him more*').

Both approaches discussed above provide trainees with a clear message regarding the trainer's views of the teaching they have carried out. The third approach trainers use to deliver negative evaluation, however, is more subtle. It involves asking questions about the feature of the lesson that trainers viewed negatively. In the following extract from CAL's feedback, the trainer focuses the discussion on classroom layout after CAL suggests that the group might experiment with the layout in future lessons. The layout had been raised as an issue because in CAL's lesson the students had been doing an activity that required them to move around the class as they took part in a reading race.

Extract 7: C7

1	*Tr*	How could how could you change the desks (.) let's talk about the
2		desks for a bit before that running activity because it was a bit
3		awkward wasn't it?

4	CAL	Well yeah
5	JEN	Yeah mm
6	Tr	Yeah
7	CAL	I mean I guess if they'd been in islands there's a lot more space
8	JEN	Mhm
9	Tr	Mhm
10	CAL	Yeah and it's such a small room it doesn't dis cos I mean our room
11		Sometimes islands were tricky because we had that thing with
12		their being by the board … but in here you are on top of them anyway
		a. [
13	Tr	mhm
14	Tr	Yeah
15	CAL	It's really different teaching in here.
16	JEN	Yeah [laugh]
17	Tr	And also just another thought on that running activity that the pairs sort of everybody got up together to look at the ta is that what you'd intended or um?
18	CAL	Erm yeah in a way cos I wanted them to stick together and and
19		because there were a lot more than I'd anticipated cos we'd sort
20		of mushroomed
21	JEN	Mm yeah
22	CAL	So I was a bit phased by numbers erm and it was almost as if
23		'oh get them doing something' [laughs] so there was perhaps
24		less less planning involved then it sort of happened like that but
25		I would have had them going round in pairs I think erm so that
26		they could talk to each other about the answers cos it was I think
27		it would have been too hard and quite lonely to throw them into
28		that reading by themselves initially. I don't know.
29	Tr	I'm just wondering how much standing was going on because if
30		you'd got two eyes erm (.) and you don't have that sense of urgency

31		if you've got to run back to your partner to tell them the answer and
32		then they've got to go and get the next question
33	CAL	I just didn't see how I could do it in this in this set up and=
34	Tr	= But I felt it was much more crowded with them all up and trying
35		to look at so if you had half the class sitting down (.) you've only
36		got one up and they can actually see the race going on
37	CAL	Yeah yeah yeah.
38	Tr	So they can say '*oh they're ahead of me*' you know so there would
39		be a bit more racing I felt it it was fairly leisurely … a bit of
40		a saunter which means then not a lot of scanning is going on really.

This extract starts with the trainer suggesting that the layout of the classroom was awkward for the running activity. Although a question, the tag ('*it was a bit awkward wasn't it?*') means that there is little that the trainees can do but agree, which CAL and JEN, at least, do. Nevertheless, the question also provides an interactional space for CAL to discuss the difference in layout between the classroom they had been previously teaching in and the one in which they had taught that day (line 10ff). The trainer, however, does not take up this topic and instead returns to the running activity and asks another question, whether CAL had intended for the students to do the reading race in pairs (line 17ff). This question is less directly evaluative; the '*or erm*' at the end softens its directness and provides a discoursal affordance to CAL to discuss this part of her lesson, and, I would argue, to outline its shortcomings. CAL's answer is equivocal ('*Erm yeah in a way*') but she goes on to provide a rationale for doing the race in pairs. However, her final utterance in this turn is '*I don't know*' (line 26) which suggests that she has not been convinced by her own rationale.

This admission cues the trainer to begin her evaluation of the reading race ('*you don't have that sense of urgency*'). Indeed, the trainer has little choice but to provide an evaluative comment at this point as CAL has been unable to pinpoint the shortcomings of her lesson despite the opportunity to do so. CAL seems at first to resist the criticism of her lesson (line 31. My fieldnotes refer a number of times to CAL being '*resistant*' to feedback and to her being '*prickly*') but the trainer interrupts CAL's attempt at justification to deliver a further negative evaluation ('*it was much more crowded with them all up*') at which point CAL capitulates and agrees with the assessment ('*yeah yeah yeah*'). However, the trainer has not finished and she goes on to complete her negative feedback ('*it was fairly leisurely*', '*a bit of a saunter*', '*not a lot of scanning going on*').

Questioning in Extract 7 has been used by the trainer to highlight weak aspects of the lesson (classroom layout and the reading race) and to provide the trainee with an opportunity to articulate what went wrong. However, when CAL is unable to do this, the trainer steps in and provides advice.

A slightly different use of questions to couch negative evaluation can be seen in the next example. Here the trainer asks a question about the pronunciation of the idioms that SEB has taught (Extracts 1 and 4). Specifically she wants to know if it is important for students to hear the pronunciation of the idioms before being asked to produce them:

Extract 8: S13

1	Tr	So possibly just you should up the challenge of the content of
2		the lesson. But as far as sort of delivering it very nice story er
3		they enjoyed it very nice er elicitation of the story matching er
4		to try and remember the the idioms and then er addressing the
5		meaning that all worked extremely well
6	SEB	Mhm
7	Tr	Erm the with the pronunciation is there any way I mean you've said
8		you've you've selected =
9	SEB	= yeah the drills
10	Tr	Yeah erm (..) do you think it it was important to for them to hear the
11		pronunciation of all of them do you think?
12	SEB	I think I think the the point of the drills was to work on stress and I
13		should have maybe offered a couple of examples in places where I
14		would naturally stress and then given them maybe two minutes to
15		go through the list and guess which words would stress and then given
16		them two minutes to go through the list and guess which words they
17		would stress and then we could have gone through those items together
18		and=

19   *Tr*   = Yep I think that is really what was needed. They needed to have a

20   model from you and then let them work it out for themselves and then

21   for you to just check they they've got it right with some drilling.

The trainer's question ('*do you think it is important for them to hear the pronunciation?*') is clearly evaluative. Within the norms of feedback, the trainer's role is to offer evaluative comment and support (see, for example, Holland, 2005). The trainees will be expecting her to do one of these two things. Furthermore, the first four lines of this extract show the trainer and trainee(s) orienting to the trainer feedback phase (see Table 8.1), as the trainer offers positive evaluation (mirroring the points she made in Extract 3), which SEB responds to with an affirmative token (line 6). It would not be unusual for further evaluative comment to follow, particularly if lines 1–5 are the positive layers of the shit sandwich. As Levinson (1992) states, '*the function of the question does not lie within [an] utterance … but in its juxtaposition with what has gone before*' (p. 84). Furthermore, teachers ask questions to which they know the answers (Levinson, 1992; Walsh, 2006). Although the feedback conference is not a traditional classroom, there are many similarities in terms of power and knowledge asymmetries. It would be expected that the trainer would know the answer to the question '*is it important for students to hear the pronunciation of an idiom before they say it?*'. Finally, the unfolding discourse supports this analysis. SEB does not answer the question directly (yes it is a good idea or no it is not a good idea); rather he takes a long turn in which he provides a rationale for the drill ('*to work on stress*') and then explains what he should have done retrospectively (given examples, allowed students to go through the list guessing where the stress came and then going over the correct pronunciation together). In other words, he orients to the underlying meaning of the question rather than to its surface meaning. The trainer's response to the answer is to agree strongly with SEB's ideas ('*Yep I think that is really what was needed*') and then for her to reiterate the stages that SEB should have gone through.

Discussion

This brief analysis of sections of evaluative talk has revealed the different opportunities that trainees and trainers have to evaluate lessons in feedback. Self-evaluation is considered to be a particularly important skill for trainees to develop as it is linked to reflective practice (see Mann and Walsh, this volume) and to trainees' ability to continue to develop as professionals once the course ends. In this feedback conference, SEB in particular demonstrates he understands the rules of the game in this regard and even his seeming parody of the genre does not undermine the strength of his self-evaluation. Of particular interest is that SEB only provides one positive comment about his lesson and this is accepted. However, it is usual for trainees to provide both positive and negative self-evaluation, as CAL does, which is more in the spirit of reflective practice where strengths are identified and retained while weaknesses are identified and developed.

Peer evaluation is peculiar to group feedback and is a difficult genre for trainees to develop as it requires them to negotiate face issues, among other things (see Copland, 2011). The example of peer feedback given here is typical in that it tends to the positive, is often hedged and is often linked to issues in the peer evaluator's own lesson. Although peer feedback can be defended on a number of levels (it develops observational skills, distributes turns in the feedback conference, supports self-development), it can also be criticized for positioning trainees as critics in a situation which many already find fraught with face issues and stressful.

Trainers, on the other hand, are expected to provide positive and negative evaluation as it is part of their job. The data here show that the trainer manages this role by providing clear positive and negative evaluation but also through engaging trainees in a more dialogic discussion of issues which she believes have affected the success of the lessons (see Mann and Copland, 2010). She does so by using questions. As Levinson (1992) suggests, questions are interactional in that they require more than one person to take part in the discussion. Through choosing to ask a question rather than passing a judgement, trainers provide trainees with the opportunity to consider the aspect of the lesson they have identified as problematic. Of course, it could be argued that what trainees are actually doing is seeking trainer approval by answering appropriately. However, as can be seen in Extract 7, such a course of action might not actually be possible for trainees who have very little experience and often struggle with basic classroom routines. In either case, the trainer is able to provide further evaluation, by suggesting a better course of action (Extract 7) or by reiterating the trainee's ideas (Extract 8).

Conclusion

This chapter has focused on one group feedback conference to investigate evaluative talk. The phase analysis and organization of feedback phases show that evaluative talk in this context is distributed between participants in the group and requires everyone to take part. Analysing examples of feedback talk has shown that evaluative talk is endemic and mostly straightforward criticism or praise. However, the questioning phase supports a different kind of evaluative talk, one that provides affordances to the trainer and trainees to discuss aspects of the lesson in more detail and to tease out trainees' understandings of the weaknesses in their teaching practice and how it can be improved. As I have argued elsewhere (Mann and Copland, 2010), developing trainers' proficiency in asking questions, particularly when these questions develop dialogic talk, is a potential area for development in trainer training and one which could support more effective feedback.

References

Adey, P., Hewitt, G., Hewitt, J. and Landau, N. (2004), *The Professional Development of Teachers: Practice and Theory*. Amsterdam: Springer.

Brandt, C. (2008), 'Integrating feedback and reflection in teacher preparation'. *ELT Journal*, 62, (1), 37–46.

Brown, P. and Levinson, S. (1987), *Politeness: Some Universals in Language Use*. Cambridge: Cambridge University Press.

Copland, F. (2010), 'Causes of tension in feedback: An alternative view'. *Teaching and Teacher Education*, 26, (3), 466–472.

———. (2011), 'Negotiating face in the feedback conference: A linguistic ethnographic approach'. *Journal of Pragmatics*, 43, (15), 3832–3843.

———. (2012), 'Legitimate talk in feedback conferences'. *Applied Linguistics*, 33, (1), 1–20.

———. (2014), 'Case Study: Researching feedback conferences in pre-service teacher training', in F. Copland and A. Creese (eds), *Linguistic Ethnography: Collecting, Analysing and Presenting Data*. London: Sage.

———. (2014), 'Examining talk in post-observation feedback conferences: Learning to do linguistic ethnography', in J. Snell, S. Shaw and F. Copland (eds), *Linguistic Ethnography: Interdisciplinary Explorations*. London: Palgrave Macmillan.

——— and Creese, A. (2014), *Linguistic Ethnography: Collecting, Analysing and Presenting Data*. London: Sage.

Edge, J. and Garton, S. (2009), *From Experience to Knowledge in ELT*. Oxford: Oxford University Press.

Erickson, F. (2004), *Talk and Social Theory*. Cambridge: Polity Press.

——— and Schulz, J. (1982), *The Counsellor as Gatekeeper: Social Interaction in Interviews*. New York: Academic Press.

Farr, F. (2006), 'Reflecting on reflection: The spoken word as a professional development tool in language teacher education', in R. Hughes (ed.), *Spoken English, TESOL and Applied Linguistics: Challenges for Theory and Practice*. Basingstoke: Palgrave Macmillan, pp. 182–216.

Goffman, E. (1981), *Forms of Talk*. Philadelphia: University of Pennsylvania Press.

Holland, P. (2005), 'The case for expanding standards for teacher evaluation to include an instructional supervision perspective'. *Journal of Personnel Evaluation in Education*, 18, (1), 67–77.

Howard, A. (2012), 'Teacher appraisal observations: The possibilities and impossibilities', in *Proceedings of the 2011 TESOL Arabia Conference*. Dubai, UAE: TESOL Arabia Publications.

————. (2013), 'Observation and feedback: Are they really necessary for teacher appraisal? in *IATEFL 2013 Glasgow Conference Selections*. Canterbury: IATEFL.

Kurtoglu Hooton, N. (2008), 'The design of post-observation feedback and its impact on student teachers', in S. Garton and K. Richards (eds), *Professional Encounters in TESOL:* Discourses of Teachers in Teaching. Basingstoke: Palgrave Macmillan, pp. 24–41.

Levinson, S. (1992), 'Activity types and language', in P. Drew and J. Heritage (eds), *Talk at Work: Interaction in Institutional Settings*. Cambridge: Cambridge University Press, pp. 66–100.

Mann, S. and Copland, M. (2010) 'Dialogic talk in the post-observation conference: an investment for reflection', in G. Park, H. P. Widodo, and A. Cirocki, (eds) *Observation of Teaching: Bridging Theory and Practice through Research on Teaching*. Munchen: LINCOM Europa.

Roberts, C and Sarangi, S. (1999), 'Hybridity in gatekeeping discourse: Issues of practical relevance for the researcher', in C. Roberts and S. Sarangi (eds), *Talk, Work and Institutional Order Discourse in Medical, Mediation and Management Settings*. Berlin: Mouton de Gruyter, pp. 473–503.

Walsh, S. (2006), *Investigating Classroom Discourse*. London, New York: Routledge.

CHAPTER NINE

Student Teacher Placements: A Critical Commentary

Neil Hunt

Introduction

In this chapter the central role of teaching practice placements in teacher education programmes is discussed. This is followed by consideration of how placements may contribute to limiting student teachers' pedagogical actions and reflections, thus constructing a minimalized, normative performance of a teacher's role.

The use of teaching practice placements and observations over the course of a programme of teacher education is the preeminent approach for teacher educators to both evaluate and develop student teachers (Marshall and Young, 2009). Observation, while a critical aspect of the process is but one stage that teacher educators generally employ. Feedback discussions and interaction with mentors from the school and the teacher education institution both before and after the observations also play a crucial role in student teacher development (Hyland and Lo, 2006). In many contexts this cycle of lesson, observation and discussion is the main approach for assessing students' teaching ability and readiness for professional licensure (Copland, 2010). As such, this cycle appears to hold an uncritically accepted and unassailable position as a vital tool in the process of teacher education.

However, while for student teachers the experience of the observation–feedback cycle can be a highly useful aspect of teacher education, it can also produce a sense of intense stress and tension (Copland, 2010; Brandt, 2008; John and Gilchrist, 1999) and such reactions may be considered as unspoken recognition by student teachers that the main aims of the cycle can be understood to be disciplinary in nature (Bernstein et al., 2000; Foucault, 1977).

In this chapter I use observation notes and transcripts of feedback discussions to explore how I, as a mentor, and student teachers co-construct their teaching practice. I argue that the central role of lesson observation is to normalize, assess and position student teachers within a regulatory framework (Toshalis, 2010) and highlight the way in which the discursive emphasis on organization of space, teacher speech and construction of disciplinary relations can restrict teacher identities.

Research context and methodology

This chapter discusses one case from a broader study which was carried out in the United Arab Emirates (UAE) while teaching the fourth year of a B.Ed. degree in English language teaching, following one cohort of six female Emirati students as they participated in sixteen weeks of school placements. The original research concerned the students' construction of teacher identities through their participation in an action research project under my supervision. However, another aspect of my role was as mentor, observing the students teach and facilitating reflective discussions.

The research subject in this paper is Badreya who taught Grade four ESOL (eight-year-olds) at a girls' primary model school in the Emirate of Abu Dhabi. Model schools, while government funded, also receive further funding through direct parental payment, albeit a relatively small amount. They are, therefore, better resourced than regular government schools and are generally considered to have higher standards. At the time of this study, the school was being managed and advised by one of several private education companies contracted into Abu Dhabi schools to facilitate education reform, so English teachers were managed by a Canadian primary specialist. The teachers at the school were mainly Jordanian or Tunisian expatriates with a minority of experienced Emirati teachers. During her placement, Badreya's action research project, entitled 'Using Graphic Organizers to Enhance Reading Comprehension', involved her investigating their use with stories and the impact on students' comprehension of narratives.

Prior to detailing how the data were assembled in this study, it is necessary to discuss the status of textual data which could be construed as being '*less a repository for what has happened than a production of it*' (Lather and Kitchens, 2007, p. 7). I take this to mean that the data should not be understood as a representation of a reality, but rather as a separate, constructed artefact upon which this chapter is created. Holliday's (2002) discussion of how collation of textual data involves stages of refinement has had a large influence in this study. Holliday describes the process of moving from the corpus of raw data, through thematic organization of this data, to the embedding of particular extracts of data with authorial commentary in the finished text. I emphasize that the data selected for this chapter is several steps removed from the raw data as collected and that I have selected and manipulated in the process of constructing the arguments I present in this chapter.

With the above framework in mind, data were collected throughout the duration of Badreya's placement by using naturally occurring opportunities for compiling texts from the regular interactions that occurred during the mentoring process. Therefore, the lesson observation and the post lesson discussion provide the two major sources of information upon which this study was based. The observation of lessons was necessarily selective because it is inevitable that only small aspects of each are actually observed and so the written representations were filtered through three interactive processes:

- Selection of what was observed, informed by biographical and socio-historical discourses

- Personal notes written as the lesson occurred: partial and constrained by time and attention

- Use of tidied up, word-processed forms as data

In addition, the observation texts were originally produced using a template which includes five categories under which students' teaching should be assessed: professionalism and understanding, planning, implementation of learning, monitoring/assessment and reflection. My experience with using this template proved limiting, as I wrote many notes in the margins because they did not fit into these categories. I decided, therefore, to write free form notes for each lesson and rewrite them for administrative purposes later.

The process of writing observation notes was not straightforward, however, as I had to satisfy the dual roles of mentor and researcher, the notes functioning to record observations of lessons and evaluative comments for Badreya's report. Therefore I attempted to create a questioning text that allowed me to be researcher, mentor and sometimes neither: an interested but curious observer. As researcher, I described the class, as mentor I evaluated my students and their lessons, as misunderstanding observer, I '*wondered*', a term which Somerville describes as '*being uncertain; not proving, but wondering*' (2007, p. 225). This is akin to '*the aside*', a writing practice that makes use of in-between space, a device '*to speak to the reader without the rest of the text hearing*' (St. Pierre, 2000, p. 271), where the discourses of my positions as mentor and researcher can be suspended. In this chapter, asides appear in square brackets.

The post-lesson reflective discussions were the second source I used for collating data and were recorded on an MP3 player, dated, named and transferred to hard disc. As with the observations, the tensions between my roles of mentor and researcher were apparent and I became concerned that if discussion tended overly towards one role or the other, either my data or my role as mentor would be compromised. It was necessary that I take into account Denzin's comment that '*the social world is best described as a parallax of discourses*' (1997, p. 46) and recognize that both Badreya and I inhabited multiple roles in conversation, not just as '*mentor*' or '*researcher*'.

The third resource for constructing data utilized texts from Badreya's college work, featuring transcripts culled from four recorded focus group discussions, three of which occurred during the course of the students' action research project and the fourth once it was completed.

Discussion

Badreya's rationale for her action research topic was based on three main impulses: an attempt to create learner-centred, communicative experiences for students that differed from the traditionally rigid curriculum, to expose students to authentic English stories and to provide them with learning activities which differed from those she was offered as a child. However, her choice of topic presented her with two major dilemmas as she progressed with her study. First, her topic raised implications concerning the effectiveness of her class management and in particular creating a student-centred learning environment, which also seemed to influence interpersonal problems with the children in the class. These intertwined issues came to dominate the data concerning her placement, together forming the central theme of this study, in which I question the extent to which teaching practice and action research contribute effectively to teacher development.

Class management: the co-construction of disciplinary practices

Throughout her placement, Badreya struggled most apparently with class management, consideration of which took up a large proportion of our post-lesson discussions and which affected Badreya's understanding of how she should be and act as a teacher and how students should be and act as students. Second, Badreya's research project represented a determination to assay what, within the school context, can be considered a relatively radical change in practice and this also placed strain upon her relations with her students and her mentor. Her attempts to use children's stories to encourage student cooperation and talk as part of a learner-centred pedagogy produced difficulties and conflicts which she struggled to overcome.

I use three scenarios to illustrate separate yet similar aspects of this theme, linked by both my and Badreya's attempts to address the difficulties she faced and co-construct a workable disciplinary practice. First, the way

Badreya and I draw upon particular discursive resources to jointly construct her identity as a teacher is discussed. This is followed by discussion of how this entails a particular positioning of students' identities. Finally, Badreya's espoused progressive pedagogy is discussed, as is the way that this is undermined by a disciplinary pedagogy with which she and I become preoccupied to the virtual exclusion of other priorities.

Three classroom scenarios

In the first scenario, Badreya had been teaching her class for two weeks, and was focusing on introducing graphic organizers in relation to '*Goldilocks and the Three Bears*'. With the students sitting on the carpet at the front of the class, Badreya read the story twice. It was during this second reading that one of the students asked her '*why Goldilocks' hair was sticking up*' (observation 8.11). Badreya's reaction was interesting as '*she seemed a little perturbed … she could have asked the class to think of reasons why, instead she just answered abruptly "she's just woken up" and moved on*' (Denzin, 1997, p. 46). A short time later (Extract 1), I observed:

Extract 1:

she was also nonplussed when one particularly talkative student asked what the name of the bird in one of the pictures was in English. Badreya replied '*crow*' and was taken aback when the girl replied that she didn't think that was right.

(Observation 8.11)

In this scenario, Badreya seems reluctant to permit students to contribute to the lesson. Rather than view their attempts at engagement with the story as a sign of interest and encourage them to join her in co-constructing a dialogue around the story, she stifles the first sign of students' appropriation of the pedagogic discourse for their own needs. Badreya appears to be caught here at the boundary between two educational discourses as she is attempting to implement a progressivist educational discourse which emphasizes experiential and interactive methods, is often considered to be student-centred (Chouliaraki, 1996) and is explicitly promoted by the college where she is being initiated into progressivist, student-centred practices. She is finding, however, that in the institutional context of school she prioritizes the regulative discourse of social order, where the practical contingencies of students' expectations and the hierarchy of mentor teachers', advisors' and school principals' priorities are more influential. The dominant regulative discourse apparent in the school completely contains and controls the progressivist pedagogic discourse (Bernstein, 1995) and, not surprisingly, Badreya appears to have difficulty attempting to involve the students actively in her class as communicative language teaching (CLT) requires and ensures that the regulative prerogative is prioritized. In this context we can understand that Badreya's attempt at CLT is an example of a Bernsteinian theory of instruction which *'belongs to the regulative discourse and contains within itself a model of the learner and of the teacher and of their relationship'* (Bernstein, 1995, p. 49). Neither Badreya nor her students were able to take on the required roles sufficiently enough to construct a learner-centred environment. Badreya's difficulties using CLT within a regulative discourse may have been exacerbated by both her and her students' lack of familiarity with the learner-centred practices, since their model of learner and teacher had been constructed within a transmission orientated pedagogy which emphasizes teacher presentation of given knowledge to students.

In the second scenario (Extract 2), there is a longer, more complex occurrence of a joint attempt by Badreya and myself to achieve reconciliation between the CLT pedagogic and regulative discourses. Badreya was finding class management to be of increasing concern and she was becoming more frustrated by her inability to focus students' attention on the stories she had selected. During the lesson, she encountered problems while reading 'The Gruffalo's Child' (Donaldson and Scheffler, 2004) and her attempt at pre-reading discussion had to be abandoned because *'there is much lost as the students are shouting out so much'* (Observation 25.2). She then moved quickly onto reading the story, but as she read:

Extract 2:

some students (about four or five) get up for a better look, others stroll for no apparent reason. Rawdha shouts out, so Badreya tells her to go back to her desk. Badreya continues to read for a while, but then says she feels the students *'are too naughty'*, stops the reading, says she will not read today and sends the class back to their desks. She then asks the class to remind her of the classroom rules – some shout out *'miss, miss'*, so Badreya reiterates them, but … while she's explaining the rules (e.g. listen, follow my instructions) – she accepts them not listening

(Observation 25.2)

During discussion, Badreya and I consider strategies she could use to address her problem for the next lesson. I then commend her for a more physical approach to managing the class, in particular how she'd *'got them to stand up and get into a line and sit down as a way of sort of shaking them up a bit'* (discussion 25.2). Badreya remembered how *'working with eye contact last semester was a very good strategy … whenever I saw (sic) them directly and said my order they would follow me … but this semester it doesn't seem to have any effect'* (Donaldson and Scheffler, 2004). She rules out a discipline chart because she tried it during the previous semester *'and they did not care'* (Donaldson and Scheffler, 2004). Following this, I suggest she should *'be more consistent … because you were saying things like listen but still allowing shouting out … you're saying don't speak Arabic but then you're responding to it'* (Donaldson and Scheffler, 2004). This leads to an exchange (Extract 3) which indicates how Badreya and I co-construct the students' use of Arabic as being a regulative issue, rather than a pedagogical or moral one. Consideration of whether students' use of Arabic can be used to facilitate learning or whether students may have a right to use their first language in their learning is not mentioned, rather we construct students' use of their first language as an impediment to the smooth management of the class and again, students attempts to speak and participate are portrayed as problematic behaviour to be limited.

Extract 3: (Discussion 25.2)

Badreya:	I noticed that whenever I speak in Arabic I respond to them … immediately.
Neil:	I have no problem with them saying something in Arabic, but is it school policy that they shouldn't?
Badreya:	no, but … whenever you allow them to speak in Arabic … their behaviour will be worse … because then they get the chance to speak … more … and together … and more jokes … but for example when I say no more Arabic, girls like Mariam and Owaya they will stop talking, less sidetracked.
Neil:	so, there's a … class control management thing about it 'cos I wondered if it was a policy.
Badreya:	no, it's not … when they are speaking within … topics I'm teaching them in Arabic I don't get annoyed … but when they are just giving … sentences which they are not supposed to say inside the classroom

I suggest other strategies to Badreya, including those based upon the quasi-behaviourist assertive discipline programme (Canter and Canter, 1992), which emphasizes a system of intensifying rewards and consequences involving repetition of key comments, separation of students, delaying break times, assertive eye contact, and use of classroom space to assert power and intimidate students.

In the third scenario (Extract 4), I observed Badreya again and strategies we had discussed were apparent in her lesson. After greeting the class, she *'emphasizes that today she wants good behaviour or she will keep the class in over break'* (observation 10/3), and gets the students onto the carpet whereupon she:

Extract 4:

shows the class a big pair of lips … *'it's Miss Mouthy – if you want to talk you have to be holding this'* … she asks the students to name 5 things and

5 colours (on the cover of the book)...starts to interrogate the students about the cover, handing out Miss Mouthy when she wants an answer. [Much of the talk is teacher-based and driven...she has her agenda and doesn't go off track]. She leads a short conversation...which leads onto some discussion of cartoons they like. [This is nice;...finally...the students have some input into the discussion]

(Observation 10.3)

However, this acceptance of students' contributions proved to be inconsistent and short-lived as, shortly afterwards, '*at the end of the reading, she says "OK, back to your seats" immediately. This interrupts a girl who is asking a question she has just started miss, why....?*'

(Observation 10.3)

In the first scenario, I positioned Badreya and her students as being in the process of negotiating their roles at the confluence of two discourses, the progressivist and the traditionalist, while finding a way for them to construct a working relationship that allows Badreya's progressivist pedagogical discourse to operate within the regulative discourse. While the three scenarios seem to show some minor progress in this regard, there are other interwoven issues upon which I now expand.

Classroom discourses and teacher and student roles

One critical feature of the data is the extent to which the developmental and pedagogical implications of Badreya's practice are not discussed. The twin issues mentioned in the previous section overshadowed her placement to such an extent that, for both Badreya and me, they became a central concern and were the focus of our post-lesson discussions. The strains that her attempt to change her practice placed upon her relations with her students and her school mentor realized themselves as a struggle with class management. I will now illustrate how Badreya's class management focused on students' bodies, both as individuals and groups, and then show how Badreya's position between discourses has an impact upon her identity as a teacher and the children's identities as students.

The manner in which Badreya's disciplinary techniques address themselves to students' bodies rather than their minds (Foucault, 1977) is exemplified by her differential positioning of students within the classroom. For example, Badreya moves the students from the collective grouping on the carpet to individual positions at their desks, changing how she constitutes the students as subjects. From being involved in collaborative learning, where all the class's knowledge and experiences are drawn upon, they are moved so they are constructed as individual subjects, whose contribution to the class is valued as individuals (unauthorized discussion is more difficult) and judged as correct or incorrect by the teacher. This move marks a shift in epistemological assumptions and power relations between Badreya and students. In the first instance, knowledge is to be mutually constructed through a social process of negotiation; in the second it is understood as a quality that students might possess and which they have to demonstrate to the teacher to attract praise. With regard to the power relations, there is a move from Badreya's use of a *'covert regulatory practice'* (Chouliaraki, 1996, p. 103) within the *'progressive'* pedagogical discourse of CLT towards a more explicit regulatory practice that constitutes a traditional pedagogical discourse. I observed a second example (Extract 5) when Badreya asked students:

Extract 5:

to stand up, continuing with *'show me your eyes, show me your ears, put your hands on your head'*. She then asks a student to be *'miss'*. The student's name is Alia, so she becomes Miss Alia and does 4 or 5 instructions, *'sit down, stand up, sit down'* [I don't know why she's doing this, but when I look up I notice she's calling some students to sit in front of her on the carpet … a way of selecting the students who respond well to the instructions to go and sit on the carpet?]

(Observation 24.3)

Neither strategy Badreya used seemed to have a clear pedagogical aim, but rather could be understood as use of disciplinary technologies, where the *'joining of knowledge and power … come together around the objectification of the body'* (Rabinow, 1984, p. 17) in order to create a *'docile body that may be subjected, used, transformed and improved'* (Foucault, 1977, p. 198) in an attempt to facilitate her implementation of a student-centred pedagogy. Badreya, paradoxically perhaps, seems to believe she needs to strengthen her role as teacher in order to implement the more student-centred approach that CLT requires.

The rationale for using such disciplinary technologies is not Badreya's alone, however, as several other excerpts from post-lesson discussions highlight how I offer advice by almost ventriloquizing her voice, saying *'when they're all on the carpet "everyone looking at me … sitting legs crossed arms crossed … looking at me" and you do that and it takes time … but after a month … it happens straight away'* (discussion 14/4). As this was near the end of her placement, I became more insistent that she show effective class management, my comments becoming more explicit, *'no don't accept it say … "I only want those who put their hands up and speak quietly" … you've really got to get them tight first … when you've got these controls and routines first then you can be a bit more flexible … but you can't be flexible to begin with'* (Foucault, 1977, p. 198), emphasizing how disciplinary strategies that focus on minor aspects of students' behaviour should be her primary aim. The pedagogical aims of the lessons are overwhelmed by the co-production of techniques for promoting normative student actions and identities. Foucault's disciplinary techniques and Bernstein's regulative discourse are co-constructed by student and tutor, pedagogical discourse is subsumed and the quality of learning is not prioritized.

A second reading of this data may construe that working within the mixed space of the traditionalist and progressive discourses has destabilized Badreya's and the students' identities, so they are more unsure how to act as they would in more singularly traditionalist or progressivist lessons. It is possible to view the overt student misbehaviour, therefore, as resistance to the change Badreya is pursuing. The data can be understood as revealing the process of their mutual negotiation and as an attempt to establish equilibrium whereby both Badreya and the students can exist within an agreed discourse. Further confusing this situation, however, is Badreya's inability to embody effectively and consistently the progressivist discourse she espouses, thus undermining her own aims from the position of successful implementation of her research and the establishment of a teacher identity in which her practice reflects her espoused beliefs.

Badreya's dilemmas are not merely the product of my and her concerns with disciplinary technologies as they occur within the broader social space of the school, as well as other social forces which influence practice. Her reactions can be understood as her attempt to break through what Britzman terms *'defensive teaching': a process whereby 'teachers maintained discipline and the consent of students by the ways in which they presented course material'* (1991, p. 45). Defensive teaching valorizes the practice of covering the curriculum rather than engagement with issues, sacrificing meaning for an illusion of progress, a pretence in which teachers and students are implicated. Badreya's problematic relationship with her school mentor can be considered a product of her mentor's concern that the material might not be covered by end of semester, an eventuality which could entail questions being asked about her teaching ability by her principal or zone supervisor. The students, however, are used to a learning environment based on the *'tacit agreement – if you go easy on me, I'll go easy on you'* (Britzman, 1991, p. 46), and resist Badreya's attempts to change the emphasis to a more constructivist approach. Such structural dynamics interact with other socio-historically constituted actions which manifest themselves as Badreya's idiosyncrasies, for example her inability to come to grips with effective class management strategies. Her struggle to reconcile these two discourses draws parallels with Britzman's (1991) distinction between authoritative and internally persuasive discourses, as the authority of the school, the local educational zone and the ministry is at odds with Badreya's subjective voice.

Social structure and teacher agency

This section discusses how the complex social nature of Badreya's placement is reflected in the discourses and practices which are co-constructed on several levels by Badreya and myself within a knowledge/power nexus (Foucault, 1980; Rabinow, 1984). We can see how Badreya exercises power over her students as she encourages them to act within the norms of a constructivist pedagogy by being open to discussion, willing to take risks, and participate in knowledge construction, so she can demonstrate her application of technique and understanding of student-centred pedagogical knowledge to myself, her tutor. On another level, as her tutor, I observe her teaching to judge to what extent her practice matches criteria of being student-centred, and, with the power this 'accredited knowledge' bestows upon me, to objectify Badreya's identity as a subject, a certified teacher.

It is necessary to emphasize, however, that both Badreya and I have been working within a broader social structure which also has a disciplining influence upon her practice. She struggles, for example, to construct a comfortable teacher identity but simultaneously appears to be accepting a 'ready-made' identity in which she is positioned by the discursive practices that existed prior to her arrival in the school. Throughout her placement, she has difficulties in accessing the discursive space that her action research may offer her, struggles to construct a sense of agency for herself or her students and appears to be unable to select discursive resources from those available so that new practices, discourses and identities may emerge.

This linkage between Badreya's potential agency and that of her students can be theorized fruitfully through drawing upon activity theory and distributed agency. For although 'agency is typically framed in terms of control' (Engeström, n/d, p. 4) in complex infrastructure and organizations where consequences of actions may be unintended and unforeseen, there have been calls for a broader, less individualistic understanding of agency where direct control is less influential. This suggests that my assumption that Badreya's dilemmas were rooted in her inability to manage the children may be mistaken, as activity theory suggests that there is a need for an understanding of agency as a multiplicity which can reside in any place within a network or within a network as a whole (Engeström et al., 1999). Within this theorization Badreya's sense of identity depends on her sense of herself within the network of the school and her ability to negotiate with, and influence, the organization to affect change. Understandably, perhaps, she is unsure of herself in this regard, exemplified in Extract 6 from a discussion between Badreya and Hessa, a peer, regarding their placement experiences in different schools. Badreya draws on her experience of working in an education authority managed school, to contradict Hessa's suggestion that such schools 'are so ... open' (Focus Group three) replying that:

Extract 6:

whether you are in a model school or a government school at the end it's your class and your strategies … if I had a government school for my project I would do the same thing … and maybe I'd have a mentor more enthusiastic about what I'm doing … but when we are in schools as full time teachers no-one will control our strategies.

(Focus Group 3)

Badreya's apparent wish to be free to pursue her practice without what she perceives as oppressive control seems to show a strong sense of her own agency, appearing to believe that her practice should remain unaffected by any outside structural or interpersonal influences. However, a few moments later, she itemizes how her practice was limited by other demands in Extract 7:

Extract 7:

we had about one or two sessions for each class … we would need to do a test on Thursday, a test on Tuesday. On Monday, the second session would be for the journals … so you don't have freedom … it's too structured.

(Focus Group 3)

As the discussion progresses, Badreya continues to challenge Hessa's assumption that the education authority schools are more open to new ideas. She also discusses how the social context in which the school operates may serve to limit individual agency, and an overly structured curriculum can contribute to limiting teachers' abilities to respond to students' particular needs and instigate curricular change in Extract 8:

Extract 8:

government schools are more interested in having … (students) … because we have new ideas that the school needs … but [the education authority] … have very structured ideas about how teaching is … they try to apply it in the schools without really thinking about what the teacher wants to do.

(Focus Group 3)

Activity theory suggests that change within social systems such as schools emerges from systemic tensions caused by contradictions and deviations (Engeström, 2008), and Badreya's struggles can be seen in this light as the beginning of a change process. However, she is facing resistance from others within the network such as her students, her mentor and the education authority advisors, so does not have sufficient power to ensure that her effort to change takes hold even within her class. Her relatively powerless position as a part-timer and newcomer in the school entails recognizing that if others in the school wish to deny her space in which to deviate from organizational norms, she is in a difficult position to do this.

Conclusion

In this chapter, the often unquestioned assumption that teaching practice placement and the mentoring cycle that accompany it necessarily contribute to teacher development have been problematized. me argue that, in this case, the overemphasis on student discipline by Badreya and I simultaneously served to limit the range of practices in which she participated and denied her opportunities to engage reflectively on them and construct a more complete teacher identity. In short, our fixation on class management serves as a disciplinary technique to construct Badreya as a teacher whose primary aim is control of children, rather than learning. Finally, I have considered how my and Badreya's work occurs in a broader social context which interacts with and also often limits the possible range of practices she can utilize and discursive resources available to her in the process of constructing her identity as a teacher.

References

Bernstein, B. (1995), *Pedagogy, Symbolic Control and Identity: Theory, Research, Critique*. London: Taylor and Francis.

Bernstein, D. J., Jonson, J. and Smith, K. (2000), 'An examination of the implementation of peer review of teaching'. *New Directions for Teaching and Learning*, 83, 73–86.

Brandt, C. (2008), 'Allowing for practice: A critical issue in TESOL teacher preparation'. *ELT Journal*, 60, (4), 355–364.

Britzman, D. P. (1991), *Practice makes Practice: A Critical Study of Learning to Teach*. Albany, NY: SUNY.

Canter, L. and Canter, M. (1992), *Assertive Discipline: Positive Behaviour Management for Today's Classroom*. Santa Monica, CA: Canter and Associates.

Chouliaraki, L. (1996), 'Regulative practices in a 'Progressivist' classroom: "Good Habits" as a regulative technology'. *Language and Education*, 10, 103–118.

Copland, F. (2010), 'Causes of tension in post-observation feedback in pre-service teacher training: An alternative view'. *Teaching and Teacher Education*, 26, 466–472.

Denzin, N. K. (1997), *Interpretive Ethnography: Ethnographic Practices for the 21st Century*. Thousand Oaks: Sage.

Donaldson, J. and Scheffler, A. (2004), *The Gruffalo's Child*. London: MacMillan.

Engeström, Y. Miettinen, R. and Punamäki, R.-L. (eds) (1999), *Perspectives on Activity Theory*. Cambridge: Cambridge University Press.

Engeström, Y. (n/d), Collaborative Intentionality Capital: Object-oriented Interagency in Multiorganizational Fields, downloaded 22nd May 2009 from http://www.edu.helsinki.fi/activity/people/engestro/files/Collaborative_intentionality.pdf

———. (2008), Cultural-Historical Activity Theory, downloaded 22nd May 2012 from http://www.edu.helsinki.fi/activity/pages/chatanddwr/activitysystem

Foucault, M. (1977), *Discipline and Punish: The Birth of the Prison*. London: Penguin.

———. (1980), 'Truth and power', in Gordon, C. (ed.), *Power/Knowledge: Selected Interviews and Other Writings 1972–1977*. New York: Pantheon, pp. 109–134.

Holliday, A. (2002), *Doing and Writing Qualitative Research*, London: Sage.

Hyland, F. and Lo, M. M. (2006), 'Examining Interaction in the Teaching Practicum: Issues of Language, Power and Control'. *Mentoring and Tutoring*, 14(2), 163–186.

John, P. D. and Gilchrist, I. (1999), 'Flying solo: Understanding the post-lesson dialogue between student teacher and mentor'. *Mentoring and Tutoring*, 7, (2), 101–111.

Lather, P. and Kitchens, J. (2007), 'Applied Benjamin: Educational Thought, Research and Pedagogy'. Retrieved from http://people.ehe.osu.edu/plather/publications-2/book-chapters/2001-present/

Marshall, B. and Young, S. (2009), 'Observing and Providing Feedback to Teachers of Adults Learning English', CAELA Network Brief, downloaded 13 October 2011 from www.cal.org/caelanetwork

Rabinow, P. (1984), 'Introduction', in P. Rabinow (ed.), *The Foucault Reader: An Introduction to Foucault's Thought*. London: Penguin, pp. 3–29.

Somerville, M. (2007), 'Postmodern emergence'. *International Journal of Qualitative Studies in Education*, 20(3), 225–243.

St. Pierre, E. (Ed.), (2000), *Working the Ruins: Feminist Poststructural Theory and Methods in Education*, London: Routledge.

Toshalis, E. (2010), 'From disciplined to disciplinarian: The reproduction of symbolic violence in pre-service teacher education'. *Curriculum Studies*, 42, (2), 183–21.

PART FOUR

Participant Responses

CHAPTER TEN

Evaluating Experienced Teachers

Mick King

Introduction

One of the aims of this book is to focus on how teachers are evaluated and supported throughout their careers but, as suggested in the Introduction to this volume, there are some attendant problems. This chapter focuses on problems which may arise when experienced second language teachers are evaluated. A rise in managerialism in education has led to extra scrutiny as stakeholders seek evidence that teachers are effective (Deem, 2003). While such monitoring may be familiar in pre-service teacher training, for experienced teachers it may be more stressful (Howard, 2012) as they might feel that it questions their professionalism and is inappropriate for their needs. This study aimed to explore via a mixed-methods approach the views of experienced TESOL (teaching English to speakers of other languages) teachers and appraisers on teacher evaluation. The rationale for this study was borne out of my own disillusionment with teacher evaluation since completing ten years of teaching English to speakers of other languages. I feel my professional development is self-driven and that the benefits of formal teacher evaluation are minimal by comparison. Therefore, I sense that existing evaluation practices may need to be examined to see if they serve the best interests of experienced second language teachers.

This study is significant as the growing body of knowledge on teacher evaluation appears to include little on experienced teachers. This research aimed to add to this body of knowledge in the particular TESOL context of the Arabian Gulf where I and many other experienced teachers and appraisers are employed. As I was unaware beyond anecdotal evidence whether my critical stance was shared, I wanted to seek out opinions on this practice which seems to have such an impact on teachers' lives. I also aimed to produce preliminary outcomes which might lead stakeholders to review the suitability of their own evaluation practices. To achieve this, I designed the following research questions:

- What are the views of experienced TESOL teachers regarding teacher evaluation?

- What are the views of appraisers regarding teacher evaluation?

Before describing how primary research was conducted, an overview is given of pertinent themes emanating from literature on this area of concern.

Motivating experienced second language teachers

Research extols the attributes that experienced teachers bring to an organization such as their wider knowledge of teaching and learning (Fabian and Simpson, 2002), their intuitive decision making, greater fluidity and automaticity (Tsui, in Richards and Farrell, 2005). In addition, Fabian and Simpson (2002) point to teachers seeking higher end engagement. The motivators for experienced teachers described above can be positioned theoretically in Maslow's Hierarchy of Needs as the higher needs of esteem and self-actualization (Quirke and Allison, 2008). Similarly, framing their motivation within McGregor's X–Y theory, where X indicates laziness and Y indicates self-motivation, Poster and Poster (1997) place them clearly in the Y camp. However, evidence suggests that many experienced teachers are not happy in their work. Stress is seen as a clear demotivator. According to Kyriacou (in Coombe, 2008) teaching is one of the five most stressful professions and Aubrey and Coombe (2011) suggest that prolonged stress can lead to poorer classroom performance, especially when caused by institutional management style, with teacher evaluation management decisions a major factor in creating disillusionment.

While effective performance management should motivate staff, evaluative practices may compromise this. For example, Riera (2011, p. 54) feels that an 'evaluative approach is fraught with risks which may damage, rather than nurture, the fragile enthusiasm and commitment to continuous improvement'. Major reasons for an aversion to evaluation are the sense that it does not promote professional growth (Howard and McCloskey, 2001) and its accountability and prescriptive conformity, which may conflict with a teacher's desire for professional autonomy (Fullan, 2007). These reasons are key factors why managerialism in education is often criticized.

Managerialism

According to White et al. (2008), managerialism is prevalent in TESOL and '*the development of appraisal systems is part of the development of a more managerial approach to education*' (Walsh in Mercer, 2006, p. 17). Its appropriation from the market-driven private sector has transformed education into a marketable commodity (Morey, 2003) with a focus on efficient use of resources (Kydd, 1997), '*quality,…improved productivity,…accountability to stakeholders and…emphasis on service*' (p. 5). However, Bush (2003) intimates a more negative perception which focuses on functions, tasks and behaviours. This has led tertiary sector institutions to become line-managed entities (Hutchinson, 1997) where '*professionals are subjected to a rigorous regime of external accountability in which continuous monitoring and audit of performance and quality are dominant*' (Deem, 2003, pp. 57–58). Mercer (2006, p. 18) points to the '*deep-seated divisions between faculty and management over the issue of accountability*' when faculty are experienced. Kydd (1997) summarizes the conflict effectively by suggesting that '*the intensification of management controls is replacing the wisdom, experience and self-monitoring of the practitioner, and leading to the devaluing of capacities which are difficult to define but which make a difference between experienced and novice teachers*' (p. 116).

Quality assurance (QA) is defined by its adherence to measureable standards and outcomes (Sergiovanni, 2001), is an integral part of a managerial approach and may be a cornerstone of the accreditation needed for institutions to open in some markets. As education has become an international enterprise, the need to ensure that trans-border standards are met has magnified its importance (Aubrey and Coombe, 2011), not just in ensuring quality, but also by providing an edge in an increasingly competitive market. QA obliges practitioners to focus on institutional requirements (Sergiovanni, 2001) and to teach curricula efficiently and effectively (Kydd, 1997). However, there are certain caveats to consider in its successful implementation. White (1998) believes that it is difficult to set standards for teaching due to its intangibility, and adds that the concept of quality can be quite abstract, so its interpretation may be contextually bound. In addition, Sergiovanni senses that the value laden constructs of '*good*' and '*bad*' teaching may translate into the formulation of badly written, and therefore invalid, standards.

Teacher evaluation

QA generally covers all aspects of educational operations including teacher evaluation via such methods as classroom observation and student evaluation. The purpose of such evaluation may include decision making on remuneration and contracts (Riera, 2011). Mercer (2006, p. 17) states that '*the faculty appraisal system of an educational institution is particularly indicative of its more general approach to leadership and management*', thereby suggesting that despite the existence of over-arching accreditation bodies, appraisal systems across the sector are not necessarily homogenous.

There are various arguments that support evaluation. Monitoring teachers can promote more effective teaching and learning (Shannon, 2003) and inform professional development (PD) needs (Riera, 2011), while Mercer's UAE study (2006) indicated that teachers were comfortable with being appraised. However, arguments against it appear to predominate. It is often seen as a time-consuming, administratively intensive task where the focus on completion means that its goal of QA is lost. Miller and Young (2007, p. 74) proffer that '*although the rhetoric of development is often present when teacher appraisal is discussed, the reality may be different*'. Indeed, in some authoritarian management settings the concept of PD as part of evaluation may be totally absent (Hutchinson, 1995), which, according to Kandil (2011), is common in the Arab world where evaluation is characterized by an accent on behaviourism, performance deficit and the passive role of the appraisee in the process. Research also questions the skills of those tasked with appraising (see, for example, Deshmukh and Naik, 2010) accusing them of bias due to poor training, poor knowledge of the appraisees and a lack of regard for contextual factors (Torrington et al., 2008). A final crucial question is whether evaluation adds value to the learning process. According to Mercer (2006), research has shown that '*the causal link between monitoring teaching performance and enhancing student learning remains tenuous at best*' (p. 19).

An integral part of many evaluation systems is observation of teaching. Howard (2011, p. 123) refers to it as a '*familiar, if not necessarily popular, part of [teachers'] working lives*' but cites its explicit goal of informing PD needs as a potential positive. Inevitably, however, literature also indicates various drawbacks of observation. A common perception highlighted is the sense of threat, which leads to feelings of intimidation, resentment and stress (Cruikshanks, 2012), while Akbari and Tajik (2007) indicate that it is extremely stressful for appraisers too. Two reasons for teachers feeling threatened are the sense of intrusion and judgement. White et al. (2008) indicate that such explicit intrusion is not practiced in other professions. As for judgement, teachers may question the validity of the evaluation instrument, particularly if it is a prescriptive checklist which may lead to conformist teaching rather than creativity and the employment of high order cognitive skills (Howard, 2011). These skills are typical attributes of experienced professionals but cannot always be seen. As a result, teachers may be appraised on basic observable skills more applicable to a novice teacher. Another issue with observation is that it is not representative of a regular class. White et al. (2008) proffer that only a few classes are observed annually and teachers may display unnatural, observer-centred traits. Howard (2011) adds that this artificial approach means that '*bad*' teachers can conduct effective model lessons, which is a further misrepresentation of reality. The final criticism of classroom observation is that observers are often unskilled, with Cruikshanks (2012) highlighting their inability to give feedback constructively.

Framing the issue

Given the high order attributes of experienced TESOL teachers and their need to be motivated by higher end needs such as esteem and self-actualization, it is perhaps understandable that teacher evaluation might be considered an unwanted and irrelevant task, especially in environments which exercise an authoritarian management style. In addition, even if an organization's sincere aim is to focus on PD in observation, teachers may reject this due to the sense of intrusion and mistrust that they have of imported concepts like managerialism and quality assurance. This rejection may be driven by negative connotations of accountability and the conflict they feel exists with the professional code of practice model traditionally associated with education. On the other hand, there is also evidence of the advantages of a focus on efficiency and quality and there are many arguments for applying this to evaluation, with some studies indicating teacher support. Summing up, when considering the value of teacher evaluation for experienced teachers, the literature suggests a partial negativity. Due to the lack of studies this research aimed to explore the phenomenon further in the Arabian Gulf TESOL context.

Methodology

The exploratory approach adopted aimed to answer the following research questions:

- What are the views of experienced TESOL teachers regarding teacher evaluation?

- What are the views of appraisers regarding teacher evaluation?

Experienced teachers in this study are those with ten years' experience of teaching as that is the point at which I started to question the usefulness of evaluation. Appraisers are defined as those persons tasked with evaluating teachers. In line with interpretive research, a mixed methods design was chosen (Scott and Morrison, 2007) incorporating an online questionnaire for teachers and semi-structured interviews with appraisers to ensure a richer, triangulated analysis of quantitative and qualitative data (Wellington, 2000). The questionnaire was designed to collect primarily quantitative data. The interview schedule mirrored that of the questionnaire before asking respondents to react to certain questionnaire results. This semi structured approach ensured both uniformity with the questionnaire design, depth and the chance to reflect on questionnaire findings (Cohen et al., 2007). The questionnaire consisted of Likert scale attitudinal questions and one short answer question to add richness to the quantitative data (McDonough and McDonough, 1997). Questions considered evaluation from the perspectives of motivation, stress, quality and usefulness before asking respondents to evaluate changing views during their career and their level of satisfaction with appraisal since completing ten years in the profession. The questionnaire sample was Gulf based experienced TESOL teachers in higher education (HE). A professional association mailing list provided fifty respondents who worked in HE and had the required experience. This sample allowed contextual conclusions to be drawn (Wiersma and Jurs, 2005). For the interviews four Gulf-based appraisers were approached who met the criteria of a minimum of ten years' teaching and appraising. Two finally consented to participate. Both were working in the region at the time of the study, had worked in TESOL for at least seventeen years and had been appraising for at least fourteen years. Standard ethical procedures were followed throughout. Questionnaire responses were analysed using descriptive statistics. Qualitative responses were coded and categorized to ascertain the most prevalent response types. For interviews the a priori coding and categorization of the questionnaires meant that only relevant data linked to the questionnaire responses were transcribed (Cohen et al., 2007). Pertinent responses which fell outside the questionnaire structure were duly noted.

Steps were taken to enhance credibility and trustworthiness in the research. While the research tools were valid in relation to the research questions, it was noted that qualitative questionnaire responses appeared to focus on observation rather than evaluation in general. While recognizing this as a potential limitation, it was assumed that the sample considered observation as the most pertinent part of evaluation and as such the credibility of findings was not deemed to be affected significantly. Interviewing more appraisers would have led to more credible findings, but time and access constraints limited this option. On the other hand, qualitative data from the questionnaire was much richer than expected so this compensated for the low number of interviewees to some extent. Finally, the global number of respondents meant that this study was limited. Therefore, as useful as findings might be to appraisers and practitioners in general, they are not statistically generalizable. These limitations aside, every effort was made to ensure the research was credible and trustworthy.

Results and discussion

The research questions of this study canvassed views of experienced TESOL teachers and appraisers on second language teacher evaluation. As interviews generally followed the questionnaire structure, questionnaire and interview responses are synthesized according to views on evaluation, changing attitudes to it and levels of satisfaction since completing ten years of teaching. For Likert scale questions, answers have been split into two groups indicating positive and negative attitudes respectively. Respondents' questionnaire comments are cited as nX where X represents the number of the respondent. For interview responses, the appraisers are referred to as John and Jane.

Current attitudes towards evaluation

Most questionnaire respondents had been evaluated (98%) in their careers. Interestingly, a large number (84%) had also observed others at some point, thereby giving evidence of being assigned more engaging tasks (Fabian and Simpson, 2002). When asked about the value of evaluation, there was strong agreement that feedback was useful (80%). Three out of four respondents felt it was an important part of quality assurance, while two out of three felt it provided useful information for management. The one factor which produced an even split was motivational impact (51% felt unmotivated) and 86% opined that it was stressful. So, generally there was a sense of support for evaluation although it did not necessarily motivate and appeared to cause stress. Interview responses were less positive. While John felt that it was useful for experienced teachers to receive a '*reality check*' via another person's perception, he also recognized that evaluation created '*tension and friction*' as teachers often had difficulty accepting criticism. Jane alluded to her own research which suggested that most teachers considered it '*a task that had to be got through*' and an exercise in '*ticking management boxes*'. John felt data from evaluation was useful but '*only part of the puzzle*' while Jane felt data were used but questioned their validity, particularly in the context of observations.

When asked to assess classroom observation in particular the stress factor and motivation levels produced almost identical outcomes to evaluation. There was slightly higher agreement for the provision of useful information for management and slightly lower agreement on observation being an important part of quality assurance and providing useful feedback. John saw observation as effective for reflective teachers but felt that other teachers questioned his feedback. He also questioned how useful observation data were for quality assurance and management given that no action was taken against '*bad*' teachers. Jane's research indicated that teachers prefer observation to student evaluation but critiqued how teachers gear the lesson '... *to the observer...so it really [doesn't] have any motivational value whatsoever*'. She concurred that this '*theatrical process*' meant bad teachers were not being '*weeded out*'. This sense of '*bad*' teachers staying in the job raises interesting questions. Could it mean that the system is badly designed or does it mean that education is a profession that feels unsettled working within a managerial framework of accountability?

Changing attitudes to evaluation

One in three questionnaire respondents indicated a consistently positive attitude to evaluation in their career. Of the 53% who had perceived a change in their views, most (39%) had become more negative about being appraised. The same question applied to observation indicated fewer respondents who maintained positive views and a slight increase in those who now felt more negative. These feelings of discontentment would concur with various commentators' views (see, for example, Kandil, 2011) that observation is an important factor in diminishing practitioners' beliefs in teacher evaluation. Interviewees shared some ideas on why this might be the case. John felt that the observation process should be more humanistic than just a checklist. He found appraisal systems often too elaborate and inapplicable, again bemoaning the fact that no explicit action was taken against poor teachers. Jane described how she questioned observation practices right from her own teacher trainee days when the lessons she enjoyed most as trainee observer were those which were considered to be poor models. She opined that observed lessons are often '*teacher fronted*' as practitioners '*like to maintain control*', and '*risk taking is minimized*' so lessons are very unrepresentative of reality. All of these factors shared by the interviewees may be reasons to question current practices, and indicate a lack of faith in the system. As a result, any semblance of motivation via, for example, good feedback may be lost if the system is considered a hoop to jump through by performing well on the day.

Satisfaction with evaluation

While one in four questionnaire respondents indicated satisfaction with evaluation since completing ten years of teaching, the majority (72%) expressed some level of dissatisfaction. When one considers that most respondents had also been appraisers, this high percentage suggests disillusionment from both perspectives and is more surprising given the generally positive responses to both evaluation and observation above. The three main reasons given for positive satisfaction levels were categorized as follows: receiving positive evaluations, receiving good feedback and perceiving the process as fair. Regarding receiving good evaluations, respondent (n13) said '*Every year I work keeping in mind the organizational needs and evaluation criteria – always the ratings were high*', which, following Hutchinson (1997), suggests that conformity is key. Of those who commented on getting good feedback, n3 stated '*I value it when it is for professional development or for mentoring purposes*'. Finally, responses alluding to fairness included that '*comments … reflected what occurred in the classroom*' (n31). The three main reasons for dissatisfaction were headed by the sense that appraisers were unskilled and biased, followed by the feeling that the system was a useless, box ticking exercise, and finally, that observation was an unrepresentative snapshot. Comments criticizing appraisers suggested they were less experienced than teachers (n6), '*inconsistent*' (n9) and the appraisal was '*a waste of time*' (n49), with some '*not qualified or experienced enough to evaluate in a non-threatening, respectful way*' (n22), thus mirroring the observations of Cruikshanks (2012). Regarding appraisal being useless, n14 asked '*If I don't know what I am doing why have I been retained for so long [?]*'. This shows clear frustration with a practice which, while costly to implement, appears to have little value. Other comments included that it '*disrupts class routine for both teacher and students*' (n23) and appraisals are '*tick box affairs conducted quickly and without thought*' (n29). Regarding the belief that observation was unrepresentative, n46 believed that observations '*are not indicative of what happens … within [sic] the classroom*' while n37 pointed out that '*Anyone can prepare and give one great class on the day of observation while being completely incompetent for the rest of the year!*'.

These reasons for dissatisfaction produced opposing reactions from interviewees. John was surprised by the level of dissatisfaction and felt it might be caused by inaction against '*dead wood*'. He continued his criticism of some appraisers by stating, '*Anybody can check boxes*' and '*Most people in administration don't want to take the time*'. With this he intimated that if management does not take it seriously, why should teachers? As a further criticism of those tasked with appraisal, he added '*Some of the people who do evaluations haven't been in the classroom for years so how on earth would they know what's going on?*' Jane was not surprised by diminishing satisfaction levels. She pointed to experienced teachers questioning the need to monitor their teaching ability when they have proven it countless times before. She was also critical on choices of who evaluated, pointing out that in the Arab world appraisers are often unaware of the environment (as indicated by Torrington et al., 2008) as they are often recruited from abroad. She added that many are not trained to do the job. These might be reasons for the appraiser stress alluded to by Akbari and Tajik (2007).

The way forward

Both interviews ended with respondents envisioning their ideas for effective appraisal of experienced teachers in Arabian Gulf tertiary settings. John wanted more action taken against poor teachers to improve learning and to validate the whole process. He also called for reflective tasks such as peer observation, self-observation via recording and journal writing to take place prior to evaluative appraisal to allow teachers to identify ways to improve on their own, which could then be appraised. John also expressed the value he placed in anecdotal student feedback to assist him in determining where issues may be arising which needed some intervention. His final suggestion was watching a class recording together with a teacher as '*that would make teachers more relaxed*'. Jane suggested that in the interests of standards '*the professional developmental aspect seems to have been lost along the way*' and believed in re-igniting the formative side of evaluation. She also felt it could be useful to sit and chat with students, and let them show what they had learned, as ultimately ensuring learning takes place is what a teacher is paid to do. Her final thought was a call for instruction in how to appraise, feeling that '*everyone needs training in evaluation: students, teachers and management*'.

Conclusion

Key findings from this study indicate that many experienced teachers are also tasked with evaluation. Despite respondents finding it a stressful part of their jobs, the majority seem to see its value and believe that it provides quality assurance and useful information for management. However, around half do not find it a motivational experience. This is highlighted by the large number of respondents who have experienced a downturn in their feelings towards evaluation throughout their careers and the large number who feel a degree of dissatisfaction with evaluation since completing ten years in the field. The main reasons for disillusionment from teachers seem to be that appraisers are unskilled and biased, appraisal systems are useless and observations are unrepresentative of reality; reasons with which appraiser interviewees concur. Both questioned the credentials and motivation of those chosen to appraise, were critical of the appraisal design and tools employed and therefore found it was potentially a useless enterprise. Jane focused on the theatre of observation while John highlighted administrative inaction and the lack of a reflective cycle, all of which allowed poor teachers to remain in their posts unchallenged. It is interesting that systems which may neither motivate nor punish appear to cause so much stress.

The implications for stakeholders are that although teachers show disillusionment with evaluation, most also seem to support it in the interests of personal development and a desire to enhance the quality of the institution where they work. Taking this into account, it would seem salient to review current practices to determine if teachers support them and make adjustments if they do not. The interview respondents both felt strongly that appraisal needed an element of professional development as part of a reflective cycle and both concurred that to validate the appraisal system in place action needed to be taken against teachers who refused to develop personally or follow institutional requirements. They also agreed that you could learn a lot from getting feedback from students, either formally or informally, when determining the value of a teacher. Finally, the need for proper training in appraisal appears to be essential. These are all potential recommendations to consider.

One aim of this study was to add to the body of knowledge on evaluation in general and more specifically in the context of experienced TESOL teachers in the Arabian Gulf. Given the limited scope of this research, it is recommended that similar studies be conducted at various levels to see if findings concur, thereby providing further knowledge in this area for analysis by the research community and other stakeholders. From a personal perspective, the findings made me aware that my questioning of the value of evaluation is shared to a certain extent in that there are signs of discontentment among the population. However, there is also an apparent belief in the purpose of evaluation if it is designed and implemented in a way which motivates teachers and helps them become better practitioners. Therefore, I may have to forego my own reservations in the knowledge that teachers often find it a worthwhile activity, as ultimately staff improvement leads to better teaching and learning and this means quality. While teacher evaluation may have negative connotations for some, quality does not, so if we all aim for quality in teaching and learning, that seems like a worthwhile endeavour.

References

Akbari, R. and Tajik, L. (2007), 'A classroom observation model based on teacher's attitudes', in L. Stephenson and P. Davidson (eds), *Teacher Education and Continuing Professional Development: Insights from the Arabian Gulf*. Dubai: TESOL Arabia, pp. 243–262.

Aubrey, J. and Coombe, C. (2011), 'An investigation of occupational stressors and coping strategies among EFL teachers in the United Arab Emirates', in C. Gitsaki (ed.), *Teaching and Learning in the Arab World*. Bern: P. Lang, pp. 181–201.

Bush, T. (2003), *Theories of Educational Leadership and Management*. Los Angeles: Sage.

Cohen, L., Manion, L. and Morrison, K. (2007), *Research Methods in Education*. London: RoutledgeFalmer.

Coombe, C. (2008), 'Burnout in ELT: Strategies for avoidance and prevention'. *Perspectives*, 15, (3), 11–13.

Cruikshanks, I. (2012), 'Observation and feedback for positive change', in P. Davidson, M. Al-Hamly, C. Coombe, S. Troudi, C. Gunn and M. Engin (eds), *Proceedings of the 17th TESOL Arabia Conference: Rethinking English Language Teaching*. Dubai: TESOL Arabia, pp. 498–505.

Deem, R. (2003), 'New managerialism in UK universities: Manager-academic accounts of change', in H. Eggins (ed.), *Globalization and Reform in Higher Education*. Maidenhead: Open University Press, pp. 55–67.

Deshmukh, A. V. and Naik, A. P. (2010), *Educational Management*. Mumbai: Global Media.

Fabian, H. and Simpson, A. (2002), 'Mentoring the experienced teacher'. *Mentoring and Tutoring: Partnership in Learning*, 10, (2), 117–125.

Fullan, M. (2007), *The New Meaning of Educational Change*. New York: Teachers College Press.

Howard, A. (2011), 'What do appraisal observations of teachers really tell us?', in C. Coombe, L. Stephenson and S. Abu-Rmaileh (eds), *Leadership and Management in English Language Teaching*. Dubai: TESOL Arabia, pp. 123–136.

———. (2012), 'Teacher appraisal observations: The possibilities and impossibilities', in P. Davidson, M. Al-Hamly, C. Coombe, S. Troudi, C. Gunn and M. Engin (eds), *Proceedings of the 17th TESOL Arabia Conference: Rethinking English Language Teaching*. Dubai: TESOL Arabia, pp. 366–374.

Howard, B. H. and McCloskey, W. H. (2001), 'Evaluating experienced teachers'. *Educational Leadership*, 58, (5), pp. 48–51.

Hutchinson, B. (1997), 'Appraising appraisal: Some tensions and some possibilities', in L. Kydd, M. Crawford and C. Riches (eds), *Professional Development for Educational Management*. Buckingham: Open University Press, pp. 157–168.

Kandil, A. (2011), 'Lesson observation: Professional development or teacher evaluation?', in C. Coombe, L. Stephenson and S. Abu-Rmaileh (eds), *Leadership and Management in English Language Teaching*. Dubai: TESOL Arabia, pp. 227–242.

Kydd, L. (1997), 'Teacher professionalism and managerialism', in L. Kydd, M. Crawford and C. Riches (eds), *Professional Development for Educational Management*. Buckingham: Open University Press, pp. 111–117.

McDonough, J. and McDonough, S. (1997), *Research Methods for English Language Teachers*. London: Arnold.

Mercer, J. (2006), 'Appraising higher education faculty in the Middle East: Leadership lessons from a different world'. *Management in Education*, 20, (1), 17–26.

Miller, L. and Young, J. (2007), 'What's in it for me? A performance management system to please everyone', in C. Coombe, M. Al-Hamly, P. Davidson and S. Troudi, (eds), *Evaluating Teacher Effectiveness in ESL/EFL Contexts*. Ann Arbor: University of Michigan Press, pp. 74–88.

Morey, A. I. (2003), 'Major trends impacting faculty roles and rewards: An international perspective', in H. Eggins (ed.), *Globalization and Reform in Higher Education*. Maidenhead: Open University Press, pp. 68–84.

Poster, C. and Poster, D. (1997), 'The nature of appraisal', in L. Kydd, M. Crawford and C. Riches (eds), *Professional Development for Educational Management*. Buckingham: Open University Press, pp. 148–156.

Quirke, P. and Allison, S. (2008), 'DREAM Management: Involving and motivating teachers', in C. Coombe, M.L. McCloskey, L. Stephenson and N. J. Anderson (eds), *Leadership in English Language Teaching and Learning*. Ann Arbor: University of Michigan Press, pp. 186–202.

Richards, J. C. and Farrell, T. S. (2005), *Professional Development for Language Teachers: Strategies for Teacher Learning*. Cambridge: Cambridge University Press.

Riera, G. (2011), 'New directions in teacher appraisal and development', in C. Coombe, L. Stephenson and S. Abu-Rmaileh (eds), *Leadership and Management in English Language Teaching*. Dubai: TESOL Arabia, pp. 49–66.

Scott, D. and Morrison, M. (2007), *Key Ideas in Educational Research*. London: Continuum.

Sergiovanni, T. J. (2001), *Leadership: What's in it for Schools?*. London: Routledge/Falmer.

Shannon, J. (2003), 'Evaluating teacher performance', in Coombe, P. Davidson and D. Lloyd (eds), *Proceedings of the 5th And 6th Current Trends In English Language Testing (CTELT) Conferences*. Dubai: TESOL Arabia, pp. 123–130.

Torrington, D., Hall, L. and Taylor, S. (2008), *Human Resource Management*. Harlow: Pearson Education.

Wellington, J. (2000), *Educational Research*. London: Continuum.

White, R. (1998), 'What is quality in English language teacher education?'. *ELT Journal*, 52, (2), 133–139.

White, R. V., Hockley, A., der Horst Jansen, J. V. and Laughner, M. S. (2008), *From Teacher to Manager: Managing Language Teaching Organizations*. Cambridge: Cambridge University Press.

Wiersma, W. and Jurs, S. G. (2005), *Research Methods in Education: An Introduction*. Boston: Pearson.

CHAPTER ELEVEN

Reflective Peer Observation Accounts: What Do They Reveal?

Wayne Trotman

Introduction

Borg (2013, p. 6) comments that although teacher research remains a minority activity in the field of language teaching, '*it has the potential to be a powerful transformative force in the professional development of language teachers*'. This chapter reports on an investigation into peer observation, an activity which meets Borg's (2013) definition of research, which, he states, should '*aim to enhance teachers' understanding of some aspect of their work*' (p. 10). Although teacher observation is a prevalent strategy worldwide for the purposes of both teacher appraisal and teacher development, peer observation differs in that it involves monitoring a lesson or part of a lesson given by a colleague, in order to gain an understanding of a specific aspect of either teaching, learning or classroom interaction. As Cosh (1999, p. 25) points out, '*In a reflective context, peer observation is not carried out in order to judge the teaching of others, but to encourage self reflection and self awareness about our own teaching*'. Cosh (1999, p. 23) argues that, '*unless they are accepted by the staff, the only relevance [of peer observation] is likely to be to accountability, rather than genuine development*'. Head and Taylor (1997) argue that since peer observations are supportive rather than evaluative, during such activities teachers are able to learn from and support each other. Basturkmen (2007) explains how peer observation discussions help teachers to reflect on their practice and explore the reasons and beliefs that underlie their classroom behaviour. This chapter therefore explains how, by implementing a programme of peer observation, teachers progressed from receiving trainer feedback from an adapted CELTA (Certificate in English Language Teaching to Adults) checklist, to writing descriptive and reflective accounts of what they had observed. It analyses accounts and locates, within teachers' personal reflections, professional development in the form of learning outcomes from observation of their peers.

Peer observation accounts and reflection

One method of writing an account of a peer observation is an observer narrative in which the most important aspects are described objectively, while any form of initial evaluation is avoided. A second approach to recording events is field notes which consist of brief descriptions of key events, perhaps one entry for each five minutes, including the observer's reflective interpretations. Checklists may also be used as a focused and systematic means of data collection, although correctly identifying certain features on the inventory may be problematic. The twelve accounts in this study contained descriptions of activities observed throughout the lesson along with observees' reflective comments on these activities. Copland et al. (2009, p. 15) point out how, '*In the last twenty years the term "reflection" has become increasingly important in teacher education contexts, [although] because of the range of interpretations provided in the literature it is not an easy process to describe and can seem a vague concept with few guidelines for implementation*'. Copland et al. (2009, p. 15) define reflection as '*the ability to analyse an action systematically and to evaluate the strengths and weaknesses of the action in order to improve practice*' and it is this definition that I use throughout this chapter. In a sense, then, peer observation involves not so much the evaluation of a colleague's overall classroom performance, but instead, the evaluation by both observer and observee of a specific and pre-arranged topic of focus within the lesson.

Methodology

Research focus

The qualitative research study discussed in this chapter involved an analysis of a corpus of twelve language teachers' accounts of a single and voluntary peer observation. The term *account* is preferred here instead of *report*, which tends to have a more judgemental tone. After submitting their accounts teachers completed a brief questionnaire. The research focus while analysing data in both accounts and questionnaire responses was first to investigate who teachers chose to observe along with their reasons for doing so, and second to locate and categorize reflective comments made in accounts and relate them to evidence, where possible, of professional development.

Context and participants

This study initially involved sixteen teachers of English as a foreign language working in the preparatory year at a state university in Turkey, all non-native speaker teachers of varying degrees of experience ranging from zero to twelve years. These teachers were chosen as they were teaching on the same programme. For data analysis purposes teachers were classified as follows novice (0–3years' experience); fairly experienced (3–5 years); experienced (5–10 years); very experienced (more than ten years). As teachers were under no obligation to carry out a peer observation, I was unable to persuade the four very experienced teachers to do so. Reasons were generally related to a lack of time or a busy schedule. Perhaps experienced teachers feel less of a need to engage in this form of professional development. Thus the eventual corpus of accounts consisted of those by five novice teachers, four by fairly experienced teachers and three by experienced teachers.

Background

In-service teacher evaluation is, unfortunately, not the norm at state universities in Turkey, being carried out principally in private universities. Possibly the degree of job security when working for the state does not necessitate in-service evaluation of teacher performance. However, on taking up a post as teacher educator at a newly opened state university I prioritized observation. This was because I had been responsible for recruiting most of the new teachers and wished to find out what might be required in future professional development sessions. In the first semester of 2012–2013 I observed thirteen language teachers, providing individual summative, that is, supportive and developmental, feedback on their lessons. The remainder were observed individually in semester two, along with several, at their request, for a second time. These observations were initially based upon an adapted CELTA checklist of a number of features a lesson might contain. Although the encouragement of reflective feedback was the aim, due to my workload I was unable to carry out such individual observations as often as I wished. I also believed that compared with peer observations, the checklist with its numerous items provided fewer potential opportunities for reflection and development. At the start of the second semester, along with continued announced individual observations where possible, I also worked with teachers to organize peer observations. As such, peer observation of a colleague was a suggested, recommended but ultimately voluntary component of individual in-service teacher self-development. It was also, perhaps, much less threatening observing and being observed by a colleague.

Data generation

Since most teachers had only rarely observed or been observed, I delivered initial background reading on peer observation (Seldin, 2012) which includes aspects such as the etiquette of observing without interrupting. I then requested each teacher select a peer to observe, acting as a go between where necessary, for example when junior teachers did not know senior colleagues well enough. To assist them I provided each teacher with a copy of a peer observation account I had previously written. The account guided teachers in their writing to create accounts that included pre-observation details and background information, a specific observation focus, details of what occurred during the observation, a section for data analysis (where appropriate), plus details of the post-observation discussion between observer and observee. Accounts varied in length, ranging from 300 to 500 words, and were treated as private documents to be read and discussed by only the author and myself for teacher development purposes. When I later analysed the eventual corpus of twelve accounts with a view to writing up the study I requested and received permission from all participants to use their data as necessary. In the final copy all names have been removed.

Data collection

Teachers were free to choose not only whom to observe, but also to select for themselves or in discussion with the observee the specific aspect of the lesson they wished to focus on. Topic selection was important as I asked teachers to both reflect on this and evaluate how observing had helped them develop as teachers. However, noticing early in the data collection phase that teachers tended to focus mainly on the general topic of 'classroom management', I led a workshop which highlighted other areas observers might adopt. The eventual list put together by myself and teachers at the workshop appears in Appendix 1. Keeping a close record of observing teachers and the observed classes involved was important to avoid classes becoming suspicious when visited on multiple occasions. For later phases of the study teachers were reminded to inform classes involved of the general reason for visiting observers. By the end of the semester, out of a scheduled sixteen, twelve peer observations had been carried out, thus providing a 75% response rate and twelve accounts to analyse. Prior to my own analysis I returned their accounts to teachers in order for them to identify reflective comments. In a questionnaire I also asked them to respond to the following:

> Who did you choose to observe and why?
> Why did you choose the aspect(s) of the lesson you focused on?
> How do you feel you benefited professionally from observing a peer teaching?

For each of the questions teachers were obliged to engage in both reflection and self-evaluation.

With regard to the third question, I requested that where possible teachers should indicate how reflective comments in their accounts related to their own professional development in terms of observable outcomes. For purposes of triangulation, member checking took place both during and following my writing up of each account analysis with regard to tabulations, perceived professional development outcomes and any conclusions drawn.

The section below details three aspects of analysis: who teachers chose to observe and why, aspects of lessons teachers chose to focus on and teachers' perceptions of the benefits of their peer observation.

Analysis and findings

Observer preferences: Who?

In seven of the twelve cases teachers opted to observe more experienced colleagues than themselves. Richards and Farrell (2005, p. 87) state that despite this tendency, in order to design future teacher education programmes '*[Experienced peers] may also benefit by observing problems less experienced teachers face on a daily basis*'. However, this study had only one instance of an experienced teacher observing a less experienced colleague, with the experienced teacher commenting in her account: '*I chose to observe (teacher X) because she always comes to me for advice and I thought I could be of more help if I saw her teaching*'. Four of the six topics of focus concerning classroom management or problems in class were chosen by novice teachers. This illustrates points made by Johnson (1992) and Tsui (2003) who note how novice teachers are mostly concerned about their survival as a teacher. Comments made by novice teachers included: '*I expected to see typical problems and solutions concerning classroom management'* and, *'She was my partner and more experienced than me'*. Fairly experienced teachers, perhaps comfortable with the amount of classroom management skills they had acquired by this stage of their careers, tended to focus on skills and grammar teaching, although still involving lessons taught by teachers more experienced than themselves. Observing a teacher covering the same material was also a popular choice and two teachers commented: *'We both taught speaking. I wanted to see the way she taught the same subjects and topics'*, and *'She was also teaching the same lessons I was giving to another class'*. In most cases observers and observees said they felt more engaged in teacher development than when being observed by myself, a trainer with a checklist, an event which observees felt was more related to evaluation. It should also be noted that due to timetable clashes teachers were limited to observing those who were available and this is a point for administrators to bear in mind when assisting with scheduling peer observations.

Observer preferences: What?

Although Cosh (1999, pp. 24–25) outlines seven potential models of reflective peer observation, it was noticeable that most study participants adopted model six: *'focusing on an area of general interest or a possible problem'*. In order to locate, code and categorize these features I used a model outlined by Saldana (2012, p. 12). Table 11.1, which contains a selection of the original data, indicates how the coding of topics of focus revealed two main categories: those with a classroom management focus (CM) and those with a classroom language focus (CL), while a single account was categorized as student focused. A closer look reveals how, overall, CM was the overriding focus in half of the accounts, while those with a CL focus were only slightly fewer. The CM category consisted of three coded features, perhaps those closest to the hearts of most foreign language teachers and most easily observed by those new to this role: giving instructions, L1 use and discipline. More than half of the language focused category indicated a concern for grammar teaching, while the remaining accounts looked at skills. From this data we may discern that the way colleagues manage their classroom is of interest to observing teachers, while within the category of a language focus the teaching of grammar is also clearly of interest. It is noticeable that four of the five novice teachers (N) indicated a concern for classroom management, perhaps reflecting a need for training in this area. Perhaps most importantly, though, in all but one of the cases the overall theme arising from coding the focus of interest was that observers were viewing the lesson only from the perspective of the teacher being observed. Teacher educators should perhaps encourage both observers and those observed to try to investigate, reflect and evaluate matters more from the perspective of the students being taught. Table 11.1 summarizes teachers' focus when observing.

Table 11.1 Categories of focus

Topic Focus	Codes	Category	Themes/Concepts
Issuing instructions/ ending the lesson (N) issuing instructions (N)	**Instructions**	**CM focused**	**Teacher perspective**
L1 use for classroom management	**L1 use**	**CM focused**	**Teacher perspective**
Teaching and revising modals/grammar teaching in English (N) L1 /L2 use for teaching grammar	**Grammar**	**CL focused**	**Teacher perspective**
Student attitudes towards a native English speaking teacher/L1 use	**Attitudes**	**Student focused**	**Student perspective**

Observer preferences: Why?

Using a follow up survey of open-ended questions to investigate their reasons, ten of the twelve teachers provided extended responses that explained why they had chosen a specific lesson focus. Table 11.2, which contains four of the original responses, reveals how the first two responses from novice teachers (N) with between one and three years' experience used peer observation for problem solving. Other categories revealed first how comparison with a colleague was the dominant feature in five of the ten cases and second how in three cases there appeared to be a perceived lack of skills on the part of the observing teacher. The other two cases were related to the development of self and other. Most cases indicated, however, a good degree of teacher self-evaluation following introspection and reflection.

Table 11.2 Reasons for the topic of focus

Topic of focus	Reason given	Category
(N) I focused on the strategies my peer used to teach reading	*to see how she gave feedback to students*	Comparison
(N) I focused on giving instructions	*because I thought my students sometimes failed to understand my instructions*	Lack of skills
My peer tried not to use L1 while teaching grammar	*and this is an aspect of her teaching she wants to work on*	Supporting development
L1 use in the classroom	*(Because) I wanted to see how L1 could be used for teaching grammar with weaker learners*	Comparison

Analysis: Observer developmental outcomes

Categories and teacher learning outcomes were established by member checking with individual teachers. Ultimately, however, teachers identified their own learning outcomes. Table 11.3, consisting of a selection from the data, reveals two noticeable main categories, both of which tend to '*enhance teachers' understanding of some aspect of their work*' (Borg, 2013, p. 395). In nine of the twelve accounts the main category was labelled '*pedagogical knowledge*', which refers to transferable skills that could be implemented in future teaching. Two of these nine were further classified as '*pedagogical/ classroom management*'. A second category, noted in three further accounts, was labelled '*affective*', as it related to '*subjective qualities of human experience*' (Saldana, 2012, p. 86). Although Saldana (ibid) breaks down affective coding into Emotion, Values, Versus and Evaluation coding, the comments in the three cases in this study were labelled '*Emotion*' since they related to recalling distinctive thoughts and psychological states (Goleman, 1995). More specifically, empathy with students was noted. As some of the learning outcomes are more easily observed, and thus more easily measured, it would be useful as a means of follow up if teachers noting these outcomes were able to implement them within their own teaching contexts.

Table 11.3 Teacher learning outcomes

Reflective comment	Category	Learning outcome
His use of the L1 seemed to make students feel more self-confident	**Affective: empathy**	Native speaker knowledge of the L1 of the target group is a desirable feature of teaching
I've had difficulties in giving students instructions (and) I made a lot of effort to get them to comprehend (but) I was not sure if they understood	**Pedagogical knowledge**	Eleven different instructions, e.g. *'Don't write them now, I'll give you time for it later'*
I liked the way she used her fingers in order not to speak but to make students speak in English	**Pedagogical knowledge**	Production and correction techniques
(She) resorted to L1 both to clarify key parts and demonstrate how sentences can be translated into Turkish.	**Pedagogical knowledge**	L1 use by the teacher is reasonable when students are low-proficiency learners

Conclusion and implications

Two important conclusions can be drawn from this study. First, it is possible, even with those who have a busy teaching load, to involve most, if not all, teachers in observing their peers. They clearly prefer this type of professional development activity compared to being observed by a trainer with a checklist, which they view more as an official evaluation. Second, teachers acquire knowledge from peer observations. More specifically, but perhaps not unsurprisingly, teachers tend to opt to observe a partner, a friend or a more experienced colleague, the latter being particularly true for novice teachers. On only two occasions in this study did teachers observe those with less experience than themselves, and it would perhaps be of use for both parties if more experienced colleagues, especially those in administerial and training positions, carried out peer observations with less experienced teachers. It is interesting to note that topics for an observer focus were divided largely into those related to either classroom management or classroom language. Within the category of classroom management, as well as giving instructions, L1 use and discipline dominated. More than half of the language focused coding indicated an interest in grammar teaching, which in a Turkish context is also unsurprising, while the remaining accounts looked at skills teaching. Since all observers but one focused on matters taking place from the perspective of the teacher being observed, it would be advisable for trainers to encourage teachers observing their peers to try to see things from the perspective of the learner. Also of interest was the fact that five cases featured comparison with a colleague while in three others there was a self-perception of a lack of skills. Development of self and other were also of interest. It was noticeable that three teachers opted to investigate the use or otherwise of L1, which would perhaps indicate a future area of research. Finally, and perhaps most importantly with regard to observer developmental learning outcomes, it is interesting to notice how they tended to be largely pedagogic, and to a lesser extent affective, with the former showing more measurable evidence than the latter. While the outcomes in the pedagogic category related predominantly to classroom management, affective factors could be further described as emotional, as they tended to be empathetic in tone. As a follow up, it would be interesting to observe the teachers in this study again in order to investigate the extent to which the more measurable learning outcomes located in these activities, such as acquiring a new vocabulary teaching technique and giving clearer instructions, had become an integral part of their knowledge base and thus something which they could demonstrate in the classroom.

References

Basturkmen, H. (2007), 'Teachers' beliefs and teacher training'. *The Teacher Trainer*, 21, 8–10.

Borg, S. (2013), *Teacher Research in Language Teaching: A Critical Analysis.* Cambridge: Cambridge University Press.

Copland, F., Ma, G. and Mann, S. (2009), 'Reflecting in and on post-observation feedback in initial teacher-training on certificate courses'. *English Language Teacher Education Development*, 12, 14–23.

Cosh, J. (1999), 'Peer observation: A reflective model'. *English Language Teaching Journal*, 53, (1), 22–27.

Goleman, D. (1995), *Emotional Intelligence.* New York: Bantam Books.

Head, K. and Taylor, P. (1997), *Readings in Teacher Development.* Oxford: Heinemann.

Johnson, K. E. (1992), 'Learning to Teach: Instructional actions and decisions of pre-service ESL teachers'. *TESOL Quarterly*, 32, (3), 397–417.

Richards, J. and Farrell, T. (2005), *Professional Development for Language Teachers: Strategies for Teacher Learning.* Cambridge: Cambridge University Press.

Saldana, J. (2012), *The Coding Manual for Qualitative Researchers.* Thousand Oaks: California: Sage.

Seldin, P. (2012), Changing Practices in Evaluating Teaching. Accessed September 2013: http://www1.umn.edu/ohr/teachlearn/resources/peer/guidelines

Tsui, A. B. M. (2003), *Understanding Expertise in Teaching.* Cambridge: Cambridge University Press.

Appendix 1: Possible peer observation topics

Compare how you and a colleague deal with the same class/topic/skill.

Focus on how a colleague deals with disruptive students: what is said and done?

For what purpose and how often does the teacher use the L1? Can you categorize examples?

How does s/he begin and end the lesson? What does s/he say and do?

To what extent and how does s/he motivate the class?

How does the teacher get the students to produce the target language?

How much authentic (unscripted) language is produced by the students? Spoken? Written?

What is the ratio of TTT (Teacher Talking Time) and STT (Student Talking Time)?

What is the ratio between the teacher and students doing the work in the lesson?

How does the teacher manage time in the lesson? Is there too much/ little focus on key aspects?

Oral error correction: how and how much? Instant or delayed? Examples? How effective was it?

How much does the teacher grade his/her language to suit the level of the class/individual students?

To what extent does the teacher rely on the course book and his/her own material?

Instructions: how many? Are they clear and easily understood? Can you label and/or categorize them?

Does the teacher make use of CCQ (Concept-Checking Questions)? What does s/he ask?

How does the teacher group the students? Any variations on the normal 'U-shape' classroom? Why?

How does the teacher organize work on the board? Is it clear and legible?

How does the teacher monitor the class while they are working on a task?

If applicable, how closely was the teacher able to follow the lesson plan?

What clear evidence of learning was there by the end of the lesson?

CHAPTER TWELVE

Giving Voice to Participants in Second Language Education Evaluation

Amanda Howard

Introduction

Observation is a key part of life in the classroom for both teachers and learners in second language education (SLE) and can take many forms. This chapter will focus on situations where the pedagogic practice of in-service teachers is observed for evaluation purposes, investigating the extent to which their input is valued and used during the observation process. In any classroom context where observation is taking place, there are three distinct types of participant: the teacher, the observer (or observers) and the learners. Each individual or group has a significant part to play in the interaction that takes place during the lesson, however, as a general rule it seems that the voice of the observer will usually predominate, as they have been given the authority to carry out evaluations by their respective institutions. In some contexts the teacher being evaluated may be offered the opportunity to provide input, but it does seem rare that the learners, who form the crux of the appraisal process, are able to take part, with the exception of the chances they have to contribute to the lesson observed. This chapter uses research data to investigate some existing teacher evaluation practices, linking them with the ideas presented in this volume and arguing that both teachers and learners need a stronger voice in the assessment process.

During *pedagogic* (regular) lessons, classrooms are the domain of the teachers and learners who are usually to be found there (Howard, 2008) and a community of practice develops as they all become accustomed to one another's behaviour patterns. However, research indicates that when an outsider, in the form of an observer, enters this domain during a *model* (observed) lesson, there is a distinct alteration in the inter-personal dynamics, as the *Observer's Paradox* (Labov, 1972; McIntyre, 1980) comes into play. This chapter is based on interview data collected during research which compared classroom discourse during *model* and *pedagogic* lessons, in order to identify whether or not the roles of teacher, observer and learners follow clearly identifiable patterns.

Teacher evaluation in mainstream education

The focus of this chapter is not on evaluation in pre-service teacher education programmes, but on that which is undergone by teachers working in schools, whether they are novice, experienced, or at a stage in between. In such contexts teacher evaluation is generally based on the confirmation of teacher quality and effectiveness: educational organizations need to know that that staff that they employ are able and willing to teach the learners in their classes effectively and meet their individual learning outcomes. Writing in 1981, Scriven argued that the following was the best definition of good teaching:

> Teachers are meritorious to the extent that they exert the maximum possible influence toward beneficial learning on the part of their students, subject to three conditions: (i) the teaching process is ethical, (ii) the curriculum coverage and the teaching process are consistent with what has been promised, and (iii) the teaching process and its foreseeable effects are consistent with the appropriate institutional and professional goals and observations. (1981, p. 248)

As with the quote provided above, much of the literature about good, or effective teaching is based in mainstream rather than SLE (Kyriacou, 2009; Moore, 2004; Muijs and Reynolds, 2005), although Tsui (2003) does investigate case studies of ESL teachers in order to understand their expertise. The importance of reflection (Schon, 1983) seems to feature to a greater or lesser extent in these books, clearly linking teaching with professionalism. This is a concept which has been identified as being of particular importance to language teachers (Mann and Walsh, this volume) and is currently undergoing something of a resurgence in SLE research. For example, Richards and Lockhart's (1996) book about reflective teaching encourages second language teachers to carry out investigations in their own classrooms in order to reflect on the effectiveness of their pedagogic practices. However, within the current context of teacher evaluation it is generally the teachers themselves who are being 'investigated' in order to establish whether or not effective teaching is taking place.

As with the discussion in the literature about good teaching, many of the books relating to teacher evaluation and appraisal also tend to stem from mainstream education, focusing on instructing the reader about the best methods to use during the process (Bouchamma et al., 2008; Danielson and McGreal, 2000; Good and Brophy, 2003; Kennedy, 2010; Montgomery, 1999; Peterson, 2000; Saginor, 2008; Tilstone, 1998; Tucker and Stronge, 2005; Watson-Davis, 2009; Wragg, 1999; Wragg et al., 1996). With the exception of Tilstone (1998), Wragg (1999) and Watson-Davis (2009), many of the texts cited above originate in North America, where the search for an effective method of evaluation seems to have been particularly driven over the last decade. However, it is interesting to note that in terms of observation and feedback, the majority of texts focus on observation, while discussion about feedback is generally limited, if it has been covered at all. The books listed here tend to give a lot of space to the classroom observation of teachers, whether pre-service or in-service, and there seems to be no shortage of advice as to why and how this should be carried out, and what methods should be used. Examples of checklists and sampling frames (Montgomery, 1999) are often provided, although it does seem that *Flanders Interaction Analysis* (Flanders, 1966) still remains popular for the analysis of verbal communication in the classroom. The checklist seems to be a common feature of the model lesson, although Scriven did not include these in his argument against teacher evaluation in the USA when he made the following claims:

> First, the visit itself alters the teaching, so that the visitor is not looking at a representative sample. The defect is exacerbated by preannouncing the visit. Second, the number of visits is too small to be an accurate sample from which to generalize, even if it were a random sample. Third, the visitors are typically not devoid of independent personal prejudices in favour of or against the teacher, arising from the fact that they are normally administrators or colleagues of the teacher … Fourth, nothing that could be observed in the classroom … can be used as a basis for an inference to any conclusion about the merit of the teaching. (1981, p. 251)

Scriven summarized by saying that '*teacher evaluation is a disaster. The practices are shoddy and the principles are unclear*' (1981, p. 244) because at that time he felt that summative evaluation had a long way to go in terms of improvement. Other voices from the USA, Withall and Wood (1979), were also arguing that the prospect of classroom observation was seen as a threat by the teachers involved, as the practice had a history of passing judgement. Weiner (1974) had previously researched this topic, identifying a need for teachers involved to have a greater voice in terms of the selection of goals, procedures, and the way in which the evaluation was to be carried out, suggesting that this might provide greater teacher commitment in terms of personal investment. Withall and Wood (1979) advocated a *Peer Clinical Supervision* cycle, which contained the key elements of many observation practices today:

i) Pre-observation conference

ii) The observation

iii) The analysis

iv) A post-observation conference

v) The critique

They argued that the agreement throughout the above stages should be controlled by the person being observed, maintaining positive reinforcement during the process. The final critique meeting was included to allow the observers to discuss what they believe went well and identify areas for improvement. It seems that the evaluation process they advocate would allow the observer and teacher a voice, but does not seem to include that of learner.

Model lessons generally do seem to have an evaluative purpose, whatever their formal label. Beare (1989, p. 15) identifies five possible reasons why teachers may be observed, which have been adapted and updated to provide the summary in Table 12.1:

Table 12.1 Rationales for teacher observation (original source Beare, 1989, p. 15)

	Model 1	Model 2	Model 3
Objective	Initial teacher education	In-service teacher evaluation	Research or professional development
Purpose	To identify teacher strengths and weaknesses and provide feedback on classroom practice	To review a teacher's pedagogic practice for reasons of appraisal, school accountability and/or improvement	To investigate particular aspects of classroom practice
Assessor	Teacher educator/mentor	Peer/supervisor/inspector/external assessor	Researcher/experienced analyst/critical friend
Result	Feedback discussion, report and/or transcript	Feedback via a personal or institutional report	A research report or constructive feedback
Audience	The observer and trainee teachers	The teacher and the institution	The profession and/or the teacher

Even in this updated version, it is interesting to note that the objective of each of the observation models above has some form of evaluative function, while the specific purposes suggest an element of judgment. In terms of the assessors, in Beare's original version no mention was made of peers, although recent research (this volume) suggests that peer observation is becoming more prevalent. However, from the evidence provided in Table 12.1, it is not difficult to conclude that observation and evaluation are closely linked. It is also interesting to note that in Beare's table (1989, p. 15) feedback did not feature significantly, although presumably there would be some form of feedback for each of the five models discussed. However, in the updated version above the links between observation and feedback are much stronger.

For many practicing teachers, observation is a fundamental part of evaluation programmes, continuing to maintain a high profile in the lists of possible assessment instruments. Many of the mainstream education texts cited above seem to firmly believe in its validity and the value placed on classroom observations by Government organizations, such as *Ofsted* in the UK (the Office for Standards in Education) does seem to suggest that they are considered to be a useful and worthwhile instrument in the evaluation of effective teaching. *Ofsted* was set up in 1992 and is an example of a national teacher evaluation programme which uses multiple observations to assess school quality. Burns (2000, p. 35) states that during research interviews with *Ofsted* participants it was found that there were five key areas where this inspection affected the school, including those where the inspection was seen as a threat and preparation for the upcoming assessment affected existing school practice. These two factors alone would seem to suggest that the teachers do not feel that they have a voice in the evaluation events taking place, although for the purposes of accuracy it should be stated that *Ofsted* does not rely solely on observations but on a range of data from both school management and classroom teachers.

It could be argued that, apart from documenting the learning that is taking place, such school evaluations also have positive effects in terms of the claim that a forthcoming inspection can stimulate positive change in a school (Burns, 2000). Research into teacher evaluation in mainstream education has been carried out elsewhere and Lasagabaster and Sierra (2011) did this in Spain among 185 teachers working throughout the education system. In this case classroom observation was turned around and instead of being a top down process, where teachers were observed by experts, a bottom-up approach was advocated in order to ensure that observation did not turn into a fault-finding exercise. The advantage of such an approach would seem to be that the participating teachers have a voice in the events that are taking place during teacher evaluation, so that this method generates discussion rather than observer-driven monologues.

The additional challenges of teacher evaluation in SLE

The range of texts about teacher evaluation, observation and feedback written from a mainstream educational perspective contrasts noticeably with the smaller number relating to SLE (Farr, 2010; Randall with Thornton, 2001; Rea-Dickins and Germaine, 1992). They tend to focus on the preparation for language teaching and teacher training: the aim again tends to be instruction in terms of what evaluators should be doing, although reflection is a key component. Randall with Thornton (2001), for example, highlights the development of feedback skills, which provides a new perspective in the observation literature and recognizes that the participants deserve a voice in the evaluation process.

Research among language teachers indicates that they have a particular way of preparing model lessons (Howard, 2008) and, for many, these lessons have a familiar format in terms of content and procedure. This often links with teachers' learned experience of desirable structures which elicited a positive observer response during their teacher education days (Howard, 2010). Freeman et al. (2009, p. 77) refer to the *'messy complexity of language teaching'*, describing assessment as a *'rich, complex and shifting exercise'*. In mainstream education, classroom observation for evaluative or research purposes is a skill that requires significant training (Wragg, 1999) and an intimate knowledge of the *content* area of the subject being taught and the *methodological* practices needed to teach it. However, it can be argued that, for TESOL professionals, an extra dimension is added in terms of knowledge about the *medium* of transmission (Freeman et al., 2009), therefore in order to understand the events in a TESOL classroom an observer needs to be aware of the following areas, summarized in Figure 12.1:

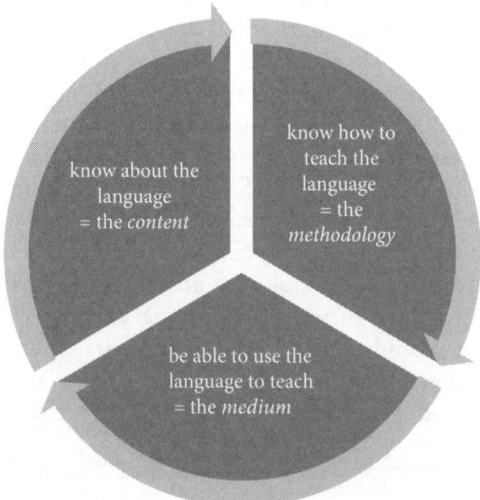

FIGURE 12.1   *Language knowledge in second language education.*

Arguably, those who teach subjects other than languages, such as chemistry, or geography, also need *content* and *methodology* knowledge, but they may not need such an extensive knowledge of the *medium* of transmission as that which is required by teachers who use the L2 (in this case, English) to teach the L2. This adds an extra dimension to SLE and that is why it is particularly important that those who are observing, or evaluating, English language teachers have a clear understanding as to exactly what is entailed in teaching such a lesson. This is a key point that SLE teachers are made aware of during their training, but once they begin working in a school or college not everyone that they come into contact with is necessarily aware of this extra dimension, as discussed by the study participants.

Research methodology

This chapter investigates participant voices in the teacher evaluation process, which include the observer/s, the teacher and the learners. The qualitative interview data has been collected during the last decade from twenty teachers, eight supervisor/observers and twelve ex-students from tertiary institutions in the Middle East. As Tierney and Dilley (2001) remind us, qualitative interviews are a fundamental part of educational research and have been considered to be the central tool in data gathering. In this chapter the interview data have been used in order to investigate the social contexts of learning and to understand the respondents' perceptions of teacher evaluation as a process. All interviews cited here were carried out in English in the United Arab Emirates and the resulting data were transcribed. The names provided are pseudonyms.

The observer's voice

The role of the observer in teacher evaluation may appear to be self-explanatory: they are there to watch and record specific classroom events as they take place, and, as a general rule, to provide some form of feedback to the teacher concerning the behaviour of all those in the classroom. The word *specific* is used because ideally observers are focused on particular areas of the classroom interaction, as there is generally far too much going on at any one time for a visitor to be able to record everything that occurs. It is interesting to note that both written and anecdotal evidence seem to suggest that the post-observation conference is more common than the one that occurs beforehand, thus focusing on the observer's voice, rather than the teacher's explanation of what the appraiser is about to see.

During a presentation I delivered about teacher observation in a Middle-Eastern country in 2012, the audience composition of teachers and observers was approximately 50:50. The assembled teachers were asked to grade their experience of classroom observation for teacher evaluation on a scale of 1 to 10, where 10 was the most stressful, and most agreed on a score of 8 out of 10. Responding to the same question, observers gave a score of 9 or 10 because they knew that much was at stake and that their own abilities were being judged to a similar extent as those of the observed teacher, so they did not want to make any mistakes. Although not frequently discussed in the literature, this point is supported by Kyriacou (1997) who writes from a mainstream educational perspective that appraisers find evaluation time consuming and difficult to set up. He also suggests that appraisers might not be doing justice to the teacher being observed as they often lack experience in the process, emphasizing the need for training in this area. The vast majority of the forty-one observers in his research had received observation training and believed that the experience had been of value to both observer and teacher. In terms of the post-observation feedback after the model lesson, they felt that:

a   It provided the teacher with objective feedback

b   It gave the appraisee the opportunity to share ideas with a more experienced colleague

c   The appraiser could sometimes see things that the appraisee had not noticed

d   Feedback gave appraisers the opportunity to be positive, reassuring and confirm good practice

e   It helped teachers to discuss and reflect on good practice

f   Appraisees could be given specific advice and guidance where appropriate. (Kyriacou, 1997, p. 38)

These points tend to illustrate the observer as an empathic, listening colleague who is there to support the teacher and give them every opportunity to share ideas and understanding of best practice in that particular context. However, the reality does seem to be slightly different among the observers interviewed for this research study.

Andrew, a British supervisor with many years of experience, has quite a summative view of evaluation. He acknowledges the importance of feedback and sees the post-observation session as an opportunity for teachers to reflect on their lessons. In Extract 1 he says:

Extract 1:

Well there is always a discussion with the evaluator afterwards, um, and the, the lesson is covered in some detail (0.5) And the evaluator would, um, ask the teacher to state what he or she thought were the high spots…and perhaps the weaker areas of the class, and through a discussion or through a process of that kind of discussion, then hopefully the poorer, less well-delivered areas would be evaluated, er by the teacher and the evaluator, and er perhaps the solutions for future competency er um discussed and um the teacher is given the opportunity to revisit the areas of their weakness

The bracketed numbers indicate second pauses as Andrew reflects. He seems to have a great deal of confidence in his ability to accurately gauge the classroom working environment and to make judgements about a teacher's performance during the model lesson. Furthermore he seems to assume that there will be areas of weakness and that these will be discussed at some length in the post-observation feedback session. The teacher therefore does have a voice at this stage. However, if Andrew encounters a lesson where he perceives there to be problems, he would ask to observe the teacher teaching an improved version of the same lesson again, but to a different group. His certainty when discussing the observation process suggests that his views on the topic are very firm and it is difficult to establish what sort of voice a teacher would have if his/her teaching was repeatedly judged to be ineffective, particularly after a second observation by an observer that might be considered to be hostile.

Katy, also very experienced, is an American supervisor with a firm view of the formative value of post-observation feedback. She sees herself as allowing the teacher a voice in the observation and feedback process, but also seems to have some very strong opinions as to what her teachers should be doing in a model lesson. In Extract 2 she talks about one of the English language lessons that she has recently observed:

Extract 2:

If I'm coming in to watch your lesson [I] don't agree that you should do a dog and pony show because I'm coming, but at the same time I don't want to see Lessons to Go (0.5) because if you're doing [coughs] that's what you did when I came to observe you that's what you're doing all week long if you don't have time to be teaching right then I have a problem.

Katy goes on to discuss the feedback session that she had with this particular teacher (Extract 3) and how they talked about the problems and made a list:

Extract 3:

I stated all *of that 'I know you've had lots of family things and been really really busy and everything else but at the same time this is what we need to see happening (0.5) so with this'* I said *'are you willing to work on some of these things?'* They actually wrote back (0.5) a whole series of points that they wanted to work on and you know it was really great it's probably one of the few times that that happened (0.5) and I said *'where do you want to go from here?'* and the person said *'I want to teach on advanced courses, academic courses'* and I said *'well right now you are an elementary six week summer school teacher is that what you want to be for your whole life?'* and and I'm sorry but I...had to be really blunt

From this example it seems that Katy's SLE teachers are allowed a voice in the evaluation process, but at the same time they need to be prepared to accept her opinions and judgements and to deal with them appropriately. She seems to feel guilty about having to be so blunt with her feedback, but does say that she always works with teachers experiencing problems in the classroom and that she has only had to *'let go'* of a few of them during her career.

Although Andrew favours summative evaluation while Katy advocates a more formative approach, both have strong voices and clear ideas as to what a classroom observation should include. Both would also allow the teachers to have a voice in the evaluation process, although it seems that this would be more positively viewed if it corresponded with the way in which the observer saw the lesson. Neither Andrew nor Katy discussed the potential expense or time-consuming aspect of this element of their supervisory job (Kyriacou, 1997) but seemed to view it as a normal part of their duties and saw themselves as positive role models. As anticipated, it appears that these observers have a relatively strong voice in the teacher evaluation process.

The teachers' voice

In a classroom observation situation it seems likely that teachers will want to establish exactly why the observer is there, what he/she is looking for and his/her potential reactions to particular classroom activities (Howard, 2008). Many teachers are likely to be aware of the feedback that they will receive after the lesson and their aim will be to ameliorate this, reducing any potential criticisms. Some teachers will also have a meeting with the observer in advance of the model lesson to discuss the learners, the lesson content and focus areas for the observer. Even if an observation is carried out for research purposes, research data suggests that the teacher's aim will be to provide observers with effective examples of the type of behaviour/content they are looking for. Similarly those teachers who profess to abhor model lessons and make a point of pursuing normal pedagogic practice when an observer is in the room will tend to be aware of the forthcoming feedback and its potential impact on their career in education. Anecdotal evidence suggests that such beliefs are relatively common within the teaching profession, but, until recently, little research had been carried out among teachers to establish whether or not this was actually the case. In order to cope with this, many teachers tend to teach what they believe to be a model lesson (Howard, 2008, 2010), often based on their experiences when they were training for a career in SLE, or on previous lessons where they have been praised by an observer.

Amelia, a British SLE teacher, supports this view when she claims that it is important to be aware of an observer's background, so, for example, when she had an observer who had not had SLE training she adapted her model lesson accordingly. She does not have a favourite lesson format, although she tends towards vocabulary lessons as she can have little groups working on different activities. In Extract 4 she says:

Extract 4:

I think it goes down well in an observation because you're (0.5) appealing to different learner types, and (0.5) you can do difficult, and a bit of that, and you know, quite a (2.0) quite an interesting lesson to watch, I think

Her perception of a lesson as being effective if it appeals to different learner types could be based on her experience several years beforehand as an RSA/UCLES DELTA candidate (Diploma in English Language Teaching to Adults). When asked if observed lessons have the same impact as she becomes a more experienced teacher, Amelia says in Extract 5:

Extract 5:

Amelia	No (0.5) no they bother me less, but I just feel very uncomfortable (1.0) in that lesson (0.5) I find its talk
Interviewer	Unnatural
Amelia	You know I'm performing, I'm like a performing sea lion
Interviewer	Yes
Amelia	Well I may do all those things when I'm normally teaching, but nobody's in there watching me do them, that's the difference

Amelia believes that the fact that she is employed as an English language teacher at a tertiary institution means that she should be able to teach without the added encumbrance of model lessons. She feels that they are a management tool and that she does not really have a voice, with which Nevo (1994) agrees:

Teacher evaluation is usually perceived as a means to control teachers, to motivate them, to hold them accountable for their services, or to get rid of them when their performance is poor. Thus teacher evaluation has the image of something that was invented against teachers rather than for teachers. (1994, p. 109)

He argues that in order to improve the situation, teachers should be actively involved in the evaluation process and that this links with the view of teaching as a profession, rather than as *'a tool of supervision in a bureaucratic system'* (p. 116). However, it does seem that there is a gap between the view of teaching as a profession, where the teacher has control, as opposed to the perception of evaluative teacher observation as a summative appraisal exercise by management. Bearing in mind that Amelia views teacher evaluation as a management tool, it would seem that she does not expect to have a voice in the process, but also wants to minimize the observer's voice (feedback) by teaching a lesson that she believes will impress within that particular context.

But teachers do not necessarily feel negatively about observation even if they do not like its purpose (Nevo, 1994). When asked how she feels when an upcoming model lesson is planned, in Extract 6, Hannah, an American teacher, says the following:

Extract 6:

Well, I think the biggest difference for me is that I actually put aside all administrative tasks, all the other little things that come in like emails, all the little 'to do' lists, and um I actually take time (0.5) to just focus on that lesson and plan (1.0) regardless of what (0.5) um of what emergency or urgent things are **there** (0.5) or somebody piling other stuff on my desk (0.5) I actually (0.5) just sit down and focus on what I (0.5) what my= beliefs are in terms of (0.5) what I want to do with this these students, what I've been working towards, but maybe not as successfully because I haven't really been planning

Hannah is very honest about the comparison between her model and pedagogic lessons and the fact that they do not have the same overall quality and focus. However, from her comments it seems that she really does feel that she has a clear voice in the observation process, which may be linked to her former experiences of evaluation as an elementary school teacher in the USA. She says (Extract 7):

Extract 7:

In the past (0.5) umm I had more time for planning and I wouldn't have had that time to think that much you know somebody walking into (1.0) say a primary class that I had (1.0) um (2.0) planning was really such an integral part of preparing for younger children that you **had** to be so well prepared and the routines were so well established (1.0) that there wouldn't have been that need (0.5) but at **this** level … I find that I I actually revel in that time to say that this is the time that I can just … put things away and focus on what I elected to do [laughs]

From her comments it might be possible to argue that SLE teachers from an elementary or primary school background could have a more positive approach to teacher evaluation, as Hannah is not only ready and willing to prepare a model lesson, but also enjoys the process. She looks forward to the opportunity to interact with the observer, her supervisor, in the pre- and post-observation conferences and feels that she has a clear voice in the events that are taking place.

The learners' voice

The teacher evaluation participants about whom the least seems to be either known, or studied, are the learners who are in the classroom at the time of the appraisal. It has been interesting to note during personal research into teacher evaluation that it is very difficult to access the students themselves, particularly if the researcher is not an organizational employee. However, access was gained to a group of teachers who had formerly been students at some of the tertiary colleges where data collection had taken place and these former learners took part in a focus group where their perception of the teacher evaluation process was discussed.

All the teachers interviewed for this research would tell their learners in advance that an observer was coming into the classroom and some argued that this was culturally based, as Middle Eastern female students might not want male observers to see their faces. Hannah says in reference to her students:

Extract 8:

And I think they think that (0.5) they're always interested in who's coming in (1.0) why they're coming in (1.0) and um you know (0.5) are they coming to see me or are they coming to you know do they want to see the students do they want to see the teachers (0.5) they they're very keen

Hannah adds that the students are on their best behaviour and there is less checking of mobile phones or ongoing communication in Arabic, which suggests that they are happy to follow the teacher's instructions during model lessons, rather than engaging in discussion among themselves. During the focus group interview with the ex-students they concur with Hannah's observations, speaking in English (their L2) about learner behaviour during a model lesson:

Extract 9:

Interviewer	How do they react?
Ex student 1	They be quiet (1.0) they thought that the supervisor come to observe them not the teacher
Interviewer	Aah so do the teachers tell them that?
Ex student 1	Yes (1.0) my feelings when I was a student also I think that they come to observe us

Interviewer	So what happens when [observers] go into the classroom then? How do the students react?
Ex student 2	They act very quietly ...
Interviewer	So do you think they answer more questions or less questions when they are being observed? (0.5) If they think that ... the observer I coming to watch them (0.5) the pupils (0.5) are they quieter or noisier?
Ex students	Mm quieter

Extract 9 demonstrates that this particular group of ex-students felt that their voice was severely restricted during teacher evaluation. They go on to say that they actually felt that they learned less during model lessons, as they are too frightened to let the teacher know if they did not understand something, for fear of losing face. However, they also say that younger children are more accustomed to being observed, therefore they would probably treat a model lesson in the same way that they approached the pedagogic alternative.

Another key point about learners in the teacher evaluation classroom is that they rarely have a voice in terms of the teaching that took place during the model lesson, although in tertiary institutions they are able to provide feedback during student evaluation of teaching (Quirke, this volume). As Tsui (2003) and Wang and Day (2002) remind us, student conduct during teacher evaluation is crucial, but they are generally behaving atypically and their voice is needed in order to establish the success (or otherwise) of the pedagogical methods being employed.

Discussion

In 1981 Scriven wrote that evaluation of educational personnel was *'usually done with amazing incompetence'* (p. 270). It is hoped that his comments have, among other factors, lead to improvements in the intervening thirty years. However, it does appear that, in many areas, there is still a great deal to be done in providing observation participants with a clear voice.

It seems that the SLE observers are those who are most able and willing to speak and express opinions during teacher evaluation, although it would also appear that observer training is a key part of their preparation for the role. However, there are difficulties for both teachers and learners in overcoming custom and practice. Danielson and McGreal (2000) draw their readers' attention to several key facts which impact on teachers' voices during the evaluation process. Among these, they claim that the communication is hierarchical and top down, taking place in one direction. They go on to say:

The climate surrounding evaluation may be essentially negative, with a prevailing perception on the part of teachers that the real purpose of the exercise is one of 'gotcha', in which administrators look for opportunities to find fault. But even when the climate is positive, the teacher's role is essentially passive; thus the teachers don't do anything. (2000, p. 5)

It therefore seems that the current view of teachers being evaluated is predominantly one of passivity: some teachers, such as Hannah, do use the opportunity to share ideas with their observer, but others, arguably the majority, view it, like Amelia, as a process to be endured, involving minimal communication. Danielson and McGreal (2000) also argue that there is little differentiation between novices and experienced teachers in the way that they are evaluated, which also has a significant impact on their desire to participate in the process. Interestingly Trotman (this volume) tells us that during his research he was unable to persuade the four very experienced teachers in his group to take part in peer observations, which seems to be part of the same problem.

One area where teachers should have a clear voice in the classroom evaluation process is in the post-evaluation conferences, when they generally receive feedback from the observer (see Copland, Donaghue, this volume). However, there seem to be several issues in terms of the way this feedback is delivered (Copland, 2008; Kurtoglu-Hooton, 2008; Donaghue and Iyer-O'Sullivan, this volume) which, if not carried out appropriately, can have the effect of reducing a teacher's desire and/or ability to discuss the evaluation experience. Research suggests that those teachers who have a pre-observation discussion with their observers do feel that they have a voice in the evaluation process, but this is still not helpful to the learners.

It is the students who have the ultimate power during a model lesson. If they choose to respond by demonstrating a lack of respect for the teacher, then he/she will be penalized, but if they behave in the way suggested in Extract 9, then an observer will probably assume that they are benefiting from the lesson and the teacher will be commended. This will happen even if the students are quiet because they do not understand what is happening: learners do not seem to have a voice in this evaluation experience. There are, however, ways in which they could be given one. At the end of the SLE lesson the observer could ask them how they felt about it, or they could be tested verbally on the lesson content in a way that did not incorporate washback on the part of the teacher. The importance of incorporating pupil perspective in appraisal has been discussed for many years (Dodds, 1986) but, as O'Leary (2006) states, learners neither expect, nor are given, a role in the classroom evaluation process.

Overall, it seems that observers, teachers and learners are all complicit in teacher evaluation and perform according to pre-determined roles.

However, it does not have to be this way, because, as Wang and Day (2002) claim, the key ingredients of effective teacher development are linked to teacher observation:

> If principals and supervisors are willing to…shift their perceptions of classroom observations from a means of teacher evaluation to a tool to promote teacher development, they are likely to make participatory roles available to teachers in the process of supervision and evaluation. (2002, p. 18)

Having participatory roles in evaluation would give SLE teachers the voice that they need in order to develop in the same way as other professionals, while an acknowledgement of the importance of learner input would provide the final triangulation point in a potentially fruitful and worthwhile process.

References

Beare, H. (1989), 'The Australian policy context', in J. Lokan and P. McKenzie (eds), *Teacher Appraisal: Issues and Approaches*. Victoria, Australia: Australian Council for Educational Research, pp. v–viii.

Bouchamma, Y., Godin, M. and Godon, C. J. (2008), *A Guide to Teacher Evaluation: Structured Observations for all Evaluators*. Plymouth, UK: Bowman and Littlefield Education.

Burns, J. (2000), *'Improvement Through Inspection?': An Investigation of Teachers' Perceptions of OFSTED as a Vehicle for Improvement*. Stoke on Trent, Staffordshire: Trentham Books Ltd.

Copland, F. (2008), 'Deconstructing the discourse: Understanding the feedback event', in S. Garton and K. Richards (eds), *Professional Encounters in TESOL: Discourses of Teachers in Teaching*. Basingstoke: Palgrave, pp. 5–2.

Danielson, C. and McGreal, T. L. (2000), *Teacher Evaluation to Enhance Professional Practice*. Alexandria, VA: Educational Testing Service.

Dodds, M. (1986), 'Those being tortured': Teachers appraising teacher appraisal. *Cambridge Journal of Education*, 16, (2), 151–154.

Farr, F. (2010), *The Discourse of Teaching Practice Feedback: A Corpus-Based Investigation of Spoken and Written Modes*. Abingdon: Routledge.

Flanders, N. A. (1966), *Interaction Analysis in the Classroom: A Manual for Observers*. Ann Arbor, MI: The Author.

Freeman, D., Orzulak, M. M. and Morrisey, G. (2009), 'Assessment in second language teacher education', in A. Burns and J. C. Richards (eds), *The Cambridge Guide to Second Language Teacher Education*. Cambridge: Cambridge University Press, pp. 77–90.

Good, T. L. and Brophy, J. E. (2003), *Looking in Classrooms*, 9th edn. Boston: Allyn and Bacon.

Howard, A. (2008), 'Teachers being observed: Coming to terms with classroom appraisal', in S. Garton and K. Richards (eds), *Professional Encounters in TESOL: Discourses of Teachers in Teaching*. Basingstoke: Palgrave, pp. 87–104.

————. (2010), 'Is there such a thing as a typical language lesson?' *Classroom Discourse*, 1, (1), 82–100.

Kennedy, M. (2010), 'Approaches to annual performance assessment', in M. Kennedy (ed.), *Teacher Assessment and the Quest for Teacher Quality: A Handbook*. San Francisco, CA: Jossey Bass, pp. 225–249.

Kurtoglu-Hooton, N. (2008), 'The design of post-observation feedback and its impact on student teachers', in S. Garton and K. Richards (eds), *Professional Encounters in TESOL: Discourses of Teachers in Teaching*. Basingstoke: Palgrave, pp. 24–41.

Kyriacou, C. (1997), 'Appraisers' views of teacher appraisal'. *Teacher Development*, 1, (1), pp. 35–41.

————. (2009), *Effective Teaching in Schools: Theory and Practice*, 3rd edn. Cheltenham: Nelson Thornes.

Labov, W. (1972), *Sociolinguistic Patterns*. Pennsylvania: University of Pennsylvania Press.

Lasagabaster, D. and Sierra, J. M. (2011), 'Classroom observation: Desirable conditions established by teachers'. *European Journal of Teacher Education*, 34 (4), pp. 449–463.

McIntyre, J. (1980), 'Teacher evaluation and the observer effect'. *NASSP Bulletin*, 34, pp. 36–40.

Montgomery, D. (1999), *Positive Teacher Appraisal through Classroom Observation*. Abingdon: David Fulton Publishers Ltd.

Moore, A. (2004), *The Good Teacher: Dominant Discourses in Teaching and Teacher Education*. London: Routledge.

Muijs, D. and Reynolds, D. (2005), *Effective Teaching: Evidence and Practice*, 2nd edn. London: Sage Publications.

Nevo, D. (1994), 'How can teachers benefit from teacher evaluation?' *Journal of Personnel Evaluation in Education*, 8, pp. 109–117.

O'Leary, M. (2006), 'Can inspectors really improve the quality of teaching in the PCE sector? Classroom observations under the microscope'. *Research in Post-Compulsory Education*, 11, (2), pp. 191–198.

Peterson, K. D. (2000), *Teacher Evaluation: A Comprehensive Guide to New Directions and Practices*, 2nd edn. Thousand Oaks, CA: Corwin Press.

Randall, M. with Thornton, B. (2001), *Advising and Supporting Teachers*. Cambridge: Cambridge University Press.

Rea-Dickins, P. and Germaine, K. (1992), *Evaluation*. Oxford: Oxford University Press.

Richards, J. C. and Lockhart, C. (1996), *Reflective Teaching in Second Language Classrooms*. Cambridge: Cambridge University Press.

Saginor, N. (2008), *Diagnostic Classroom Observation: Moving Beyond Best Practice*. Thousand Oaks, CA: Corwin Press.

Schon, D. A. (1983), *The Reflective Practitioner: How Professionals Think in Action*. London: Temple Smith.

Scriven, M. (1981), 'Summative teacher evaluation' in J. Millman and L. Darling-Hammond (eds), *The New Handbook of Teacher Evaluation: Assessing Elementary and Secondary School Teachers*. Newbury Park, CA: Sage Publications, pp. 244–271.

Tierney, W. G. and Dilley, P. (2001), 'Interviewing in education', in J. F. Gubrium and J. A. Holstein (eds), *Handbook of Interview Research: Context and Method*. Thousand Oaks, CA: Sage Publications, pp. 453–471.

Tilstone, C. (ed.) (1998), *Observing Teaching and Learning: Principles and Practice*. London: David Fulton Publishers.

Tsui, A. B. M. (2003), *Understanding Expertise in Teaching: Case Studies of ESL Teachers*. Cambridge: Cambridge University Press.

Tucker, P. D. and Stronge, J. H. (2005), *Linking Teacher Evaluation and Student Learning*. Alexandria, VA: Association for Supervision and Curriculum Development.

Wang, W. and Day, C. (2002), 'Issues and concerns about classroom observation: Teachers' perspectives. *Paper Presented at TESOL Conference in St Louis, USA, 27th March 2001.*

Watson-Davis, R. (2009), *Lesson Observation Pocketbook*. Alresford, Hampshire: Teachers' Pocketbooks.

Weiner, B. (1974), *Achievement, Motivation and Attribution Theory*. New York: General Learning Press.

Withall, J. and Wood, F. H. (1979), 'Taking the threat out of classroom observation and feedback'. *Journal of Teacher Education*, 30, pp. 55–58.

Wragg, E.C. (1999), *An Introduction to Classroom Observation*, 2nd edn. London: Routledge.

———, Wikeley, F. J., Wragg, C. M. and Haynes, G. S. (1996), *Teacher Appraisal Observed*. London: Routledge.

INDEX

Note: The letters 'f' and 't' following locators refer to figures and tables respectively